FINDING HOME

An Irish American Story

To Maureen —

♡ Lois Farley Shuford

Lois Farley Shuford

To request permissions, contact the publisher at
information@antobarbooks.com

Paperback: ISBN 979-8-9853518-0-4
Ebook: ISBN 979-8-9853518-1-1

Library of Congress Control Number: 2022900545

First paperback edition March 2022.

Cover and interior design by Jess LaGreca, Mayfly Design

"Children in the Earth" is reprinted by kind permission of Karen
Wingett. First published in *Nebraska Life*, March/April 2001.

Printed by IngramSpark in the USA.

anTobar books
Evanston, Illinois
AnTobarBooks.com

To all who take the risk to find a safe and welcome home.

Contents

Foreword vii
Introduction ix
Prologue xi

Part 1: Beginnings

1. Born at Home 3
2. Iowa, 1964 9
3. Iowa, 1988 16

Part 2: Ireland

4. Transatlantic 23
5. History Lesson 33
6. How Did We Get Here? 44
7. My House 50
8. Diaspora 59
9. Dig a Little Deeper 64
10. Hunger 71
11. Parliament's Response 81
12. Maps 88
13. Paying Respect 95
14. Skibbereen 99
15. I Heaved a Sigh and Said Goodbye 104

Part 3: America

16. Philadelphia 115
17. Panic 121
18. Enlistment 125
19. US Archives 130
20. Civil War 134

21. The Regular Army 138
22. Peninsula Campaign 145
23. Standing on Battlefields 149
24. Fredericksburg 154
25. Return 160
26. Strange Land 168
27. What Did You Find? 172
28. New Haven 176
29. Migration 185
30. We Found Bridget 198
31. Identity 206
32. Norfolk 218
33. Reunion 222

Part 4: Home

34. Blessings 229
Epilogue 233

Timeline 235
Further Reading 237
Acknowledgments 240
About the Author 242

Foreword

ABOUT TWENTY YEARS AGO, I stood with my dad's first cousin in the humble cemetery by the grand Knock basilica in Ireland's County Mayo. My Philadelphia family had lost connection with my paternal cousins in Mayo for decades and were just getting reacquainted. I stared at the grave of my great-grandfather Thomas O'Brien, and in that moment, the sadness of Ireland's history of emigration struck me with a pain that was real and visceral—not like the facts and figures from the books I had read. I felt the actual impact on my own extended family, the heartbreak of siblings and cousins separated by an ocean, of a family torn in two by colonialism, bigotry, and poverty.

This is the kind of experience you have with Lois Farley Shuford's *Finding Home: An Irish American Story*. In her book, Ms. Farley Shuford explores a tragedy suffered by many Irish Americans, the lost connections, the broken links, the suffering immeasurable and often unmentioned. The mystery of *Finding Home* remains unsolved for millions with a genetic connection to and longing for Ireland but without the name of their ancestor's townland or even county of origin.

With dogged persistence, luck, and perhaps a little help from some of Ireland's "thin places" of coincidence, Ms. Farley Shuford uncovers the story of her great-grandfather Patrick, who emigrated to Philadelphia, and the sad tale of his wife, Bridget, who later accompanied him to Nebraska. She tracks down the details of the lives she investigates, draws the outlines, and colors them in with her vivid historical imagination.

With lithe, swift-moving prose, Ms. Farley Shuford puts you in the fields of an Irish farmer at the time of the Great Hunger and into the marching shoes of a soldier in the American Civil War. She takes you to the hospitable townlands of County Cavan, the streets of burgeoning Philadelphia, the battlefields of Virginia, and the plains of Nebraska. She continues her hunt until she discovers the fate of her great-grandmother, whom her family had never talked about.

Through privileged eyes, Ms. Farley Shuford envisions the experiences, thoughts, and feelings of the Great Hunger generation and empathizes with them, pulling no punches in assigning blame to the colonialism and callous policies of the nineteenth-century British ruling class. She then extends her empathy to the migrants of other countries and cultures treated callously today.

Since that day in Knock cemetery my families in Philadelphia and Mayo have been reunited and have formed real bonds. We get together for weddings, family reunions, and any reasonable excuse. I have written plays and books about Irish America, given readings and talks in Ireland, and even had a play produced in Dublin's Liberty Hall. My connection with my Irish family and with Ireland is strong. Perhaps someday I can be as determined as Ms. Farley Shuford has been and find the connections with my lost maternal ancestors in Counties Cork and Tipperary.

Ireland's history of family separation is indeed sad. But we can take comfort and pride in the fact that we have survived the calamities of the past, and with examples like Ms. Farley Shuford's, we can have faith and hope that if we keep looking, we can, eventually, find home.

—John Kearns,
author of *The World*, *Dreams and Dull Realities*, and *Worlds*, and dramas including *Boann and the Well of Wisdom* and *Sons of Molly Maguire*; past salon producer and treasurer of Irish American Writers and Artists, Inc.

Introduction

THIS IS A STORY about a disaster of epic proportion, injustice and intolerance, mass movements of people, governmental mismanagement, and hatred and divisiveness strong enough to tear apart a country. Somehow in the midst of it—in spite of it—ordinary people continued on, striving for a better life, a better world. I did not expect to finish telling this story during circumstances that echo so strongly the times in which it took place. It has seemed at times that nineteenth-century events were replicating themselves in my own twenty-first-century world.

As I write these final pages, the United States is struggling to emerge from the ravages of a pandemic that has cost the lives of hundreds of thousands of its people. On our southern border the number of people fleeing from physical and economic devastation elsewhere is surging. Our cities are receiving new refugees from war-torn countries and the effects of climate change. All this as our government is endeavoring to address the deep wrongs of past generations and to calm the roiling waters of political turmoil. Perhaps there's no better time to look at our own ancestors' lives to see what they can teach us.

It happened for me like this. At a family reunion I picked up an old photograph of an old man and asked a simple question: who was he? That question led me on a path—his path and mine, as it turned out—to another time, to another country, and back again. I'd like to tell you about it.

Prologue

ONCE I CAME OUT of the rain into a place so otherworldly that it still feels like a dream. It was a day at the end of a trip to Ireland. My husband and I had taken the ferry to the Aran Islands: three slivers of land—small, medium, and large—laid in the sea like stepping-stones off the Galway coast. After a forty-minute ride over rollicking waves, we stumbled off the boat onto Inis Mór, the largest of the islands. We handed our luggage to a man who would deliver it to our B&B later that evening, steadied our land legs, and stopped at a small restaurant for a cup of coffee. It was late afternoon.

No cars are allowed on the islands, save for a few small delivery vans. Bikes, horses and carts, and your two good feet are the modes of transportation. Right next to the dock is the bike rental stand. We perused the row of well-used bikes and chose two that mostly fit us, then set off on the circular island road for the cottage where we would spend the next three days. I'd booked it months before we left—a nineteenth-century traditional cottage well off the beaten path. The photos on the website were postcard perfect: whitewashed stone cottage, thatched roof, sea in the background, smoke from the chimney. It was a lovely day. We looked forward to a lazy ride along the narrow, meandering roads bordered by low stone walls, sheep grazing in the small grassy fields.

Rain can come up suddenly along the western coast, particularly on the offshore islands. We knew that as fact and were prepared, we thought, zipped up in our rain jackets. We tooled along, impressed by the myriad stone walls that crisscross the island, the ruins of an old abbey off to the side, a few cows sleeping in its shade. After pedaling a few peaceful miles, I felt some drops on my face. *This is part of the picture*, I thought. *It's Ireland, it's appropriate to have a little rain.* But soon, what started as a soft, romantic Irish mist changed mood without warning. We found ourselves battling a full-force gale, the rain pelting our faces. Seeing even a foot ahead became difficult. It was starting to get dark. No cottages in sight, no one else on the road. I yelled at Bob, "Did we take the right road?" but my words were lost in the wind. We had passed some crossroads—had we missed a turn? We were far from the village and now deep in what the Irish fittingly term "a lashing rain."

Our lightweight American jackets were no help; the rain had soaked through them. I couldn't lift my face. My eyes stung and my vision blurred, and the rain kept pelting down. The gears on my bike wouldn't work. It hurt just keeping my eyes open enough to stay on the road. No streetlights here: it was pitch black. I was desperate. How much farther? Were we lost? We must be lost. It felt as if this furious storm would never end.

And then, like a mirage, two faint lights shined through the hazy dark. Across a small inlet, the outline of a cottage began to appear. It was our B&B. I was never so glad to see shelter. A turf fire's incense floated up and out the chimney into the dark, rainy night.

We dismounted at the bottom of a low hill and walked our bikes up a stone path toward the door, as drenched as if we had emerged directly from the ocean just to our right. We could have been selkies, the seal-like creatures in Irish myths that become human when they reach the shore.

The red door was unlocked. We shook off our soaking jackets and entered, dripping rain onto the grey slate floor. I pushed the wet hair from my eyes to take in the scene: before us was an open fire, with a pot of hot tea and two cups placed beside a plate of biscuits on a small table in front of a couch. From the other room, unseen, I could hear a woman softly singing in Irish.

It crossed my mind that this might be what entering heaven would be like—the difficult transition from death to afterlife and then, all at once, the surprise of a simple, profound welcome.

From time to time, I think about that day. It holds a kind of comfort for me. It makes me wonder about the idea of home and welcome. It was a stranger's place, but it was home the minute we entered. If we're lucky in our time on Earth, we find moments or places like that. They may not be our actual place of origin, but they have for us a deep resonance. When we experience it, we know it for what it is because we're born searching for it.

PART ONE
Beginnings

Chapter One

Born at Home

I WAS BORN AT HOME in my parents' bedroom during a February blizzard, unusual for St. Louis. My mom, ever the efficient nurse, set out clean linens, towels, and hot water between contractions, making sure everything was ready before she lay down on the bed to give birth. A doctor friend of my dad's stood by in case of trouble. He wasn't needed, for no trouble ensued—It was an easy delivery.

Ordinary life happens amid extraordinary times. Most of us grow up oblivious to the state of the wider world we enter. But it still informs us, seeping into our being and carrying us along in its wake as history unfolds.

Far beyond the safety of our small house on our quiet street, as I took my first breath, the world was in tumult. It was winter 1945. Franklin Delano Roosevelt had been inaugurated only a month earlier, beginning his fourth term as president. Dresden was still burning from Allied bombings, and soon the battle of Iwo Jima would begin. Allied forces had liberated France and Belgium, and American forces would soon begin the liberation of the death camps in Nazi Germany. In two short months, FDR would die unexpectedly and Harry Truman would become the thirty-third president of the United States.

All of that was worlds away from the February snowstorm on the north side of St. Louis. The family story goes that my mom didn't want to go to the hospital—the war was on and the hospital was full, she said; there might not be enough beds. My sisters, my only siblings, were fifteen and nineteen. My mom hadn't had a baby for fifteen years. She was turning forty, a time when most women she knew were done having their children, and my dad, a doctor, was forty-seven: old enough to be my grandfather. Having a baby after all those years was unexpected for my mom, to say the least. I think she was embarrassed. It was a bit of a weird way to grow up—having parents who could have been your grandparents and sisters who seemed more like aunts. I once went shopping with my oldest sister, Mary, and the clerk referred to me as her daughter. My sister was not pleased.

My dad, second of five children, had grown up on a small family farm in Indianola, Iowa. While most of his siblings stayed in Iowa, he left for medical school after college. He had black hair, olive skin, and an Irish appreciation of the mysteries of life. He played violin, embracing music as language on a higher plane, and loved books about nature, poetry, and history. Above all, he cherished his family. His formality hid a quick sense of humor and ability to tell a good story.

My mom—red haired, green eyed, and the ninth of eleven children—was born in Litchfield, Illinois. Her family moved to St. Louis when she was still young, and she started nursing school as soon as she completed her schooling. Reserved, but appreciative of the human condition, she never knew a stranger. Since most of my mom's family lived in St. Louis, I had cousins nearby to play with. There was always room at the table at the Gerhardts'.

Part of the Greatest Generation, my parents valued character, humility, honesty, and family above all else. Their whole lives were dedicated to caring for others. And they were inseparable, a real team, deeply respectful of each other and as in love at eighty as they were at twenty. I think of them almost as a single unit. They worked together in my dad's medical office, where my mom—with her Germanic sensibility of keeping things in order and running smoothly—was the nurse and business manager. My dad began his practice long before managed care, and many of his patients lived in our neighborhood. It was a time of true family practice. When my dad ran into his patients on the street or somewhere in town, they would often stop him and ask, "Doc, I've been having this problem. What do you think?" He knew their lives and had his own sliding scale, sensitive to his patients' economic situations.

Arriving so late in the game, I didn't get to know my grandparents; all four had died before or soon after I was born. My sisters spent their childhood summers on my dad's family's farm in Iowa, but I missed that experience. I had an only child's fantasy about how great it would be to have a big brother to look out for me or a sibling close to my age to play with. There were definite advantages to this onliness, of course. My parents were more financially comfortable than they had been when my sisters were young and they were just starting out in practice. I didn't lack for material things or attention, even though my mom had gone back to work when I was very young. But I always felt a little disconnected, a little lost and unsure of where or whether I belonged. Where exactly did I fit in my family, in the world? Was I just a late-in-life surprise or mistake? I envied big families. I loved being at my girlfriend's house down the block, which overflowed with siblings of all ages. I loved the warm, chaotic messiness of her home, filled with noise and babies toddling around in diapers, bottles hanging out of their mouths. My house was quiet and tidy. It's not that I lacked a happy family or that I had a bad childhood. I knew my parents loved me, and I had everything I needed. But I always felt like an odd appendage to the family, never quite at home.

Children have a natural hunger for connection. It's the human condition. I don't think my feeling of being an outsider had as much to do with being born late in my parents' lives as it did with being the only child in a sort of second family, one that was generationally different from the first. When my mom went back to work, my parents hired a warm and loving woman who stayed with us during the week. Hilda was like a second mother. She lived on a farm west of St. Louis, and often I got to go home with her on weekends and for longer stays in the summer. I loved waking up early to farm sounds and smells. Out in the country I could run free, bang up my knees, and get my clothes dirty. At the farm I had small jobs. Even as a little kid, I could be useful: collector of eggs, washer of cantaloupes, feeder of pigs and chickens. Sometimes I got to be the farmer-helper girl, carrying iced tea or lemonade in an old graniteware pitcher and a basket of graham-cracker sandwiches with thick chocolate icing out to the men working in the field. I could climb high up in the hay-loft in the barn to look for newborn kittens, explore the woods that bordered the fields, or sit on the three-legged stool and milk a cow. I learned to drive a tractor at thirteen. I was an active part of the whole scene—not fussed over, just a small girl in the big outdoors. It felt like freedom, an alternative version of life, and I soaked it up. But I knew that eventually my parents' car would come up the long drive between the barn and the farmhouse to collect me, and I would go home to sleep in my bed in the little white brick house in the city of St. Louis, where the only livestock was my dog and the only field our backyard.

We lived in a homogenous working-class neighborhood on the north side of the city, where small brick bungalows and a few older two-story frame houses lined the streets. Any diversity came from European country of origin: there were no people of color in my neighborhood. Most of the families my dad cared for were second- or third-generation Italian, German, or Irish. He knew their world, their extended families, their joys and troubles. He could speak openly to them about their smoking habits or if they were drinking too much. He was someone to talk to if there was trouble in the family. His first office was a little red-brick storefront that opened right onto the side-walk; inside was a small waiting room he shared with the dentist next door. My dad's treatment room was off to the right, and behind that was a small storage and X-ray room. Our house was an extension of his office; at home the phone could ring at any time, day or night, and my dad would leave to see a patient. When it rang, I learned to answer "Dr. Farley's residence" and never just "Hello." He was an ENT spe-cialist, but primarily a family doctor who did everything, from emer-gency house calls to eye surgery at the hospital. Doctoring for him was a 24/7 profession. He had opened his practice in the Depression, a challenging time to start anything. My sisters remembered times when they were little, when people brought food to the house for payment, baskets of potatoes or tomatoes, and once, left on our back steps, a beautiful yellow lone star quilt.

There was an unspoken question about why I was such a latecomer. I mean, really, why have a baby a full fifteen years after your last child? Many years later, when my mom was in her nineties, I asked her, knowing that people are sometimes less guarded as they get older. She didn't blink as she told me that they wanted to try once more for a boy. Whoops. That didn't work out, but it rang true. They'd only had a boy's name picked out. And my parents gave me room to be a tomboy, climbing trees and playing pickup games of baseball in our backyard. I had my own glove and my own basketball and hoop up on our garage. They made the best of it without ever making me feel that I was a disappointment.

The summer when I was ten, my dad pulled off an amazing feat. He found a way to take our whole family to Europe for two weeks. There were eight of us: my sisters and their husbands, my parents, me, and Hilda. My memories of those two weeks are the memories of a child; I can't tell you what museums or cathedrals we saw. I have a few blurry memories of buses and trains, hotel rooms, and walking, walking, walking. Was the whole experience lost on me? Not quite.

The trip ended with several days in Ireland. My dad had always wanted to see the country. We're Farleys, after all, and Ireland is the homeland, even though back then we didn't know exactly where in the country we originated. We spent some days in Dublin and then took the train to County Kerry, on the west coast. After a couple of days in Killarney we would board a plane home from the Shannon airport. The adults spent time in the village shops, and we all watched a group of Irish dancers—young girls my age—and saw a castle and some gardens. But the tour de force for me was a long horseback ride through the Gap of Dunloe, a narrow, breathtaking mountain pass that slices through the Purple Mountains and Macgillycuddy's Reeks, the highest mountain range in Ireland. Put a ten-year-old girl on a horse and all bets are off.

This one day stands out in my mind, sharply in focus. I can close my eyes and bring back the creak of the saddle, the smell of my horse and the warmth of his shoulder, the constant mist on my face, the light and shadows playing on the hills, the brilliant blue of the lakes coming into view as we rounded the mountain path. It was exhilarating. The mix of fresh air and burning turf and the small white cottages and green hills flecked with sheep and stones were mystical. Eventually we reached a large lake. We tied up the horses and in small groups got into rowboats that took us across the three lakes of Killarney: upper, middle, and lower. Weathered and muscled Irishmen in caps, their sleeves rolled up above their elbows and cigarettes hanging out of their mouths, told stories as they pulled at the oars until we reached the opposite shore. And then, suddenly, it was over. But not in my mind. I'd fallen in love with the place.

CHAPTER TWO

Iowa, 1964

FAST-FORWARD TO ANOTHER SUMMER. I was nineteen. Ireland, the Gap of Dunloe, and that sense of freedom and exhilaration were a faded memory.

It was a hot, dry July day in Iowa. The still air carried the faint sound of bees hovering over hydrangea bushes, the giant white blooms like summer snowballs. We were at my aunt and uncle's white clapboard house in the small town of Indianola for a family reunion. Aunts and uncles filled the living room, talking, laughing. The creak of a wooden rocker and the whir of an old fan created a constant drone under the conversation. Younger cousins played in the yard, the older ones chatting on the steps or leaning on a car parked in the driveway beside the house. The back screen door slammed and slammed again. Someone brought out a pitcher of lemonade and paper cups and placed them on the front steps where I was sitting. Through the window I could pick up snippets of conversation, the adults laughing and telling stories: "Do you remember . . ." and "When did . . ."

I poured a cup of ice-cold lemonade and swallowed it down in one gulp. It was getting uncomfortably hot on the concrete steps, so I went inside. Immediately the air changed. My eyes took a minute to adjust from the bright sunshine to the cool, dark living room. Over on a long table by the window was a collection of family memorabilia: letters, photo albums, a book of poetry, and a pair of moccasins. Not ready to join in the conversation with my parents, aunts, and uncles,

I perused the family treasures and artifacts. I slid my hand inside one of my grandfather's old leather moccasins. My cousin Erik said you could feel the imprint of his feet inside them, find where each toe fit. Our grandfather said the moccasins had been a gift from an Indian friend—possibly Santee Sioux or Oglala Lakota—back when he was a teenager working as a cowboy in Nebraska. They were his everyday slippers, and he wore them all his adult life.

I never knew my grandfather, George Thomas Farley, or G. T., as he was called. I never got to ask him about this part of his life, which seemed so exciting to me and my cousins. I put the moccasin down and moved along the table to a book of poems that he had written and a stack of photo albums of people gathered at earlier reunions, some familiar and some not. And then I stopped. Off toward the back of the table, a small black-and-white photograph in a simple frame caught my eye. I reached over and picked it up.

It was a rather formal photograph of an old man. He was seated in a Morris chair with a big book open on his lap, his hand resting on one of the pages. *Who is he? What's the book?* I wondered. The text on the page was blurry below what looked like pictures of trees or plants. He was handsomely dressed in a three-piece suit over a striped shirt, with flyaway white hair and a neatly trimmed beard. He looked sort of stern, but I saw no anger or sadness in his face. He seemed to be looking right at me with his piercing eyes—asking? inviting? I was mesmerized by his eyes.

I brought the picture over to my aunt Ruth and asked her who it was. "That's Patrick Farley, your Irish great-grandfather—your dad's grandfather. Haven't you seen this picture before?" No. I'd never seen it. I held on to the photograph for a while, searching his face, looking back at those eyes. One of his eyelids drooped a little, just like mine. I put it back on the table, intrigued. Who was this guy?

The next morning, before we drove back to St. Louis, I asked Aunt Ruth if she had any copies of the photograph of Patrick. She did and was happy to give me one. "I'm afraid this is the only picture we have of him," she said. "You know, he fought in the Civil War!"

PATRICK FARRELLY (FARLEY), COLUMBUS, NEBRASKA

That following September, when I returned to college, I tucked the photo in my suitcase pocket. The weather was unusually warm, the sky a sunny haze over central Illinois, and the leaves on the trees hadn't begun to turn. The day after I got back, I walked to the bookstore and bought a big piece of canvas and framing wood. I was an applied-art major focused on drawing and painting. The campus was still pretty quiet; classes hadn't begun and the painting studio was empty. I unrolled the canvas, stretched it over the frame, stapled it tight, and spread on white gesso to prepare the surface for paint. It was nice to have the room to myself. I carefully tacked Patrick's photo at the top of the easel, then stood back and looked him in the eye. I opened my paint box and chose the palette: muted browns, greens and grey, maybe a little blue somewhere. The photo was black and white, I had to imagine the colors.

I laughed. I had no idea why I was doing this. An old, white-haired man wasn't the type of thing I typically drew or painted. But there he was, and here I was—as if we had an appointment. When the gesso was dry, I roughed out his head and suit, his face, the folds of his sleeve on the armrest. My eye and pencil followed down his arm and along his knotted fingers to the blurred pages of the book whose words I couldn't read. I liked working on this, trying to get it right, trans-porting this guy, this mystery ancestor, right here onto my canvas, larger than life. I liked having him around. For the next few days, I'd wake up and think about it, how I would work on it that day. We'd begun to have a relationship.

The fact was, at this point he was just an interesting-looking old man in a photo. I asked my dad a few questions, and he told me that his grandfather Patrick was eighty-five when he died in 1921, so judging from appearance, the photograph must have been taken not that many years before. Age is hard to tell in old photos. But someone clearly wanted his picture to keep. He's so carefully dressed and posed. Why did he feel it was important to have that book on his lap in the photograph? Maybe he felt it defined him in some way—or maybe it was just the photographer's idea. Maybe he often sat around with a book in his lap. I realized I knew almost nothing about him. I hadn't known any of my grandparents; my knowledge of the people on my family tree stopped after my parents. No deep roots. I'd missed the family history lessons and the sense of connection, of belonging, that I might have gotten from grandparents.

So I asked my dad for a little more information. His full name was Patrick Farrelly (the spelling was different from ours), and he came to America from Ireland because of the potato famine, and he fought in the Civil War. He was my father's own grandfather, but my dad didn't seem to know him very well either. Growing up in another town in another state, he had only met his grandfather once, when he was ten. I thought it was strange that I hadn't heard about him before. Maybe it was just too long ago. Maybe if I'd known my grandparents, I might have asked them about their parents. I suddenly felt like I had missed this whole world of people and relationships and experiences, and now they were dead and that door to their world had closed.

I worked on the painting over several weeks. It was a decent enough endeavor—more personal and representational than most of what I drew or painted. I brought the painting home with me at the end of the semester, and my parents had it framed and hung in our downstairs family room above the fireplace.

And that was that—or so it seemed. My days in college and after were a time of awakening to the antiwar movement, to women's rights, to racial injustice. Life went roaring on through the turbulent sixties and seventies, and at times my own life was a rough ride on choppy seas. Less than three short years after graduation I found myself a divorced single mom with a two-year-old daughter. But Becky brought the sunshine every day as we began a new life with just the two of us. I found an apartment, a good caregiver for her, and a job for me. While working full-time and trying to be the best mom I could under the circumstances, I entered grad school, taking courses in the evenings and on weekends.

One weekend my across-the-hall neighbor hounded me to go to a party so I could meet her fiancé's brother. I didn't want to go. I had put together a nice life for Becky and myself, and I had no interest in meeting anyone's brother, thank you very much. But she was persistent, and I finally relented when she said she'd find me a babysitter. So I dug out a dress, brushed some dry shampoo on my hair, and got myself to the house where said party was happening. To my chagrin, I found this brother guy, Bob, to be interesting, attractive, and funny—someone I wanted to get to know. He was finishing up a doctoral program at Northwestern. He asked me out, and he wasn't put off by my being a single mom. In fact, the first time he met her, he fell in love with Becky. Bob became my truest and best friend, and less than a year after that unwanted party we got married.

We set out on life's adventure together, adding three more children to our family: Gabe, Jessica, and James. Each one brought more joy to life. Our little house stretched to hold our family of six and all the laughing, crying, fighting, hugging, singing, playing piano and baseball, skating and dancing, reading and drawing, building Legos and ideas, and mostly growing up way too fast. When I think back to those early years now, I realize it was not unlike my friend's house down the street growing up, where I liked to hang out amid the happy chaos and the evident love. Looking back, through all the good times, the hard times, the kids growing up, job changes, moves, and even a bout with breast cancer, I found some hidden source of strength and resilience when I needed it.

I also managed to hang on to Patrick's photograph. I uncovered him one day as I was rearranging storage in the basement. Wondering what might be hidden in a box labeled *old photos*, I pulled it off the shelf, blew off the dust, and opened it. There he was after all this time. It seemed to me that anything worth keeping shouldn't be hidden away, so I took his photograph to a nearby art store and found a simple black frame like the one I'd seen back at Aunt Ruth's. My parents had both died by this time, so along with photographs of them, I corralled pictures of a few ancestors that I'd never known in life and got them all together on the wall—a little family reunion in two dimensions.

Maybe it was walking past them and making eye contact with Patrick every day that made me pay more attention to that piercing look.

Sometimes I think that buried questions are like dormant plants that sleep until they have light and water and warmth enough to awaken. That question I had asked so many years earlier at Aunt Ruth's, "Who is this guy?," emerged from hibernation and demanded an answer.

Part of the answer came on another trip to Iowa, this time with Bob and our children in tow.

CHAPTER THREE

Iowa, 1988

IT WAS SUMMER and we were at the front end of the Family Trip West. It was a classic comic-strip scene: the packed-to-the-roof burgundy Plymouth Voyager minivan, a mom and dad and stair-stepped kids, suitcases, juice boxes, cookies, and a million childhood accoutrements. We were heading out to see the wonders of the American West.

The plan was to make our first stop in Indianola, Iowa, for a visit with Aunt Ruth, now older, widowed, and living by herself in the same little house that had held all the summertime Farley reunions. We took her to lunch at the local diner, brought her up to date on the kids, and chatted a little about the family. My dad had died six years earlier, at almost the same age Patrick had been when he died. Ruth was my dad's younger sister, and they had been close. It was good to be with her—hearing her voice and her laugh was a little like being with my dad again. We went back to her house after a good, unhurried meal. Before we left for our hotel for the night, she said, "I've been meaning to ask you: do you have copies of the letters?"

"What letters?"

"Patrick's letters. Your folks surely had them."

No, I didn't have copies of his letters, and yes, I would love to have them! I hadn't even known they existed. Ruth went upstairs and brought down a folder of pages of typed letters. She had the originals, handwritten, faded and getting hard to read. A former librarian, she had carefully transcribed, typed, and mimeographed them.

In addition to the letters, she also put together a family tree. It was lopsided: the maternal side of our family had lots of branches, but the paternal stopped with Patrick. Ruth had given each of her siblings copies of the letters, and now, with a smile, she handed them over to me, tucked in a manila envelope, saying, "I know you like history. I think you'll be interested in these."

There were ten letters. Patrick had written nine of them from his home in Columbus, Nebraska, to his oldest child, Mary, after she had moved back to New Haven, Connecticut, around 1890 as a young woman. The tenth letter was written to Mary by her younger brother, my grandfather George. I had the clear sense that I was being handed more than the envelope. Ruth was passing the family history baton.

We checked out of the hotel in the morning. The kids were still sleepy and content to look out the window. As Bob drove, I opened the envelope and took a quick peek at the contents. Here were the words of someone who'd lived a hundred years ago, but not someone in a history book. This was my guy, Patrick—still a mystery, but my own flesh and blood. The letters were a fascinating glimpse into the experience of the westward movement. They mentioned blizzards, drought, grasshoppers, Native Americans, militias. Lions and tigers and bears, oh my! I was excited to share them with the kids. It would be like reading our own *Little House on the Prairie*, perfect timing as we headed west toward South Dakota.

I skimmed through them and picked out parts that might interest the kids while we drove west on I-80. In the first one I read, dated January 1891, my grandfather told Mary, "I suppose you have heard about the Indians. There is some excitement in South Dakota and at Northwestern Nebraska. I think the report is 1600 warriors on the warpath. The Militia (State) have been called out. There have been some 300 or 400 Soldiers killed and maybe as many Indians." (Much later, when we were back home, I looked up that date and realized that my grandfather was referring to what we now know as the massacre of the Lakota at Wounded Knee. I shuddered.)

I read from another, dated August 1894, when Patrick wrote to Mary, "There will be I fear much suffering this winter out here on account of the drouth. Everything is dried up, no corn, no hay, no potatoes. The whole surface of the ground hot and dry as ashes. People are going through here every day with their teams and all they possess, after fighting the drouth for several years without success. The oldest settlers say they never seen anything like it. The grasshopper time was a plentiful time compared with the present."

The kids were impressed that someone in our family had lived through the same events as Laura Ingalls Wilder. I told them to try to imagine those scenes as we drove along the highway from Iowa to Nebraska to South Dakota, on our way to Yellowstone National Park in Wyoming and eventually to the Pacific coast. I wanted them to know that this territory was steeped in family history.

The ten surviving letters span a time period from November 1890 to March 1912. Aunt Ruth had explained that when Patrick and his wife came to the United States after their marriage, they settled first in New Haven, Connecticut, but the family moved west in 1878 to Nebraska. When Mary died, someone had found the letters and sent them back to George, and when he died they went to Ruth. I wondered why Mary had moved back to New Haven. She must have written back to answer his questions, to talk about her life and ask about her siblings, and there must have been more letters—what happened to the rest? Were they read and discarded? Did someone decide what was kept and what was not?

It seemed to me that Mary—the oldest child, the only one who moved back east—would have kept all the letters from her family. Those missives were all she had of them. Nebraska was over a thousand miles away, and travel was expensive and difficult. No one seemed to know of any other letters from Mary's other siblings—just that one from her brother. And there were these gaps in time. The letters stop nine years before Patrick died. What happened to the others?

As I read, Patrick began to come alive. He was no longer just a two-dimensional person in a photograph. When you read a letter, you can hear something in that interior voice, something unique and personal. The limits of time and place fall away. A handwritten letter communicates so much more than email or text, or even phone calls.

Taking the time to write a letter leads the writer to a more reflective perspective, and as it's read, the handwriting brings to mind the person. Reading old letters is like stepping into the writer's mind. It's a lost art today. I was glad that I'd had the sense to save a few letters from my dad and mom.

Ruth told me that when Patrick got older, he moved in with his youngest child, Lizzie, and her family in their house in Columbus. It's possible that any letters he had saved were thrown out after he died or when his house was sold. I had only half of a conversation, and I desperately wanted to hear the other side. Especially, I wanted to know what Mary had asked him that gave rise to this response in a letter dated December 28, 1891:

> Now in relation to my luck in this world. It might be better and it might be worse. When young, my ambition was to see the world and I have succeeded pretty well from all I have seen and learned, in every way I am satisfied with the path that fate marked out for me. It might have been more smooth but it was not too rough to conquer me. If I met with adversity Heaven gave me hope to stand it. Prosperity does not try anybody. It takes adversity to do it. Notwithstanding that my path was a little rough betimes, it was not so bad as it was for thousands who were probably more deserving.

Now I wanted to know more about this path—his path—the one that "fate marked out for me."

My own world had been so easy, so comfortable, in comparison. My parents weren't wealthy by any stretch, but I'd never had to worry about basic survival or, for that matter, fear or loss or prejudice of any kind. We always had enough to eat, we had a warm house, and my parents had dependable work. I knew I would go to college. I had what I needed, but not everything I wanted. I wasn't a spoiled child, but I lived with the assumption that life would be good to me. My parents' own childhoods and values had created a good balance about material things. Unlike Patrick, I met with little adversity.

In my twenties I experienced self-inflicted hard times and their consequences, but none of that was the result of my immigration status, religion, name, or skin color. I never worried about being arrested or deported or denied a job because of how I looked or where I was born. In high school and college, like many in my generation, I had pushed against my white, middle-class life, which kept me safe and, as I perceived it, isolated from the real world. I felt a mix of guilt over my family's privilege—a word that I wouldn't have used or understood back then—and an acute sense of the injustice of racism and poverty. It was the height of the civil rights movement, and as I watched it unfold on TV in the spring of my senior year in high school, I was repulsed by the violence against the marchers in Birmingham. I still remember how I felt watching the news, seeing the police dogs straining at the leash, their mouths open and snarling, threatening the marchers as I sat with my hand on my own beloved dog curled up beside me. I hung on the words of Martin Luther King Jr. and Robert F. Kennedy and felt devastated by their assassinations. I embraced the antiwar movement and celebrated the first Earth Day. In those intense days of the sixties and seventies, I wrestled with how I could truly be part of the human family when I had had it so easy. Now I wondered if Patrick's path, the one that "might have been more smooth," had something to teach me. Famine, emigration, and a bloody civil war made a pretty rough road for him, it seemed to me. I don't know how I would have survived it. Maybe that's why he was so intriguing, why I had hung on to his photograph.

PART TWO

Ireland

Chapter Four

Transatlantic

4:00 A.M. *Somewhere over the Atlantic Ocean.*

I've been trying unsuccessfully to sleep for the last few hours, stiff neck, achy legs, that nauseous all-nighter feeling. The plane's interior lights are off—just the small reflectors along the aisle and a few glowing iPads. I'm watching the tiny airplane on the screen move slowly toward Europe. It's still in the dark shadow, but not for long. I gingerly raise the window shade a few inches, trying not to wake my seatmate. Outside my window the silver wing stretches out, and through the nook between body and wing, I look down into the night sky. Tiny dots of light shine below on a peninsula that juts out into the ocean. Before me is a darkened stage. And then the night curtain begins to rise.

Each time the plane approaches Ireland, the sudden emergence of land still surprises me, as if the ocean and the night would go on forever. Far below, rivers, roads, new developments skirting old villages, lakes, mountains, and the ubiquitous stone walls—all are quiet, sleeping. Now coming slowly into focus, growing larger, more real. Then, as if on cue, the sun emerges, pink and golden.

It's a startling thing to leave one world and emerge in another in the breadth of seven hours. Wheels down, disembark, and then the long walk from the plane, the wait in line to get the passport stamped, keeping watch for baggage rolling off the carousel, and finally, the first step out the airport doors. From the first breath outside I know I'm somewhere else. The light and air are different, fresh, new. This is my world now for a while. I inhale deeply, breathe it all in.

I wait in line for the bus to Dublin's city center, still foggy from the jet lag but excited. It's not quite six in the morning. Out the windows of the Aircoach, I see the city begin its day, and I begin my pilgrimage in the midst of it.

This is the part I like best, the moment of arrival with all possibilities before me. The challenge of getting from one place to another, finding my way by foot or bus or car, excited for an adventure. The surprise of waking up the next morning, transported. The freedom of it.

I've made this trip many times in the last twenty years, sometimes for the university where I work, but more often for myself. Sometimes alone, sometimes with my husband. There are many ways to approach travel, one can be a tourist who visits a range of places in the world or a pilgrim who returns to the same place, each time going deeper. Most of my travel has been of the pilgrim sort to the country of my family of origin, looking for Patrick's path. As often as I've done it, it always feels new.

My first trip to Ireland as an adult was a celebration of Bob's and my twenty-fifth anniversary. It was going to be our once-in-a-lifetime trip. We had saved our money and vacation days and planned for months, wanting to take in as much of the country as we could. A few weeks before we left, I ran into an Irish transplant in Chicago who asked how long we were going to be in Ireland. "Three weeks," I answered. She smiled and replied, "Ah, you'll not want to come home." She was prophetic.

Travel guides can't do the country justice. All their beautiful photographs can't explain the way the air feels after a morning rain, the smell of the earth, the way turf smoke and music wind around each other in an old pub, the way streams fall down the mountainsides like silver tears, the way the small, meandering country roads force you to slow down, to really see. Nor can they come close to describing the Irish themselves. The country has its issues, as every country does, but there is a basic humanity, a concern for others, and lack of pretense that make it easy to feel welcome. I fell in love with the place all over again.

We wanted to see as much of the country as our time would allow, and our carefully planned itinerary promised to do that, but I also wanted to find out whatever I could about my family before they emigrated. A month or so before we left home, I had contacted a genealogist who worked at the National Library of Ireland and sent her the facts that I had. Helen agreed to meet us. The day after Bob and I landed in Dublin, the three of us met for breakfast at a little café across from the library. As we talked, I tried to flesh out the basics of Patrick's story, a common one for famine emigrants who landed on the shores of North America. I realized I was reciting what she had probably heard a million times. I was just one more American, Canadian, Australian coming to the National Library with a name— or, with luck, perhaps a county or better yet a village or parish. All of us wanting answers, wanting connection, wanting our history. Without someone's help, there's a high strikeout rate.

I knew the name of Patrick's parish, Lurgan, because he had listed it as his birthplace rather than just writing *Ireland* on his US Army pension records from his service in the Civil War. Location, location, location. It's as important in family history as it is in real estate. I had access to that information thanks to Aunt Ruth's research years before. But I was about to learn how much I didn't know.

"I want to find the place he came from, where his family lived," I told her.

Helen said she would help us. "But don't be satisfied as so many are, with just names and dates on paper," she said. "When you drive out there, get out of the car and walk along the country roads they walked." Her voice softened. "I really believe that for those souls who left in such desperation"—she paused—"that when their descendants, like yourself, return and walk those same roads, they can finally be at peace." I had not thought of the spirits of my ancestors hanging around somewhere, waiting for me to show up. But her words struck something deep.

The next morning, we took a taxi back to the airport, picked up our rental car, and headed west toward County Cavan. I navigated while Bob adjusted to driving on the other side of the road and shifting with his left hand. We had no GPS on that first trip in 1998, just the map that came with the rental. Eventually we managed to find our B&B in a village not far from the area where Patrick's family had lived. County Cavan is part of the rural Irish Midlands, not often visited by tourists who don't have a connection there. The tour buses hug the coasts of Ireland, where the most spectacular scenery is found. But the counties in the middle of the country have a peaceful, quiet beauty that is not unlike parts of the American Midwest: fields in shades of green and brown, winding roads, stone walls, rolling hills, and lots of lakes. It's an area good for fishing, for growing crops and raising cattle. It's out in the Midlands that you can get a feel for Irish rural life.

After a good night's sleep and a full Irish breakfast of eggs, rashers, toast, and coffee, we headed out to the countryside. Our B&B hosts, the O'Reillys, had suggested we might want to stop by an old abbey in the parish where Patrick was born. They gave us directions, and after a couple of wrong turns we saw the first landmark, the small white church of St. Patrick that they had told us to look for. We took the turnoff just beyond it and continued down the narrow road until we saw the ancient abbey ruins on our right.

Enclosed by a stone wall on a small hill, the abbey sat alone in the surrounding fields. It was early May, the air was fresh, and flowers and trees were just beginning to bloom. The fields were a million shades of green, and in the distance we could see scattered trees heavy with white blossoms. We pulled the car off the road, climbed over the stone stile, and entered the abbey's cemetery. There was not much left of the abbey itself, just a few ruins surrounded by gravestones.

As Bob and I gingerly walked around this ancient cemetery we looked for gravestones bearing my last name, Farley, but spelled the Irish way, Farrelly or O'Farrelly. I had a jump start on my research: I knew the name and location of Patrick's parish, and several years earlier, my uncle had discovered the names of his parents and siblings. When I told our hosts that I was looking for the family of my great-grandfather, Patrick Farley, Mr. O'Reilly said with a sigh, "Ah, the place is pickled with Farrellys." And, for good measure, the given name of Patrick was hardly a help in the land of the patron saint.

The abbey was established sometime in the twelfth century as an offshoot or subsidiary of the Abbey of Kells, the origin of the famous Book of Kells. The monks at Lurgan had built a small church and a dormitory-like residence and worked the lands that surrounded them. I tried to imagine them in their coarse robes, gathering wheat in these fields, extracting honey from beehives, maybe tending to a few cows or sheep. But this abbey, and so many others like it, was destroyed in the 1590s by soldiers of Henry VIII in his attempt to dissolve the monasteries and root out Catholicism in Ireland and England. Many of the stones from this little church had been carted away to build the Protestant church in the nearby village, and the abbey lay in ruin. What was left was nearly buried in the weeds. Only a small arched wall of the church remained, with a tiny window still open to the light. My feet sank into the uneven ground as we explored. No one had cut the grass; gravestones were slanted and sinking in the earth. I made out some of the dates on them, many from the 1700s, with names common in the area: Farrelly, Reilly, Brady, Clark, Sheridan, Smyth. The grass was high and damp, and I could feel the squishy mud seeping into my boots. But seeping into my brain was the fact that I knew so little of this country. What is it that good detectives say? You have to put aside all your expectations before you can see the reality of a situation. It was dawning on me that none of these grave markers could have been erected by a tenant family living in a one-room mud or stone cottage. Patrick's family were small tenant farmers. These stones had been purchased and placed by families of means or, in several cases, erected on behalf of the deceased's emigrant descendants. Lesson #1: Poor tenant farmers and laborers from the nineteenth century do not have carved stones to mark their graves. They were lucky if their cottage walls were stone rather than mud and thatch. I had a lot to learn.

I stopped trying to read the gravestones and looked out beyond the enclosure walls. We had an almost 360-degree view of the countryside. It was all so green and quiet and peaceful. We were the only people around. There were no other cars on the road, no other houses within sight. On the slight breeze I caught the scent of the junipers and cedars that surrounded the cemetery. A single bird sang. The air felt soaked through with the past.

Breaking my reverie, Bob suggested we might learn something from the local priest. We climbed back over the wall, knocked the mud from our shoes, and drove back up the road. At the main cross-road, a couple of teenage boys were practicing with hurley sticks outside their house. We stopped and asked where we could find the parish priest. They caught our American accent.

"It's Father O'Dowd you're looking for," said one.

His friend or brother interrupted, "No, send 'em to Father Tom. The rectory is just up the road there in Virginia. Across from the old mill. Father Tom'll help you out."

The parish rectory was an aging, grey, two-story building at the end of the main street of the village of Virginia—not to be confused with the American Virginia, although both were inspired by the same person, Elizabeth I, the "virgin queen." This Virginia was one of many towns built in the seventeenth century by the British, to encourage settlement by British citizens who had been given land confiscated from the Irish. Called plantation towns, they all have a similar look: carefully laid out with a wide main street and the Protestant church as the focal point of the town. In Virginia, the Catholic church and rectory were situated at the end of the street, across from the old mill, just as the boys had said.

We walked up the steps to the rectory door and were about to knock when a short, athletic-looking man with light brown hair walked up behind us and invited us in. It was Father Tom. I made a mental note of the providential timing. Inside, the rectory living room was comfortably worn and unassuming, a couple of unmatched stuffed chairs on either side of a small fireplace, a faded red couch in front of the window. A Gaelic-football trophy held pride of place on the mantel, a cross hung on the wall.

The hurley boys were right. Father Tom would help us out. Over tea and biscuits, I explained who we were and what we were trying to find. These priests must hear these stories all the time, the returned

American looking for their roots. I wondered if they ever get tired of it or if they're glad we've come back. Father Tom seemed genuinely glad to see us, glad that we cared enough about our people, our ancestors, to ask questions. We agreed on a time to meet the next day.

At 10:30 the next morning we drove up to the rectory to meet with Father Tom, who suggested we ride out in his car to see what we could find. We offered to drive, but he wisely suggested that the roads weren't great and the rental car might suffer. We took off, leaving the village behind and heading into the countryside, into the old Ireland.

We were getting better acquainted with the country and by now I had learned a few things. People here never ask "What do you do?," which would be considered rude. Instead, they ask "Where are you from?" or "What is your name?" If you're Irish, the answer to those questions delivers the most important information.

To understand the country, it's important to understand the land. The island nation is divided into 4 provinces, 32 counties, and at last count, 61,098 townlands. Townlands are the smallest Irish unit of land division but the most important in understanding history as it was and is lived in the life of a community. The townland division has its origins in the old Gaelic order, going back to the Iron Age. Most townland names are in the Irish language or a kind of bastardized Anglo-Irish. Their names may reflect a geographic marker, a simple description of the area, or an ancient story sometimes remembered, sometimes lost in time.

A parish is composed of many townlands. Each one might include as few as six families or many more. The townland is comparable to a neighborhood; it's the place you are from. More than that, it represents family, almost clan. Townlands function like mini zip codes full of deep history. In rural areas or small villages, townland residents know who lives in which house and who lived there before them, who emigrated, who stayed, and who they married, when they died, where they're buried, and where the vanished cottages once stood. They know the history of the place, the seemingly small details that tell the story of the community. Marriages often happened between residents of neighboring or nearby townlands. Place was so important to an

Irish emigrant's identity that in some American cemeteries, the older gravestones identify not only the person's name and dates of birth and death, but also the county, parish, and townland where they originally came from.

We were in the country of Ireland, in the province of Ulster, the county of Cavan, the Catholic parish of Lurgan, and we were looking for the townland of *Curraghmore*. That was where my great-grandfather was born and baptized—his place of origin—and where my paternal roots lay deep in the soil.

We left the main road and entered a thinly populated area. Small rolling hills called drumlins predominate the topography; we saw lots of hedges but few trees. The land here is rough, good for sheep but not easily tillable, and poor by most agricultural standards. Translated to English, Curraghmore means "the big marsh," which tells you what you need to know.

THE BRIDGE TO CURRAGHMORE, LURGAN PARISH, CAVAN, IRELAND

Father Tom's old red Renault bounced along the rutted single lanes of the back roads. The three of us were now in "the back of beyond," as locals say. We passed no cars or houses until finally we stopped by an old, two-story, grey stone house belonging to Phil Reilly. After a knock on the door, a thin elderly man in a sweater with more holes than thread answered. Father Tom greeted Phil and asked if he knew of any Farrellys around here. No luck: "There was a Matt Farrelly," he said, "but they've all gone now." He didn't know of any left. We struck out.

Back in the car, Father Tom mentioned that there was a holy well around here somewhere, but he was not sure where. The roads were narrow, and overgrown hedges swiped at the car doors on both sides. After a while, a tractor came into view and stopped in front of us. A very short red-haired farmer hopped off, and Father Tom whispered that this was "wee Benny Farrelly." Wee indeed, but no relation that we could ascertain.

"Benny, these folks are from America, and they're looking for their family's place in Curraghmore. Isn't there a holy well around here somewhere? St. Patrick's well, is it?" Holy wells abound in Ireland. Each has an ancient history originating in pre-Christian times, holding a curative power for various ailments in addition to being a source of clean water. They now carry saints' names, often the patron saint of the area. They tend to be in out-of-the-way places still visited by locals.

"I'm going there myself now," said wee Benny. "Got a sick cow. Turn the car around and follow me."

We managed to turn the car, which was no small accomplishment, and followed Benny's tractor across a narrow crossing and down an even narrower road. When the tractor stopped, we parked, got out, and walked back to what looked like more hedgerows and a low stone wall. There was a small opening in the wall, and from that we followed four stepstones leading down toward an open well in the ground. It was not visible from the road. A small corrugated-metal roof placed on top of a low, circular wall of stones covered most of the opening. Trees cast heavy shade around it, and it took a few seconds for my eyes to adjust. A shallow stream flowed nearby, the water singing as it ran along the bed of rocky soil under a canopy of trees. Off to our left was a narrow stone bridge that led to Curraghmore.

"We may not find the cottage where your people lived," said Father Tom, "but you can know that they came here to this well many, many times, perhaps every day."

I bent down, dipped my hand into the water, cupped it, and took a drink. It was surprisingly cold. I felt the cool, clear water run down my throat. It was a seminal moment. I was aware that I was standing on ground where my great-grandfather Patrick—the guy I'd only known from a photograph—and his parents and their parents had stood, going back hundreds of years, drinking from a source that had once eased their thirst. This well, Toberpatrick, became a baptismal font, my entry to the past.

Chapter Five

History Lesson

WHEN WE CAME HOME from that first trip, after I dipped my hand into the well, I set out on my own independent study of Irish history. If I was going to follow Patrick's path, I needed to learn much more about his country and its history; I needed to know the backdrop of his life.

I love history. I've always felt a need to know the history of any place I lived, apartment, house, or town. When was it built? What did the first inhabitants see when they looked out the same window I was looking out? I want to know who and what came before, what they lived through, what their hopes and fears were. I think about the people who built our little house in Illinois 140 years ago. They kept a horse in a stable out back, where our garage now stands. Bits from a bridle emerged when we turned over the soil for a garden shortly after we moved in. When our house was built it had no electricity, no running water. I imagine those early residents waking up on cold mornings and cracking the ice in the basin to wash their faces. I wonder what they thought the first time they saw a car go down the street, how amazed they must have been when they could turn on a light with a switch, how they felt when the world wars ended.

Now I wanted to know why Patrick had left his homeland when he did. On our first visit, I was so awed by the beauty of the land that I asked a man how people could leave it. He said simply, "You can't eat beautiful."

I knew that Ireland had a long and tortured relationship with England. When Patrick was born, Ireland was tightly controlled by the British government, as it had been for hundreds of years. He left in the last year of the Great Famine. But how could it happen that a small country, ruled by a mighty empire just across the Irish Sea, lost nearly half its population in the span of five or six years? How was it allowed to happen?

What I knew at the time of our first trip was basic travel-guide history, but soon I saw that learning about the so-called potato famine wasn't a simple matter. That common term for the catastrophic period of 1845 to 1852 is misleading. *The Great Hunger* (*An Gorta Mor*) is the accurate title. A true famine indicates a total absence of food, and there was no shortage of food in Ireland at the time. But there was an extreme shortage of potatoes. So why did people starve? Why did they flee their homeland?

I quickly learned that I couldn't understand Irish history without learning something about English history. The two countries have a fraught symbiotic relationship that they can't seem to resolve even now, as the Brexit decision has made clear. It would be like trying to understand the United States without learning about slavery and the Civil War.

The event that drove Patrick and two million others to emigrate to North America was the result of centuries-long power struggles, invasions, and conquest. This small island—the size of the state of Indiana—was invaded for centuries. Vikings, Normans, and the British Crown have all taken their turn at dominating the land. Ireland was England's first colony.

When Patrick was born in 1836, his homeland had been colonized for over two hundred years, built on what was essentially a feudal economy. The conquest of Ireland began in earnest under Henry VIII in the 1500s. Henry, deeply in debt, not only lopped off the heads of two wives but also aggressively confiscated Irish land. After Henry's unsanctioned divorce, Anglican Protestantism became the official religion of England and therefore of Ireland as well. Henry saw Catholics as a threat to his power. He dissolved Catholic monasteries throughout England and Ireland to eliminate resistance to his reign.

The monasteries in Ireland, such as the Abbey of Kells, were centers of learning and art, producing illuminated books and highly decorated crosses and chalices of gold and silver. As Henry plundered the monasteries, he helped himself to what the Vikings hadn't taken, enriching himself to pay off his debts and reward his friends. He confiscated land and turned it over to loyal English and Scottish families to "settle" the country. This turned the Irish tradition of shared clan land into private property, bestowed by the king and now under British management.

The Irish did not submit quietly. Rebellions and resistance movements, small and large, simmered for hundreds of years. When Oliver Cromwell came to power in England a century later, a second wave of confiscations followed. Irish resistance and rebellion were brutally put down by British forces. Massacres, hangings, and forced transportation to the West Indies raised Cromwell to the top of Ireland's list of most-hated Englishmen. Like Henry, he rewarded his supporters and soldiers with massive tracts of confiscated Irish land. Overnight they became the landlords of nearly all Catholic Irish. A few who could prove they had not been involved in the rebellions and who swore allegiance to British rule were allowed keep their land. All others had to pay rent on land that had once been their own. They were also required to pay a tithe to the Anglican Protestant church. Because this did not sit well, intermittent and continuous uprisings by tenant farmers and laborers increased, and England responded by increasing its already heavily militarized occupying force. The goal was to keep the lid on Ireland at all cost.

The land confiscations upended Irish social and political order. In the old Gaelic order, Irish clan chieftains—the O'Neills, the O'Donnells, the O'Reillys, the McKennas—did not own personal land, but held it for the use of the whole clan. It might change hands through clan wars or mergers, but families shared the land on which they lived. After Cromwell's confiscations, 95 percent of Irish land was now owned by five thousand Protestant landowning gentry. Their estates were virtual fiefdoms.

I learned about the notoriously restrictive Penal Laws that Patrick's grandparents had lived under. *Penal* means "penalty." These laws prohibited a Catholic from voting, attending school, owning land, owning a horse worth more than five British pounds, or marrying a Protestant. Catholic priests were expelled from the country and could be executed if they returned. Use of the Irish language was discouraged and in some cases forbidden. For many years the Catholic Church operated underground. In the countryside where the Farrellys lived, priests moved from house to house, dressed as farmers or laborers to avoid being found out and arrested. Mass was held secretly in homes or barns, at large Mass rocks that served as altars, or behind hedges. In Lurgan parish several Mass rocks or lookout places are still remembered. Priests and lay teachers taught Catholic children in secret at hedge schools—held literally behind a hedge or in a sympathetic farmer's barn, where students would gather out of sight. The result was a number of poor Irish Catholic children (usually boys) who might not have shoes, but who could quote Virgil or conjugate Latin verbs. Several of these schools existed in Lurgan parish.

By the time Patrick was a small boy, things had improved marginally. The church had emerged from the underground. Priests were no longer hunted down and hanged, and Mass could now be held without fear in a simple building called a chapel, as long as it didn't have a transept or a steeple, which were reserved for the official church. National schools were built and were now open to every child. But the curriculum was controlled by the British government: no Irish history could be taught, and no Irish could be spoken.

Many landlords were absentee, keeping primary homes in London or Dublin, but their Irish country estates—often managed by a local agent—were a measure of wealth and power. They held palatial homes, used for entertaining and hosting others of the privileged class. Unrest continued. Sporadic tenant uprisings and stories of violence didn't make for good night's sleep. Landlords often held peerages: they were lords, earls, barons, and viscounts. Tenant farmers worked the land and paid rent to the landlord. It was the agent's job to collect the rent and keep the buildings, grounds, and herds well managed and safe. The estate holdings ranged in size from impressive "big houses" to massive castlelike estates with great ballrooms, stables for horses readied for hunting, and thousands of acres with stunning gardens of imported trees and plants.

One late afternoon on our second trip to Ireland, on the drive back to our B&B, Bob and I noticed what looked like a large, deserted house standing alone off the road, falling to ruin. We decided to investigate. We parked, got out of the car, and peered over a high wall. We could see that this was part of a large abandoned estate. No one was around. We climbed over and ventured up a grassy path toward the big house. As we got closer, the ruins of great wealth became clear: through broken windows we could see the plaster crumbling. Vines grew inside the entry. On the walls, faded but ornate wallpaper was peeling off in strips; the broken stairway had once been beautiful, gleaming woodwork; ornate decorative plasterwork was still visible in places. I thought about the craftsmen who had labored on this place to meet the standards of the inhabitants and wondered who had lived here. As we walked around to the back of the house, dusk was approaching and a rush of blackbirds flew out of the empty windows and up to the trees lining the walkway.

Perhaps this place belonged to some midlevel member of the gentry or the agent of a greater landlord like Lord Farnham or the Earl of Bective, who had massive estates near here. Their agents, or middlemen, also paid rent. They often lived in impressive residences such as this one, covering as much as one hundred or acres or more. But that was still a fraction of the holdings of the primary landlord.

Patrick's family, like all Irish tenant farmers, lived on a small parcel of land, often subdivided among family. Spinning and weaving provided cash to purchase clothing, flour, or oats. At the bottom of the social pile were landless laborers, who traveled the country looking for work. They had no homes of their own but would lodge with a family while they helped work the crop. The big landlords, many of whom served in the English Parliament, sat at the very top. The peasant tenantry—laborers and small farmers like Patrick's family—supported this hierarchy. Their work paid for the extravagant lives of their landlords. The precariousness of tenant life ultimately caused the entire system to crumble. In the end, no one was safe.

At the base of this economic pyramid was the simple potato. An easy-to-grow monocrop, it required only a small bit of land and thrived in boggy fields or rocky mountainsides—almost anywhere. It was surprisingly nutritious, filled with vitamins, potassium, and iron. One potato variety was predominant: the Lumper, a prolific type that thrived in poor soil. What it lacked in taste it made up for in quantity, supplying the calories that nourished a healthy, robust population. By the eve of the famine, Ireland's population had swollen to more than eight million. (For reference, the population today is under five million.) Prefamine visitors to the island often commented on the sturdy build and healthy appearance of the poor.

Potatoes were the food of the poor. But Ireland produced all kinds of food. It was England's farm: wheat, oats, pork, and dairy flowed out of the country to feed the British. The financial return on agricultural exports during the Napoleonic Wars was especially good. But the conflict, which had powered an economic boom, ended in 1815. Around the same time, industrialization was beginning to decimate the cottage linen industry. The small-scale spinning and weaving that had been such an important cash buffer for countless tenant farmer families dried up as mass production moved to industrial Belfast.

Stop for a minute and imagine that you are an Irish tenant farmer in the mid-1800s, living on a small plot of land with a patch to grow your potatoes. The pattern of your life would go something like this: In the spring, near St. Patrick's Day, planting would begin with the seed potatoes saved from last year's crop. Small bits of potato—each with at least one eye, the growing part—were dropped into the ground in a row and then covered with a small mound of dirt in a long ridge. In the summer the young plants would sprout, grow, and flower. In the "hungry months" of July and August, the previous year's potatoes began to run out before the new ones came in—a hard time for families who had no other reliable food source. But it was a regular thing: you expected it and made accommodations as you were able. Perhaps you had planted a secondary crop, some turnips or cabbage, as insurance. You might need to pawn a blanket, shawl, or coat, or a pair of shoes, to purchase oats (assuming the price was within reason). You knew you'd get your blanket or coat back when the potatoes came in. Or perhaps you begged your neighbors or even strangers for enough to survive.

You had survived lean times in the past, using your wits to get by. In September digging would begin, and out of the earth would come the new potatoes. You could sleep well again, knowing that this year's supply of food was covered with straw and buried in a pit next to your cottage or right under the dirt floor where you slept. Next spring, the whole process would begin again. This was how life went—until the Great Hunger began.

Stay in the mind of that Irish tenant farmer or laborer or spinner. It's September 1845. You had heard rumors about a new blight showing up in the countryside outside Dublin city. A neighbor told you that on his way home from town he'd stopped in the pub and heard the publican read from a British newspaper, the September 13 issue of the *Gardeners' Chronicle*. He read aloud to all who gathered around: "We stop the Press, with very great regret, to announce that the Potato Murrain has unequivocally declared itself in Ireland. The crops about Dublin are suddenly perishing. . . . Where will Ireland be, in the event of a universal potato rot?"

At first you weren't especially worried. The year's harvest hadn't been a total disaster, and Dublin's countryside seemed far away. But stories quickly spread that there was trouble in much of the country. Of course, you couldn't foresee how this new blight would progress nor the devastation it would reap.

During that first year a sense of dread slowly began to grow—people were shaken by the stories of the unusual way some potato plants were so totally destroyed. The way that perfectly healthy crops would be obliterated overnight. It was strange. But still, no one could know, in that first autumn, that the destruction would return relentlessly for six years in a steady march, taking its deadly toll.

Ireland had seen potato crop failures before. Through the eighteenth and early nineteenth centuries, it would descend over an area like a dark cloud. In her excellent book *The Great Hunger*, Cecil Woodham-Smith wrote, "The unreliability of the potato was an accepted fact." But those early failures had not encompassed the entire country.

Stories were passed along and theories bandied about of how the new blight began. An ominous change in the air, plants destroyed in a seemly random manner. It came without warning. "The blight's sudden, inexplicable recurrence seemed almost supernatural: one day 'the potatoes were clean and good,' remembered a peasant from Sligo, 'but that morning a mist arose up out of the sea, and you could hear a voice talking near a mile off across the stillness of the earth. It was the same . . . for three days or more; and then you could begin to see the tops of the stalks lying over as if the life had gone out of them. And that was the beginning of the great trouble and famine that destroyed Ireland'" (Miller, *Emigrants and Exiles*, 281–82).

The real cause of the mysterious rot was a fungus, the HERB-1 strain of *P. infestans*, likely brought by ships carrying goods to Europe from the Americas. There were no herbicides to prevent it, no understanding of crossbreeding that might have reduced the loss. In the years of the Great Hunger, it remained a mystery. This strain of fungus thrived in cool and moist environments and quickly found a receptive host in the potato fields of Ireland. The fungal spores settled on the leaves of the potato plants, multiplied, and spread throughout the country on the wind and mist. The consequences were severe. That first year, 50 percent of the potato crop across the island failed in bizarre patterns. One family's potatoes were destroyed and the plants of their neighbors spared.

The next spring, planting began again for those who had seed potatoes, with the hope that the last year had been an aberration. Potato ridges were dug and rebuilt. Mothers and fathers walked along the ridge lines with their children, dropping the little seed potatoes into the ground, covering them with soil and a prayer. Then the waiting began. In 1845 there was no starvation; small government relief measures reduced some of the pressure, and people could always sell a pig if they had one or pawn more clothes and blankets. Getting by. Getting through the hard time. Placing their hope on a good crop in the coming year.

The potato crop of 1846 emerged full and healthy, the little white flowers brightening the fields. But in the fall the blight returned with a deadly vengeance, and this time it destroyed virtually the entire crop. New plants sprang up strong, but within days their green leaves would blacken and their stalks crumple to the soil. New potatoes came up sound and firm when first dug out, but within minutes they turned soft and rotten. Now, slowly, the realization would hit that there were no seed potatoes to plant for next spring. The realization that your family had no food at all. No one could escape the smell of rotted potatoes. It permeated everything, like death itself.

People panicked. It was a madman's mystery. Why was this happening? Was it God's vengeance? For what horrible sin?

Far away in London, Parliament spent a great deal of time and energy attempting to discern the cause. Was it dampness or a watery vapor? In Ireland there was less concern about cause and a frantic concern about what to do. Anyone—tenant or landlord—who had seen potato failure in the past could project ahead. Priests and pastors wondered what and who would provide relief on this scale. How would the country get through this? Would Parliament support work programs? They had done so before during a previous short-lived potato failure. Would the party in power change the market rules that governed food exports and set prices? Surely they would see that people needed food and prices had to be stabilized.

In the midst of this calamity, Ireland kept producing vast quantities of wheat, oats, cattle, pigs, butter, and milk. But ships filled with Ireland's bounty carried that food away to feed English families. British soldiers guarded the docks, armed to prevent theft or riots. Small amounts of oats and wheat were still sold in the village shops, but Britain's laissez-faire economy meant that as food became more scarce, prices skyrocketed and starving tenants—the very laborers and small farmers who had grown the wheat and oats loaded on those ships for export—had little or no money to buy what food *did* remain in the country.

And then, as if a spirit of darkest malevolence had been summoned to this one small place on Earth, the winter of 1846 to 1847 was the worst in living memory. Patrick was ten years old. Fierce cold, normally not seen in Ireland's temperate climate, invaded the cottages and hovels of starving and sick men, women, and children. Storm after storm, snow, sleet, and brutal winds buffeted those on relief work, breaking stones to build roads to nowhere without the overcoats, shawls, and blankets pawned to buy a pittance of oats. People caught fever and collapsed and died on the roadside. The blight returned in full force in 1848 and again in 1849. There seemed no end to it. Now the opportunistic diseases—cholera, typhoid, and relapsing fever—swept in to do their deadly work.

There are stories of compassionate landlords who depleted their own resources in an attempt to help. A landlord in Blacklion, Cavan, is said to have gone out on the roads to bring starving tenants back to his house to feed them. But others saw this moment as an opportunity. They began to evict tenants unable to pay their rent. These clearances were referred to as "land improvement." The goal was to replace people with cattle. Some landlords provided assisted emigration, paying for passage for tenant families who still had to walk miles to the ship that would carry them to Canada or America. The fortunate ones survived the Atlantic journey. Others, now homeless, wandered the roads or crawled to the workhouses if they were able.

Central Europe, especially Belgium, Germany, and the Netherlands, contended with the deadly blight as well, but none of these countries had been colonized. None was built on the feudal-style economy that existed in Ireland. Continental governments that were not frozen in adherence to dogmatic economic philosophies or hindered by an inherent distaste for colonized populations took action to mitigate their citizens' distress.

In Patrick's small townland of Curraghmore, tenant families fought to survive. The Farrellys were small farmers, only one step up from landless laborers. Tenants in a one-room cottage on marginal land, they may have raised flax to pay their rent. But what they didn't have by 1847 was potatoes, or any sound method of getting cash to buy other food. Some farmers in the area had begun to grow turnips in place of potatoes, which may have lessened the worst extremes of starvation. It may have been how Patrick survived.

In Cavan, one-third of the population was lost to starvation and disease. The parish of Lurgan shrank by nearly 40 percent. At some point, the Farrelly family vanished from the parish. Father Tom said, "They seem to have fallen off the rolls." What happened? Where did they go? I knew that Patrick emigrated, and later on his younger brother, Andrew, joined him. But where were the others?

The changes in those seven years of the Great Hunger were stark. Cottages sat deserted, their chimneys cold and smokeless, and the roads filled with wanderers and the daily procession of coffins or carts bearing the dead. Perhaps the biggest change was the quiet that descended on the land, the buzz of community replaced by numbness and fear. The traditional fabric of community began to unravel. Death became commonplace. Priests and doctors, exhausted, could not keep up with the spiritual or material needs of their parishioners, some succumbing to cholera or typhus. Disease, no respecter of class, reached the landlords and their families too.

CHAPTER SIX

How Did We Get Here?

IT'S A STRANGE THING to know that my country of residence on planet Earth was determined by a blighted vegetable. But that's only a partial truth. It was not the potato's fault—nor the fault of the fungus that afflicted it. It was the fault of colonialism and the hubris of those in power. A familiar story.

The lives of ordinary people living through extraordinary times and events are largely forgotten. It's the famous ones, the people of means or stature, who populate the history books, inhabit documentaries, and show up in classroom texts as names to remember, with events and dates attached. We take ordinary people for granted, but they are the backbone of the world.

Today in Syria, Somalia, El Salvador, or Honduras, a woman or man is summoning the courage to leave home—to escape the danger and deprivation of war or famine or gang-driven violence. They have finally realized that this is their only hope. They are ready to risk it all. They will leave, done with just talking about it. They will somehow find the money, pay the man, and get on a sketchy boat and cling to the side as the waves swell in the dark, or walk for miles toward the border, sleeping along the roadside with eyes half open to keep watch. Some on their journey will be sick, screaming, crying—some will be lost. But this one particular man or woman will make it to shore or safely across the border. Somehow, they will make their way to a welcoming community in Europe or Canada or a safehouse in the US Southwest. They will count on the kindness of strangers for shelter and help figuring out how to navigate the asylum labyrinth, and perhaps two or three years later they will be on a plane to New York or a on bus to Chicago or Ottawa. Then the long process of finding housing, a job, a friend begins. They will endure prejudice and suspicion. But they know their children will be safe at night and able to go to school in the morning. They will have food and shelter. There will be no bombs going off in the street, no gangs taking their daughters and sons away, never to be seen again. Eventually they will apply for citizenship in their new country. They will become Germans or Canadians or Americans. And years from now, one of their grandchildren will look up and ask, "How did we get here?"

I'm here, born in the USA, because of that kind of courage. The fungal blight that destroyed the primary food source of my Irish ancestors set in motion the largest single population movement of the nineteenth century. The historical event we erroneously refer to as "the Irish potato famine" was in fact a cascading disaster caused by the indifference, malevolence, and ineptitude of the British government. Those in positions of power mishandled the crisis until it was a cataclysmic event.

And, in the end, it was simple courage and sheer luck that fueled the survival of those who left. Many who crossed the Atlantic Ocean to North America wanted to begin a fresh new chapter. They closed the book on the past. For many Irish emigrants, including my ancestors, the dark years of the Great Hunger were not to be mentioned, although some were determined that there would be retribution. For some the past held a kind of shame, felt in both the old country and the new. It may have been the stigma of poverty or of otherness, or the guilt of having survived when others perished.

Survival in this new world relied on the kindness of strangers, especially fellow immigrants from home. Adjusting to the new country involved looking forward, not backward. The accepted theory about immigrant family generational tasks is that the first generation is focused on survival, the second on assimilation, and the third and fourth on identity: understanding origin, culture, and history. Those categories are generalized and frequently blur, but they are roughly accurate in my own family. I'm fourth generation; my cousins and I are the ones who asked, "How did we get here?"

Here's another question: beyond the family members we live with, the ones who gather around a Thanksgiving table or come together for reunions or weddings or funerals—parents, grandparents, siblings, aunts, uncles, cousins—does it matter who or where we come from? Many of us live out singular lives with little thought for the generations before us, the people whose DNA we carry, whose personal or cultural history may affect our way of seeing the world. Does that matter? For most of my life I didn't ask that question. But gradually, with the nudging from Patrick's photograph, it moved to the front of my mind.

"The story is interesting, but what's more interesting is, why does it so compel you?" I struggled to answer this question from a writer friend. Why indeed? She was right: I did feel compelled. I have felt so strongly drawn to the life of this man, Patrick. He came from the shadows of our family story, the details of his personal history largely ignored, except for his service in the Civil War. I was surprised to learn that my dad had only met his grandfather once, when he was ten. Why was I so intrigued with him? Do the dead call to the living? Or was this call just my own search for connection, a sense of belonging that had eluded me? Maybe it didn't matter. Maybe none of those questions mattered. Maybe if I just followed the call, I'd find out why.

I've never been one of those people trying to make an elaborate family tree, adding names and dates and looking for a link to Charlemagne or some other figure of royalty. I was just looking for this one guy's story, and it has taken me on quite a journey.

I started with just that photograph. Then fragments, puzzle pieces of his story bubbled up to the surface. And soon I was hooked. Family history always involves some mystery, and maybe that's what intrigues people. Isn't it a natural human thing to try to understand who we are and why we do the things we do? Who do we think we are?

An individual life is just a small pinpoint on a long cord, braided from the life strands of that person's ancestors. The cord will stretch far beyond that one life as more strands are added to the braid. When I'm sitting in my favorite café, working on my laptop, sometimes I look around at the rest of the people sitting at their tables, talking, working, sipping their coffee. Each of us carries the invisible stories of multiple generations. The place is crowded with ghosts in a riot of gene pools. If they could all speak out, wouldn't it be wild?

Genealogy had a bad rap for a long time. In many people's minds it was stuck in the era of proving a person's pedigree (as we still do with purebred horses and dogs, even cats!). It got tangled up with the destructive eugenics movement in England, which spread to all of Europe and North America in the late nineteenth and early twentieth centuries. It was used to create categories of people, to judge and exclude. The word *eugenics* comes from the Greek, meaning "well born." The concept of excluding genetic groups deemed inferior fueled Nazism in Europe and slavery and racism in America.

Fortunately, science emerged from those darker times and genealogy has taken on a new life. It has become more inclusive than exclusive. The discovery of the human genetic code proves that we are far more alike than we are different. Thanks to globalization, the internet, and rapid advancements in gene-sequencing technology, more people are getting interested in their roots and their family origin story. Today DNA testing is affordable for many people—it's not just for forensic technicians solving a crime, but for regular people wanting to learn about themselves and their families. Send in a spit sample and bingo! suddenly whole worlds of cousins emerge.

This human need to reach out and to reach back makes sense to me. The world has grown smaller, and yet with increased societal mobility comes a loss of community. We've gained independence and lost interdependence. What passed for success—a kid makes good, departs the small town for the big city—has frayed the threads of our connectedness. And that loss is costly, on a personal and a national level. The great irony of *America First* is that as a nation, the United States is made up of individuals descended from multiple countries, multiple cultures, and multiple histories of struggle and triumph. If any nation's population reflects the whole mass of messy global humanity, it's us. Without that recognition, our identity—what it means to be an American—is a lie.

When we lift the lid on our ancestors and their history, we get a glimmer of who they were, their challenges in life, the ways they survived. As we learn about the world they lived in, we gain perspective on our own world and time. We start to see how the gardener working on the lawn down the block, drenched in sweat, could be our great-grandfather; the stressed and tired checkout girl at the grocers could be our great-aunt at her day job, the same woman who goes to night school after work to get her degree; the eighteen-year-old enlistee who sees the army as his best chance at finding acceptance in his new country could be our great-uncle. In the pictures of refugees fleeing their homes we may see a shadow of the faces of our own great-grandparents fleeing famine or war or economic deprivation.

As important as all of those reasons is this: when we get to know our ancestors, we honor them. We give their lives and their struggles new meaning. And we can begin to understand that none of us stands alone.

The film *Amistad* tells the true story of mutiny on a slave ship in 1839. While out on the ocean, the captured people of the Mende tribe broke the chains that held them below deck. Freedom seemed to be at hand. They took control of the ship, but the Spanish navigators tricked them and brought the ship to shore along the eastern coast of the United States instead of returning to Africa as the Mende had ordered. Once on shore they were recaptured, but now their status was unclear. Were they escaped slaves or free people? Remarkably, they were granted a court case to determine the answer. The case moved up through the courts until it reached the Supreme Court, where John Quincy Adams got involved.

In the film, the court scene is a dramatic conclusion to a heroic story. When Adams warns that the test ahead will be difficult, Cinque, the leader of the Mende, states that they will not face it alone. Adams assumes that this is a reference to the American judges and lawyers, but Cinque clarifies with a profound statement about our connection to the past and the present: "I meant my ancestors. I will call into the past, far back to the beginning of time, and beg them to come and help me at the judgment. I will reach back and draw them into me.

And they must come, for at this moment, I am the whole reason they have existed at all."

For at this moment, I am the whole reason they have existed at all.

We are all walking around with our ancestors. Everywhere we go, throughout our lives, their blood flows through us and their DNA shapes us. Their life experiences influence our own. We carry them with us, and perhaps they carry us. We owe them recognition. And as we acknowledge them, we begin to know who we really are.

Chapter Seven

My House

ALONG A NARROW COUNTRY ROAD in the small townland of Skearke, near the village of Moynalty in County Meath, are the ruins of a deserted cottage. A low stone wall overgrown with briars separates it from the road near a small outbuilding. A line of beech trees makes a shady spot for sleeping cows. The cottage is easily missed when driving past, but if you aren't in a hurry and look through the tall, overgrown hedges that line the road on your left, you might catch a glimpse of stone wall and a corrugated-metal roof. There's an old iron gate hanging off-kilter, the latch held with a bit of frayed blue plastic rope.

You might pull over to the side of the road, carefully making sure you don't get stuck in the ditch, and get out of the car for a closer look. If you peer over the gate you can see better. There. It's a house, an old cottage. Nobody is home. They haven't been for years. So I don't feel too presumptuous calling it "my house." I wasn't the first to call it that—it was Margaret.

I first heard of Margaret Flanagan in 2000, the first time Bob and I visited Moynalty. It was the final days of our second trip to Ireland. We had gone to Mass that morning at Moynalty's parish church, where Patrick married Bridget McKenna. Leaving the service, a woman asked if we were visiting. I said yes and explained that my great-grandparents had been married here and I was looking for Farrellys and McKennas. "Well, you're looking at a McKenna right now," she said with a smile. She told us that all the McKennas are related in some way, so she was

McKenna/Lynch cottage, Moynalty, Meath, Ireland

probably a distant cousin. "Be sure to visit the cemetery and look for the McKenna stone. It's a big, tall cross, right in the center, you can't miss it." She added that we should be sure to pick up a copy of the millennium book before we left town. "Stop by the credit union—it's in the old Church of Ireland building—and ask for Joe McKenna."

For the new millennium the village had produced a book with a history and photos of parish families. Irish parishes often create such local history books, but typically they don't publish many copies. I knew that if we wanted this one, we would need to get it now. These gems contain local history that would be entirely lost without them. Joe McKenna wasn't in at the credit union, but the woman at the desk told us we could get a copy from Mrs. Mahon, cochair of the book committee. I asked for a phone number so I could set up a time to come, but the woman said, "Ah, sure, don't worry, just stop by. She'll be home. Here's the address."

We stopped by the Mahon house and knocked on the door. Mrs. Mahon, a slight, friendly woman with grey-brown curls, greeted us with a welcoming smile. She brought us into the living room for a cup of tea and biscuits. Boxes of books sat in the next room. As she handed a copy of *Moynalty Parish: The Millennium Record* to me, she asked about our connection to the area. I told her what little I knew: that my great-grandparents had been married in this parish and my great-grandmother was Bridget McKenna, from the townland of Skearke. I hadn't had any luck yet in finding out what direct relatives of hers might still be around. "Skearke. Hmm," Mrs. Mahon said, "I don't know of any McKennas from Skearke. But you're talking about a long time ago." She said she'd give it some more thought. Just in case, I gave her the number for the Jurys Inn in Dublin, where we were staying that night before our flight left the next day.

We were packing up after dinner when the hotel desk put a call through. It was Mrs. Mahon. "Lois? You must call Margaret Flanagan. She lives up in Skearke," she said. "I was thinking about this and remembered she knew something about McKennas back there." Now, I am not a fan of calling people I don't know. I hesitated, but I dialed the number she gave me.

"Is this Margaret Flanagan?" I asked when someone picked up.

"Yes?" said the voice on the other end, the word drawn out and rising at the end. I explained why I had called. "Yes, Tommy's great-granny, down the road, was a McKenna. When can you come see me?" My heart sank. Our flight was leaving the next morning, and there was no way we could get back to Skearke before we left. So near and yet so far. I promised that I would call on her the next time, hoping there would be a next time, and I said I would write, and she gave me her address.

When I got home, I wrote to tell Margaret all I knew about Patrick and Bridget. She wrote back with an invitation to come see her anytime. Then, in a stroke of good luck, I had a work assignment in Dublin two years later. Part of my job involved administering an international residency program for graduate students in journalism, and I was overseeing our media sites in Dublin. So, I added a few open days at the end of my duties in Dublin, rented a car, and headed northwest.

I had been to Moynalty with Bob, of course, but I had no idea where Skearke was. I was driving alone, getting used to staying on the left side of the road and reading the signs. My only guides were the map that came with the rental car and my own fuzzy memory of landmarks. Once I got out of Dublin and into the country, I breathed a sigh of relief. The roads became smaller, and everything seemed to slow down. I stopped at a hotel in Kells for a cup a coffee and confirmation that I wasn't lost.

Margaret had given me directions, and I set off again, looking for the landmarks she had described. I followed a sign to the village of Mullagh and its one-block-long main street, lined on both sides with old buildings, turf smoke rising from their eighteenth-century chimneys. At the beginning of the street—which was the beginning of the town—I spotted an unmarked road beside an old cottage that Margaret had told me to watch for. This should be the Lislin road. I took the sharp turn and followed the narrow, hedge-lined road as it wound along, past a few new homes and some deserted cottages, and over a stone bridge just wide enough for one car.

As Margaret had described, just past the bridge and on my left was the country manor house named Annesbrook. Built in the 1700s, it had a long, curving entrance drive, bordered on each side by ancient, arching trees, and horses grazing on the expansive grounds. It was a complete contrast to everything around it. Far back on the opposite side of the road were the remains of what looked like an old mill. I turned left at a T intersection. According to Margaret's directions, this should be the Skearke road. Just after the turn I thought I saw an old cottage through a tall, brambly hedge.

I had the windows down, and the air felt cool as I drove through the shade of tall oak trees. I was the only car on this one-lane road. Bordered by hedgerows, it narrowed and gently rose and fell, eventually leveling out into a sunny little valley banked by little hills. On each side of the road were fields, sleeping cows, small houses, and utter quiet. The sweet smell of fresh-mowed hay drifted in through the windows. Up ahead I saw a small white house that I was fairly certain was the Flanagan cottage. I turned into the drive, parked the car, and came around to the back kitchen door as I'd been instructed.

It might as well have been two days and not two years since that first phone call at Jurys. Margaret opened the door with a smile and gave me a hug. "Mrs. Mahon told me about you. I don't know why she didn't think of me when you was there. But that's done and dusted. Sit down and I'll make us some tea."

Thus began years of having tea at Margaret's kitchen table. The scene is always the same. The kitchen table is pushed up to a window that looks out onto the field where Black Angus and Friesian cows graze, so close they may as well be joining us for tea. A low wall separates the field from the path around to the back door. Across the room is a great white-and-black stove that serves up heat for the house and warm brown bread for all visitors and inhabitants. Along one side of the room is a dark red couch that at one time must have had pride of place in the sitting room, on the other a matching stuffed chair. I wondered if that had been Tommy's chair—Margaret's husband had died of cancer about ten years before she and I met. They raised their four children in this cozy one-story, three-bedroom house. Pictures of the grandkids are lined up on the window ledge. The sacred heart of Jesus hangs high on the wall above the calendar from Pat Reilly, Family Butcher.

I learned that my connection to the Flanagan family is through Tommy; in fact, I'm related to him through both Patrick's and Bridget's families. One of his great-grandfathers was a brother to Patrick's mother, and a great-grandmother was Bridget's sister. The cottage down the road—the one Margaret calls "my house"—belonged to Bridget's sister and her husband in the mid-1800s. She was living with her sister when she married Patrick.

I had finally found some of my family in Ireland.

Over the years, Margaret's home became Bob's and my home away in Ireland. Welcomed as family, we sit and talk about family and local history, listen to stories, and ask what the grandchildren are up to. There's always some talk of how the world is changing, how Ireland's changing—and yet, this place seems caught in a time warp. Margaret and I talk on the phone and exchange letters. She asks when we're coming home. I feel I have known her all my life. It is a gift beyond measure.

On that first visit, Margaret and I drove back down the Skearke road to the old cottage. I parked the car and untied the blue plastic rope that held the old gate to the post. It creaked open. As we walked around outside, she explained that Tommy had been born there in 1929, in a small back room that had been added for his parents, Molly and Michael Flanagan, when they were married. His mother had been raised by her grandparents in this small cottage. The cottage and land had long ago passed out of the family, and the current owner was using it for a cow shed. Cows slept or stood at the back wall along the grove of trees. Behind the hedges, level with the road, the cottage sat up on a rise above the manor house I'd passed on the way in. Annesbrook had been the home of the local landlord, Rathborne, when Bridget lived here with her sister Catherine. Catherine McKenna and her husband, Edward Lynch, were Rathborne's tenants. As Margaret and I looked down toward the estate, I wondered if those living in this cottage ever felt a little superior. They clearly had the better view.

We were trespassing, but Margaret wasn't concerned. The cows were the only witnesses, and they didn't mind. It was overcast and cool. Dodging mud and cow pies, we walked back to the house and entered where a half door had once been. The dirt floor was covered with straw to keep it dry. A corrugated-metal roof replaced the original thatch. The walls were a foot thick. Bare stone now, they would have been whitewashed back in the day. The room was maybe fifteen feet in length and twelve in width. Two windows on either side of the door brought the morning sun inside. The house had no formal hearth or chimney, just a slight indent along the back wall where a turf fire would have been banked up. I stood still, trying to memorize every stone.

Margaret broke the silence. "You know, Tommy's sister Nan was here not long ago. She was after saying, 'I wonder if anyone will ever care about these old stones.' And now you're here!" Trying to take everything in, I had to focus to absorb all that Margaret was saying.

She recounted what Nan had told her about the house: "The main house was just this one room we're standing in. Nan said there were two trundle beds on either side of the hearth—they folded up along the wall in the morning and made a kind of bench. The floor was dirt with straw covering. There was a table at the front of the room—they called this the upper room." Margaret laughed. "Nan said there was a stool, but she didn't remember any chairs. And the table, for the store."

"The store?" I asked.

"Yes, they had a little store in the cottage. The mill is just across the road from Annesbrook—you drove past it—and they bought and sold flour that was ground there. Sometimes they had eggs and sugar. There were two bowls on the table, one for bills and one for coins. It was all on the honor system; people took what they needed and left their money in the bowls."

Margaret added, "It was a ceili house in the evenings."

"What's a ceili house?" I asked. I had heard the word, but I thought it referred to an Irish dance.

"A ceili is . . . you know, people come and sit around and visit and tell stories and talk. They'd sit around the fire and talk and smoke."

"Was there music?" I asked.

"There might be. It's just people coming together. When I was younger, we would always go ceili-ing. You always knew which houses to go to."

The clouds broke and the sun came through the windows as we talked. The place smelled of animals and straw and damp stone. It was early November, but I didn't feel cold. I ran my hand down the back wall where the smoke and the stories had drifted up and out to the sky.

Then it was time to get back to Margaret's and start dinner. That night I slept like a stone in the bedroom that had once belonged to Margaret's daughters. No street noise here. An unfamiliar bird's song woke me up. After breakfast, I walked the long road up to the cottage by myself. Clouds hung low in the sky, and the trees were losing some of their leaves. But birds were singing, and the air was fresh and clean. It was good to be out walking. The Skearke road rolled along like ribbon candy. Somebody's border collie barked but then decided to walk alongside me. I was glad for the company. He stayed with me until we reached the cottage gate, then turned and went back home to whatever farm he was responsible for protecting.

I untied the rope, lifted the latch, and went in. The morning breeze was picking up, and the sun came and went behind the clouds. Weather is so changeable in Ireland. I paid more attention to the whole area this time. Across from the cottage were two small stone outbuildings, sheds no taller than four or five feet. The cottage had been here at least since the early 1800s, but the outbuildings might have been added later. The remnant of a stone wall was overgrown with yellow ragwort, its roots weaving through the stones. Nature takes over when humans leave. Around the back of the house, the cows had gone to graze somewhere else. Wildflowers were plentiful here: pink valerian, goldenrod, blue speedwell, and bright red fuchsia. It was a truly beautiful place.

I sat down on the low side wall and looked back at the little cottage, snug in its setting. Bridget lived here when she married Patrick, before she left Ireland forever. Did she work for the Rathbornes or help her sister with her growing family? Their parents were dead by then; they just had each other.

I got up from my perch and went back into the cottage. A shaft of light shined through the two small windows and door, making a bright triangle on the dark wall. *This is how it looked in the mornings a hundred and fifty years ago*, I thought. *The sun would have come in just this way.* I leaned on the window ledge to the right of the door and looked out. The window framed the piece of wall I'd been sitting on. Bridget might have looked out this same window, seen this same view. An old, moss-covered alder tree stood behind the wall. Of course, that tree wasn't there when she was here, I reminded myself. But maybe it had grown from an old stump. I was trying to travel through time. *How odd*, Bridget would think if she were here, *that some woman is standing in my cottage, looking out my window, and wondering about an old tree.* Before I left, I picked up a small stone that had fallen from the cottage wall and tucked it in my pocket.

After two more nights with Margaret, I packed up, carefully bubble-wrapping two jars of her homemade blackberry jam and tucking the little stone from the cottage inside one of my shoes in the suitcase. Margaret gave me a hug, and I waved from the car window as I pulled out of the drive and headed toward the Dublin airport. It had been such a good visit, so much packed into these few days.

Chapter Eight

Diaspora

On the flight home, I thought about my time in Moynalty and my days with Margaret. I tried to hold on to the way the air smelled, the rolling green hills, the little streams, cows lying the shade of old trees, the total quiet of the countryside. The way people are so welcoming, the way everyday conversation is an art, the focus on a person's character rather than career. The wry humor from a cabbie or a farmer. The way people greet each other on the street. How a cup of tea and a slice of warm brown bread can lift your spirits on a rainy day. I wanted to keep it all safe in a drawer in my mind that I could open when I needed it. I knew that once I got home, life and time would speed up: the holidays were coming, our kids would return home, and I'd get so wrapped up in things that I might forget. And I didn't want to forget any of it.

Our family makes wish lists for Christmas, and that year I asked for a DNA kit. Bob, not even thinking that was weird, lovingly went ahead and ordered one for me. On Christmas morning, there it was, wrapped up and tied with a bow. I was thrilled. On a cold Chicago night in early January, after things had settled down from the holidays, I opened the box and read the instructions. Abstain from food and drink for at least an hour. Spit into a little tube so it is filled up to the line on the side. Add the included preservation fluid, cap the tube, seal tightly, and shake for thirty seconds. Replace tube in box. It all seemed very Hogwartsian.

The chemical makeup of my identity sat overnight, sealed in its prepaid box. In the morning, I took it down to the post office, where it would be loaded into a truck, then onto a plane, and then onto another truck, and eventually reach the lab in California. Several days later, the company emailed to say it had arrived. I felt a little surge of excitement. In four to six weeks I would get another email with the results of how my personal strands of DNA break down into percentages of global ancestry, get a little health information, and maybe find some unknown cousins.

Why did I, and thousands of others, want to know this? Would it make me feel more complete? I imagined a miniature family tree unfurling before my eyes. My own piece of human history.

DNA testing is big business, and there are several good companies to choose from. I used one of the first brands in the market, 23andMe. Why are people willing to pay approximately a hundred dollars to find out where their ancestors originated or locate distant cousins both generationally and physically? Across Europe, Asia, and Africa, it's not unusual to know that your parents, grandparents, and great-grandparents came from within the same twenty-five-mile radius. For many North Americans it's another matter. Anyone here without indigenous ancestors—Native American or First Nations—has ancestors who left a generational home somewhere else in the wide world because they wanted to leave or were forced to by physical or circumstantial forces.

Before the results came in, I knew I had a classic Northern European genetic makeup. My grandfather on my dad's side was full Irish and my grandmother on that side French and English. My maternal grandfather was full German; my grandmother, we're not sure—maybe English. Perhaps because my surname is Irish, I've always identified with that slice of my makeup. And I'd always assumed my ancestors were somewhat recently off the boat from the great nineteenth-century European migration: the classic tired, poor, huddled masses, homeless and tempest-tossed, yearning-to-be-free types. I liked the thought that my ancestors had arrived more recently. But then a cousin shared some research he had done on my mom's family about Shadrack Greene. That was his actual name. And yes, before you ask, he had two brothers:

Meshack and Abednego. Not kidding. Shad and his sons had settled in the southern half of the country all the way back in revolutionary times.

When it comes to family history, one should always expect surprises. But no matter what we discover, learning the history of our family—knowing what shaped our ancestors—matters in how we come to understand ourselves.

Interesting research from Emory University has investigated the effect on children of knowing their family's story. Dr. Marshall Duke and Dr. Robyn Fivush found that knowing family history strengthens children's self-esteem; children who learn it are better able to handle stress from external events. From their research—part of the Family Narratives Project—Duke and Fivush have found that storytelling about parents, grandparents, and great-grandparents and their triumphs and failures gives children powerful models. These events and stories create an intergenerational self that is associated with an increase in resilience, and children with it tend to show better adjustment and an improved likelihood of overcoming challenges (Judy A. Rollins, "The Power of Family History," *Pediatric Nursing* 39, no. 3 [May–June 2013]: 113–14).

Almost six weeks later to the day, I got an email from 23andMe. My spit had given up its secrets. It felt like getting my grades or college acceptance letters in the mail. I paused before opening the email.

Then, one click and there it was. Boom. One hundred percent European. I laughed out loud. No surprises. The geographic breakdown of my ancestry going back five hundred years shows:

60% Irish & British
33% French & German
4.7% broadly Northern European
1.8% Spanish & Portuguese
.04% Greek & Balkan

So very white. No Italian, no Swedish, Finnish, Asian, Middle Eastern, or African. No presence of Ashkenazi or Native American markers, two groups I thought might have mingled with my Northern European ancestors somewhere in time. But no. European through and through.

The second email came a day later; this provided a list of my DNA relatives among those who had submitted samples to 23andMe. There are 1,521 of them as of this writing. We could fill the Vic Theatre in Chicago or the Olympia in Dublin. My newly found relatives are listed in order of closeness of relationship, name, family surname, and location. Online profiles allow me to contact them to say "Hi, cousin!" and ask if they would like to share genomes. How odd that we can look at one another's chromosomal makeup, right? But this is where we are today, from the world of "Want to grab a beer?" to a world of "Would you like to share genomes?" So far it's been hit and miss, with some responding on the "Hi, cousin" level and others sharing to determine just how we are related.

In one of my wilder experiences, I was scrolling down the list of cousins, which is ordered by estimated cousin relationship (e.g., first, second, third, and so forth), I found a fourth cousin who had included New Haven in his family's locations. I knew that Patrick and Bridget had first settled there when they arrived in the United States, so I clicked on his profile. And just like that, the world got a whole lot smaller. Mr. Flanagan lives in New Jersey, but in his profile he writes, "I am descended from Flanagans in Killeeter, Cavan." Whoa. Killeeter is the townland across the road from Margaret Flanagan's farm, the townland of her husband's family. I contacted the New Haven Mr. Flanagan, and we arranged a phone conversation. He told me to have an Irish map handy, and while we spoke, he directed me to follow along the map's roads with a pencil and thus brought me (on paper) to the original Flanagan farm. The world felt large and small all at once.

Tommy's father had moved across the road to marry. Now I had DNA confirmation that my family roots from both Bridget and Patrick are right there, in bordering townlands from bordering counties—one in Meath, one in Cavan, separated only by a quiet country road.

At the beginning of my search for Patrick's path, I had expected to learn about the places and history that surrounded his life. I had hoped but never really expected to find living relatives in Ireland. There's been too much death, too much migration and lost Irish records and family dislocation. But there they are, in this one little spot on Earth.

A link by blood. Now, when Margaret asks, "When are you coming home?" it means so much more.

Since then, I've found a few more Irish cousins thanks to the magic of DNA, more links to this small spot on the island of Ireland. Bob thinks I'm probably related to everyone in the parishes of Moynalty and Mullagh somehow. A nice thought, indeed.

CHAPTER NINE

Dig a Little Deeper

ONCE I DISCOVERED living family in Ireland, I made more frequent trips. Now, driving out into the country and onto the little winding roads of Cavan and Meath truly feels like coming home. Bob and I have visited every two years on average, and I've made a few solo trips. It never grows old, but much has changed since that first trip. When we first visited twenty years ago, the many eighteenth-century buildings and pubs with their multiple chimneys were plain and grey; now they are often bright with color, and flowers are everywhere. In Dublin it's easy to find a new coffee shop or a wine café, often next door to a pub that may have been in business for two hundred years. What has stayed the same is the Irish welcome.

Today it's a quick hour by car from Dublin to rural Cavan on the efficient EU motorways. In 1998 it took an hour and a half or more. Back in Patrick's day, it would have been two days by coach with a stop along the way for those who could afford it and God knows how long on foot for those who couldn't.

The place my Irish ancestors left was, and to an extent still is, a world away from cosmopolitan Dublin. The British colloquialism *beyond the pale* originated many centuries ago in relation to Ireland. From the fourteenth century on, Dublin was essentially an outpost of London. The English Pale was the area in which "civilized" people could count on a degree of safety and Britain's version of socially acceptable behavior. My ancestors came from the wild country, the area beyond the Pale.

Long, long ago, County Cavan was called East Breifne and ruled by the O'Rourke and O'Reilly chieftains under Brehon or Old Gaelic law. When you left the Pale, you also left all the laws and institutions of England behind—civilization itself, as the British saw it. There's no Pale today, but out in the country, there's still the feeling that Dublin is different. Young people who work in the city but are priced out of housing there can sometimes find a place in the Midlands. Some in the older, rural community call them *the Dubs*. I once heard someone say, "They just sleep here—they don't *live* here." That's not everyone's feeling, of course, but it's an example of worlds still colliding across old borders.

Many things can change the culture of a small community. The famine certainly did, but affluence and modernity leave their mark as well. On our first trip to Cavan, the county was mostly open fields and uniformly grey buildings in sleepy villages. Then the rapid rise and fall of the "Celtic Tiger" in the nineties and the housing boom and bust that undergirded it left rows of often uninhabited McMansions looking very out of place in the landscape. Ubiquitous quick-marts sprang up and threatened the livelihood of local grocers. Saddest of all were the for-sale signs on local pubs, the places that, along with the parish church, had always been the heart of the community. Rural pubs especially were driven out of business by new and stricter drunk driving laws, which came with social ramifications that no one predicted. Now it's easier to pick up a six-pack from the quick-mart, bring it home, and not worry about the Garda than to go into town, grab a stool, and have the publican pull a pint and ask, "How've you been keeping?" Much like the loss of church authority through scandal, it's one more tear in the social fabric.

No one wants to go back to the slick bank deals and shoddy overbuilding of Ireland's economic boom. But no one wants to go back to the poverty that gripped this island for centuries, either. The Irish are realists. Some in the American diaspora romanticize the old Ireland.

Misty views of tidy white cottages nestled in heather-covered hills, smoke drifting from chimneys, and families sitting around the hearth telling stories make an idyllic, nostalgic picture. But I wanted to know the real one, and that meant looking squarely into the eye of history. Like an old song says, I needed to dig a little deeper in the well.

The countryside where my ancestors lived and worked and had their being, as my dad liked to say, is steeped in history, but it can be reticent about giving it up. After a while I learned that some of the story was in the land itself. Like a language, if I could pick up on the hints, I could start to learn to read and understand it.

When I began my research in Ireland, I searched through written records, both civil and church. Anyone looking for family history in Ireland hears about the destruction of nearly all census records during the Irish Civil War of 1922, and many give up, thinking they'll never find their family. For a long time there was next to nothing online. But I was fortunate: I had an assortment of written material from my own family. My uncle Bruce set foot on Irish soil back in the eighties. He'd taken his whole family around the island in a van, headed toward County Cavan and Lurgan parish. Bruce obtained the baptismal records for Patrick and his siblings from the priest at St. Patrick's church in Lurgan parish and Patrick and Bridget's marriage record from Moynalty parish, just over the border in County Meath. By the time I arrived many years later, armed with that information, I knew the name of the townland where the Farrellys had lived. From there I found land records and eventually old census data. Every bit of information led to another, and the picture started coming together.

In one of my favorite mystery series, detectives stick Post-it notes on a large board and draw lines between the evidence they have to solve the crime. That's what I was trying to do. In the plot of any good mystery, there's always a missing element that must be found to solve the puzzle. It often comes as a sudden recognition of something that might have been staring you in the face all along. In Ireland, it helps to understand the physical setting and the history behind it if you want to know the full story. You can't do that from an ocean away; it makes all the difference to go there yourself.

Ireland has secrets right beneath your feet. Maybe every place is like that, but it seems to me that Ireland has left more hints of its past untouched. The Irish have great respect for what and who came before. The island's climate and geography are also friendly to the past, and the wheels of economic progress have turned more slowly there, all the better for preservation.

For example, there are many stories in the bogland. Irish bogs are not like cranberry bogs in the United States. From the road, they look like nothing more than mushy brown fields, but they've been quietly growing upward for ten thousand years or so. Created from waterlogged masses of partially decayed vegetation—trees, moss, grasses, whatever—these sections of acidic, low-oxygenated, spongy soil go down deep, to twenty-five feet or more, and cannot support crops. In ancient times, some resourceful local discovered that dried chunks of this matter, called peat, can make a very nice fire. It's been harvested for fuel for millennia. When cut into bricks and dried, peat becomes turf for warming homes, pubs, and hearts, these small glowing sods huddled together, burning slowly in the hearth, sending their ancient, earthy smell up and out the chimney. The scent of this incense as you drive on the back roads tells you immediately that you are in the heart of rural Ireland.

A treasure chest of the past, bogs have hidden many things. For example, more than 270 wooden containers of butter dating back hundreds or even thousands of years have been discovered in Irish bogs. It was a good cold-storage solution unless you forgot where you put your cask! Bogs also hid precious objects from pillaging Vikings or carried offerings to ancient gods. Bogs have given up brilliant Bronze Age ornaments made of gold, tools of war, sacrificial offerings, jeweled liturgical chalices from the Middle Ages, and ornate brooches of gold and silver. They have preserved the work of the cloistered medieval scribes who meticulously wrote out the Psalms or the Gospels in tiny stone huts, decorating page after page of calfskin in intricate spiral designs with ink made from oak galls gathered nearby and lapis lazuli imported from what is now Afghanistan. And there are bog bodies. The oldest, found in County Laois, dates to 2000 BCE. A man sank into the peat, where he fell or was sacrificed, and lay there silently as the bog grew over and around him. Digging turf, Irish farmers have been finding these wonders for decades. When they do, most of them know that the first call to make is to the National Museum of Ireland in Dublin. Many of these important and beautiful discoveries end up on display in its Treasures Room or in the permanent exhibit simply called *Ór*, the Irish word for gold. The museum is one of my favorite places to visit in Dublin.

The bog offers up its secrets after preserving them for centuries or millennia in its own unique, boggy way. Then it's up to us—the present earthwalkers—to be the new caretakers.

Bogs are not alone in preserving the past. Away from cities, towns, and villages, the rural landscape itself offers plenty of clues hiding in plain sight. Stones are everywhere: in the field walls and hedgerow supports and ruins of cottages or castles—shelters for the poor or the rich, the lowly or the mighty. Piles and piles of stones, abandoned by death, eviction, emigration, or war. Brambles and vines grow up, over, and through them, sometimes disguising their identity.

In the countryside, history lies in layers, partially exposed. Sitting unmolested in farmers' fields are ancient tombs and monuments that once held the bodies of those who were revered: megalithic dolmens, stone cairns, passage graves. Many sit right in the open. Then again, I've driven along a small country road past a mound of stones covered in brambles that looks like nothing but a messy pile. But beneath that growth one might discover a hearth, a foundation, the tumbled stones that once sheltered a family, or perhaps the site of an ancient burial. You just never know. A young tree, reaching deep down in the mound, grasping a stone for stability and spreading out its fingerlike roots, might cover the place where someone slept, built their fire, fed their children, laid to rest the bones of a loved one.

The point is, a chapter of the past might lie just below the surface. In the summer of 2006, for instance, in a rain-soaked bog of County Tipperary, the great maw of farmer Eddie Fogarty's digger dipped down and scooped up a 1,200-year-old mystery. Only a tiny, tempting glimpse of half-uncial script on the corner of a piece of golden-hued vellum hinted at the value of this mass of brown mush.

The glint caught Eddie's eye as it dangled off his front loader, and he jumped out to retrieve it. Now dangerously exposed to the open air, it had fallen—literally—into safe hands. Eddie knew immediately that it looked important, and he did the right thing: he put it right back in the soggy bog and called to the property owners, who placed a call to the conservation experts at the National Museum.

It was a real mess. Preservation technicians referred to it as alphabet soup or lasagna. But this wet brown mush would become known as the Faddan More Psalter. A book of psalms, it was estimated to have been written around 800 CE by monks in a nearby monastery. The inside of the cover was lined with papyrus, confirming links between early Irish and Egyptian churches. It is so historically important that it has its own display room in the National Museum.

When John Gillis, the museum's senior conservator, first saw the psalter, he described the condition of the manuscript as "a mass of disintegrating vellum with letters floating in the gelatinous mess." The letters were made with iron-gall ink, which held up better than the vellum it was written on in the acid environment of the bog. Gillis's task was to separate the letters from the gelatinous mass one at a time and then—after replacing the bog fluid so the surface of the remaining vellum did not shrink and distort when dried—put the Latin words back together. Piece of cake.

No one knows why the psalter was in the bog. Was it hidden there by monks for protection from warring clans? Dropped in flight by marauding Vikings? But there it lay, undiscovered for more than twelve hundred years, while Ireland grew up around and over it. It missed centuries of historic and cultural changes as it slept.

I had read about this discovery before I left for a work trip to Dublin. It was years after the initial discovery, and the special Faddan More exhibit had opened in the National Museum. I stood mesmerized in the dimly lit display room, spellbound by fragments and floating letters and the incredible chance that this thing had come to light after a dozen centuries of darkness.

On this trip I had set aside time for family research as usual, still hoping that *my* shovel might pull up some bit of my own manuscript.

The physical analogy of a squashed, undecipherable mass hidden in a bog was not lost on me. I thought about all this in my hotel room that night—the discovery, the history, the curious museumgoers like me who want to understand its place in time. The Faddan More Psalter still holds its mysteries, a life in the past that no one today can really know.

In a similar way, every human being is a DNA stew, the composite of histories of thousands of people who lived before, each with no idea of their place in their line of progenitors. I find it fascinating, this unknowing connectedness. Each person who came before played a role—their experiences, their choices, the time in which they lived, the flukes and flights of history—and all of it has filtered into my life, my very being. All of it plays a part in who I am, who I might become. I've sometimes wondered if the fact that some people loom larger to us than others might be for reasons both physical and spiritual.

Chapter Ten

Hunger

SOMETIMES I THINK IRELAND has locked part of its story away just to keep the diaspora coming back to look for it. For many of us whose ancestors left during the Great Hunger, there is no bit of information too small, no factoid we would dismiss when learning about our Irish roots. It's another kind of hunger.

A few years after that visit to the museum, I was back in Dublin for a vacation. I had arrived a few days early, and Bob would join me at the end of his work week. It was a good opportunity to do some research at the National Archives of Ireland (NAI). All surviving Irish census records are available online today, but at the time of this trip the oldest fragments of census were only available on microfilm, so I had to go to Dublin if I wanted to see them. I had emailed ahead, so I knew the archive's hours and policies. My hotel was across the street from St. Stephen's Green, and I looked forward to crossing it every morning on my way to the archives. Stephen's Green is Dublin's version of New York's Central Park, and much of the city's population finds a way to cross it on the way to work or on a lunch break. It's beautifully designed with walking paths, flower gardens, and benches to rest on or watch the swans and ducks swimming about in the ponds. It's a peaceful oasis in a busy city.

The National Archives are housed in a modern building on Bishop Street, about a twenty-minute walk from the green. I arrived early, signed in, got my card (good for two years), placed my coat and purse in a tiny locker, and took the elevator to the second-floor reading room. This space holds large wooden tables with seats for six, each section numbered and lit by an overhead banker's lamp. Behind the tables are the head archivist's office and rows of microfilm machines. An assistant in a small room will make copies of records upon request. The main room is lined with books and catalogs. It has a feeling of quiet, important work being done.

At the main desk I submitted my requests for material, and then I found a seat at one of the desk stations and waited until the records were brought to me. Researchers are allowed only a notepad and pencil. When using any archive for research, it's critical to make a plan, write out your questions ahead of time, and bring along your notes. The better organized you are, the more you'll get done. But sometimes, digging more broadly can show you something you hadn't thought about. Each discovery often leads to a new question.

The Irish census records have a sad history linked to the country's tumultuous past. Until Ireland won its independence, the census count was done by the British because Ireland was under British rule. The first official census was taken in 1821. This record and those of the next three decades contain details about life before the potato blight that are hard, if not impossible, to find anywhere else. But only a few fragments of those records have survived. The census records from 1821 until 1901 are almost entirely missing. In June 1922, eight hundred years of recorded Irish history burned in an explosion at the beginning of Ireland's civil war. The yearlong war followed Ireland's War of Independence from England. The British Parliament had offered to cease hostilities on the condition that Ireland be partitioned: six counties in the north would remain part of England and the remaining twenty-six counties in the south would gain their independence. Irish leadership split on whether to accept the British offer, thus bringing about the short but brutal civil war. Suddenly, Irishmen and women who had been fighting together against Britain were now at war with one another.

Patrick must have read or heard about the start of Ireland's War of Independence in 1916; its opening salvo, now known as the Easter

Rising, made the news across North America, where so many Irish immigrants had settled. He died just five years later and was spared the knowledge of his birth country's own civil war. He'd surely had enough of civil wars.

In 1922, men and women who had fought together had now broken into two groups, pro-treaty (Free State) and anti-treaty. Skirmishes had happened throughout the country, but now the conflict developed into a true civil war. It would be far shorter than the US Civil War, with far less loss of life, but the issues divided families and friends just the same, causing deep and painful divisions that lasted long beyond the bloodletting.

The political rupture began as soon as the Anglo–Irish treaty was signed in London. Should Ireland take the deal offered by the negotiators, a qualified independence contingent on splitting off six counties in the north and retaining allegiance to the British queen, or go for broke to keep united all thirty-two counties as an independent Irish republic? On the evening of June 28, the anti-treaty side was hunkered down in the Four Courts, a complex of separate courthouses that faced the Liffey. At the back of the complex was the Public Records Office, which housed public documents and the records treasury. The walls were thick, seemingly impenetrable. Thinking of the future, not the past, the anti-treaty soldiers had stored munitions, gasoline, paraffin, and a large amount of the explosive gelignite there. They blacked out the windows with old record books containing wills and court, parish, and government records going back to the Norman invasion. Their headquarters, which also contained explosives, was in a larger building next door to the office.

The pro-treaty side fired away for two days to no avail to force the anti-treaty side to surrender. On the second day of the siege, the British government sent assistance to the pro-treaty soldiers: two large cannons and a howitzer. These guns were set up across the Liffey and aimed directly at the anti-treaty headquarters. Their massive shelling started multiple fires and ignited the stored munitions and fuel. By the third day of the siege, the fires had spread to the Public Records Office. A tremendous explosion destroyed the records buildings, leaving a crater and rubble in their place. Amazingly, while many were injured, there were no fatalities from the explosion. It did, however, turn a thousand years of recorded Irish history into a towering mushroom cloud rising two hundred feet into the air. Paper rained down like confetti. A staffer at the National Archives told me her mother remembered walking outside the Four Courts building the day after the fire. Her mother had told her, "It was the end of June, and tiny fragments of paper were still drifting down from the sky, covering the ground like snow."

Miraculously, a few fragments of those early census records survived, among them a small section from the very first census of 1821. That fragment included a section of County Cavan. It seemed like a lot to hope for, but the genealogist at the archives gave me the good news that the records for Lurgan parish were part of that fragment. How on earth did anything survive? Who gathered up the pages blown free of the fire? With a silent thanks to whoever it was, I hoped I might be lucky enough to learn about my family in the years before the potatoes failed and everything changed.

The record was on microfilm. Working without an index, I began the tedious job of scrolling through the roll, trying to stay focused and decipher the writing of the census taker. Eventually I found it: Lurgan parish, townland of Curraghmore. I let out a quiet gasp. A little window had opened, and I could look back in time. Curraghmore was a very small townland, with only thirteen dwellings. The twelfth contained the Farrelly family: Thomas, Patrick, Rose, Ann, Mary, and Elizabeth, names that have been passed down in our family for almost two hundred years. They were small farmers, living on nine Irish acres that they shared with the Smyths. (An Irish acre is a land measurement traditionally derived from the amount of land that one man with an ox could plow in one day. It is roughly equivalent to 1.62 English or standard acres.) Every woman in both families was a flax spinner. In fact, as I looked down the list, I found that nearly all the women in Curraghmore were flax spinners. Granddaughters Mary and Rose, ten and eleven years old, were at the Farrelly cottage the day the census taker came by.

A census is just a snapshot in time. It lists everyone who is present in a dwelling on the actual day of the census. In 1821 it revealed the relationship people had to each other, their ages, their occupations, how much land they lived on, and who owned it. In Curraghmore, the last dwelling on the list was on a much larger amount of land. This dwelling had a name, Lurgan Lodge, and was occupied by the Nixons, a prosperous Protestant family. The Nixons had four house servants listed in the census: Elizabeth Farrelly and two of the Smyths, Catherine and Michael, and a James Briody, all in their teens or early twenties. The Nixons also owned the mill down the road. The Farrellys and most of the townland families paid their rent to James Hunter, an agent who collected rent for the local landowner, who then paid his rent to a larger landlord. So on and so on, money flowing from subtenants and tenants up to a greater landlord. This was the snapshot of one small place in 1821, flourishing for those at the top and challenging for those at the bottom.

I'd had a successful morning at the archives, but I needed a break from the microfilm and time to digest what I'd found. I planned to come back the next morning, but before I left, I asked the archivist if there were any records from the time of the famine by locality. There were. She explained that at the beginning of the famine, each county was ordered to create relief committees to organize, collect funds, and provide relief to the local population in need. I asked if there was anything from either Patrick or Bridget's area. "Yes, you'll be wanting to see the famine committee letters. Fill this out and we'll have them ready for you first thing tomorrow."

The next morning, I grabbed my notebook and headed out, glad once again for the walk through Stephen's Green. It was a warmer day, and the green was already filling with students lounging on the grass, couples in conversation, tourists taking photos. I greeted the ducks in the pond, left through the gate, and walked up the five or six blocks to the NAI. It was another glorious day—so tempting to spend it outside—but I only had these few days with access to the archives, so I'd spend them inside with my head in the past. I stopped for a quick cup of coffee, wrote out a list of questions, and got to the NAI as the doors opened.

The night before, back in my hotel room, I had looked up Irish Famine Relief Committees. In 1845, at the beginning of the famine, small groups consisting of a few landlords, gentry, and priests and pastors from towns or villages had been given the unenviable task of overseeing government relief programs for the afflicted tenants in their areas. The committees were to advise the British government on the local situation. Their main task was to establish and collect for a fund that could be used to purchase and distribute food and create and regulate small outdoor work-relief projects. The committees were required to create meticulous records of funds and expenditures to be sent to the British commissioners in London, where decisions would be made. It was a classic example of bureaucracies far removed from human suffering deciding how and whether to alleviate it.

A smattering of committee correspondence has survived, including letters from Virginia and Moynalty, the villages closest to Patrick's and Bridget's townlands. I checked in with the main desk to see if my requests were ready. I took a seat at the table and waited. Minutes later, a clerk handed me a large green folder. Inside were letters, pen on fragile paper, well over 160 years old. This was not microfilm, not

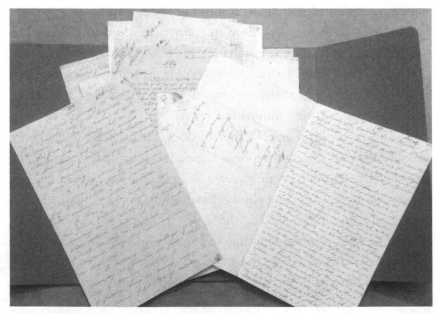

FAMINE COMMITTEE LETTERS,
NATIONAL ARCHIVES OF IRELAND, DUBLIN, IRELAND

fragile vellum locked away in a case; these were the real thing. I could hold them and read them. Touching these letters (no white gloves required!) was a portal to one of the most catastrophic events in Ireland's history. I took a deep breath and began to read.

The first letter was dated November 6, 1846, the second year of the blight, when the entire potato crop had failed. Robert Sargent, the chairman of the Virginia Relief District (where the Farrellys lived), wrote, "We find from what we daily witness, that the distress, and impending famine, is absolutely beyond our power to fully describe. It is a state of things which none of us has had any experience: from time to time partial distress has occurred in Ireland, but to behold nearly an entire population suddenly deprived of the food they have all their lives depended upon, is to our minds perhaps the most awful calamity that can be conceived."

This letter is addressed to all the local landlords. Mr. Sargent pleads, "I pray God to dispose your heart to give largely and willingly, to save a multitude of our fellow-creatures from the misery and danger they are now in." He explains that many are too weak to work on the few public projects that have been allowed. The rules set by Parliament are very strict about who is allowed to work for food, he notes, and therefore eliminate many in severe need: "Arising from the scant allowance of food we have seen instances on our works of poor men becoming quite unable to continue—some have fainted, and many have been obliged to absent themselves from downright weakness. At this moment, every man holding any land beyond a little garden is excluded from the work—although we believe in many cases, these men are as poor, if not poorer, than the mere laborer."

Mr. Sargent continues, "We have on our lists of working people nearly one thousand, allowing some of those to be without families, we have at least FOUR THOUSAND SIX HUNDRED HUMAN BEINGS to be provided with food or means to purchase it for many months to come."

Virginia was a very small village. This committee was responsible for not only those in the village but also those in the countryside surrounding it. The laborers and small farmers who hung their hopes on this committee's action must have included nearly everyone living in the area.

I placed the letter from Virginia gently back in the folder and took out another. This one was from the village of Moynalty, in County Meath, just across the border from Cavan, where Bridget grew up and where she and Patrick would later be married. Dated December 14, 1846, it was written by the Moynalty Relief Committee and addressed to the secretary of the commissioners of the Relief Office in London. The signers were all local landlords. The increasing frustration is palpable as the writer tries to express to well-fed London officials the severity of what he saw as starvation and fever began to overwhelm the land:

> Sir: At our regular meetings we have attended scrupulously to the Governments instructions in the awarding of tickets for public works and are satisfied that many have abstained from importuning us as long as they had any means of support. However, the constant applications for tickets increasing weekly and oftener and the number of laborers convinces us that these means are fast failing. We have at the beginning of the famine examined with our own eyes, the conditions of the laborers and small farmers in each townland of our populous parish, and can consequently speak with strict accuracy of their position and prospects. We feel it is our duty to give expression to our convictions.

The writer seeks to explain to those who made the rules that the wages are far too low for the hungry people hired on the work-relief sites (which generally set workers to breaking stones to build roads) and the rules of who could be hired are much too strict:

> The price of labor wages is now 10 pence per day to able bodied men. One of the rules of the Commission Relief board, is that where the family does not exceed 5 in number, only one ticket is allowed. To that rule we have closely adhered, but cannot without outrage to our feelings and with safety to the public

peace. The fact meets us at every point that for such hire as 10 pence per day to the head of a family representing five, even supposing he can work six days in each week and be blessed with uninterrupted good health, he cannot properly support himself and his family. We find that many in such circumstances are perishing. Earnestly we solicit the attention of the government to this state of things, becoming daily worse by the daily increase in the price of food and the bodily deterioration of the people. The groups of applicants importuning us on this point makes our position very painful.

We are, Sir, your obedient Servants,

Rich. Challoner, esq.

Chas. Lambart, esq.

William Garrett

The three signers were landlords, men of privilege in Ireland's suffering countryside. But their status did them little good in Parliament, where the motto persisted that "Ireland's property should pay for Ireland's poverty." The Moynalty Relief Committee received a short response from the Relief Office, telling them that their request for flexibility on the "only one ticket for a family of up to five rule will be forwarded to the Board of Works for consideration." In the meantime, they should try to get more money from the local landlords, noting, "We trust they do not deceive themselves of their liability to repayment, as every shilling of the outlay must be assessed and collected in the proper proportionment field by law."

These letters are only a sample. I read several more, all expressing with growing desperation the impossible situation in Ireland. The physical presence of the actual letters in my hands made it feel immediate, as if it was happening today. They painted a vivid picture of the feudalistic scaffolding as it teetered under the weight of calamity.

In 1849, the very man who had been put in charge of dealing with these requests had had enough. Edward Twistleton, the chief poor law commissioner, resigned. The grounds for his decision were explained in a statement: "The destitution here is so horrible, and the indifference of the House of Commons to it so manifest, that he is an unfit agent of a policy that must be one of extermination."

I thought about the superficiality of my high school textbooks, which summarized the great wave of Irish emigration in words to the effect of "a large number of emigrants from Ireland flooded into the United States in the nineteenth century because of the failure of the potato."

Potatoes. It was about so much more than potatoes.

CHAPTER ELEVEN

Parliament's Response

FLOODS, DROUGHTS, FIRES, HURRICANES, tornadoes, pandemics. How do countries handle national and global disasters? How does a government respond to a crisis when it affects the poor in an outsized manner? The United States may not "colonize" other countries these days, but we allow the same stratification of our own citizens. It's tempting to look back at Britain during the Great Hunger and see nothing but mismanagement at best and cruelty at worst. There is truth to both. But in the United States today, how do we care for the "least of these"? Crises, whether Katrina or Covid, strip away the veneer many so comfortably live with and force us to see the underlying structures of inequity.

Think about this: Before the potato blight struck Ireland, the country had a population of eight million people, approximately the size of New York today. What if, in the span of five or six years, more than a million New Yorkers died of starvation or disease and another two million fled the city, desperate for a chance at survival? What would we do? What would we feel? How would the government respond?

The archive staff made copies for me of the 1821 census section that included the Farrellys and some of the famine committee letters from their area. That night I sat in bed, rereading the letters and thinking about Patrick's family, trying to put myself in their place. The next morning I went to the National Library to try to understand how things had gotten so bad. How did a mighty empire, geographically so close, allow part of its own kingdom to dissolve into chaos? The answer is complicated. The political and economic theories of England in the mid-1800s had a strong undercurrent of discrimination and mistrust, particularly in their colonies. Patrick and his family were caught in those particular wheels of power in Britain's first and nearest colony.

As the crisis unfolded, the British government debated numerous responses. Should Parliament provide direct relief and feed the starving poor? Should it create relief-work projects to make people earn their food? Should it change the laissez-faire market laws so substitute foods such as oats would be affordable?

The market rules were sacrosanct. And, sadly, it was nineteenth-century British dogma that you should not give anyone—especially the Irish—something for nothing. Parliament insisted that doing so would create dependency on government and reinforce the habits of "a lazy and petulant people." Charles Trevelyan, the British secretary of the treasury and decision maker on relief, famously said, "The judgement of God sent the calamity to teach the Irish a lesson; that calamity must not be too much mitigated."

Parliament did allow direct food provision, creating soup depots for a short time in a few areas. It was the most successful method of abating starvation. But London demanded constant reports of eligibility, which slowed the effort. The ministers wanted to be sure that the people getting soup really qualified as starving poor. If those men had crossed the Irish Sea, they wouldn't have needed a report: they would have seen the lines of ragged people who had walked miles for a small amount of watery gruel. But Trevelyan and others continued to blame the victims: "The real evil with which we have to contend is not the physical evil of the Famine, but the moral evil of the selfish, perverse and turbulent character of the people."

There were instances, however, when human compassion overruled bureaucracy. Individuals and private associations abroad offered compassionate help. Relatives who had already emigrated sent the largest amount of funds directly to family back in Ireland. The Society of Friends (Quakers) in the United States delivered a remarkable amount of assistance, raising the funds to send 118 ships to Ireland with supplies. People of the Choctaw Nation in Oklahoma, nearly destitute themselves and grieving the loss of their own native land by forced removal only a few years earlier, contributed $170. Two Jewish synagogues in New York—Shearith Israel and Shaaray Tefila—together raised over $1,000 for Ireland, the equivalent of more than $80,000 today. The US Congress, riddled with nativism and devoted, like the British Parliament, to a laissez-faire economy, could only agree to send two decommissioned warships with supplies but no funds. The ships were to leave from New York and Boston in 1847. The Boston Irish Relief Committee and others stocked the first ship with food and clothing, and it arrived in Cork to a deeply grateful reception. When the New York ship was delayed, with no monetary support from Congress to stock it and hire a crew, Captain George C. DeKay used his own money to fill the ship with food and deliver it to the Irish Quakers for distribution.

The Quakers in Dublin organized their own relief committee in the fall of 1847. They provided direct relief, food, and soup kitchens through the end of the next summer. Parliament requested that they continue, but they declined, pressing the British government to take responsibility for relief on a larger scale. It didn't work.

Outdoor relief meant work projects. The rules precluded any projects that would enhance a landlord's estate, so the starving Irish broke stones to build roads to nowhere in order to earn a few pence to buy what little food they could. As unregulated prices rose, their wages bought less and less. Traveling through the Irish countryside today, especially along Ireland's westernmost coast in Mayo, Donegal, Clare, and Galway, you can see the faint remains of useless roads wandering halfway up mountainsides.

Parliament pondered and argued about these questions but supplied no consistent approach to the snowballing disaster. The government opened soup kitchens in 1847 and then closed them before the year was out, began outdoor work relief and then suddenly ordered all projects to close, opened food depots and closed them.

The main concern was money. Who would pay for any kind of relief? In 1838 Parliament had passed the Irish Poor Laws, the first laws to deal specifically with the poverty rampant on the island. The laws divided the country up into sections called Poor Law Unions and established boards of guardians for each. The board would receive funds by taxing landowners: "Irish property will pay for Irish poverty." The revenues would then fund the building and maintenance of workhouses to deal with poverty-stricken people, whose numbers were increasing even before the famine. Workhouses had a long and notorious history in England and Ireland, existing since the 1700s as the last resort of the destitute and immortalized by Charles Dickens in *Oliver Twist*.

Families had to enter intact, which in Ireland allowed landlords to clear the property of those unable to pay rent. When a family entered, they were separated, men on one side and women on the other, with children above the age of two in yet another space. By spring of 1846 some forty-seven thousand people had entered workhouses. Three years later, more than a million people were crowded in what was referred to as *indoor relief*. By then, the Irish workhouses had become charnel houses, disease-infested buildings dooming their guardians or managers to an impossible task and their inhabitants to a horrific and lonely death.

By January 1847 the government was receiving 100 reports a day of starvation deaths. In Ireland's workhouses the number of reported deaths climbed to 2,700 per week. Many more deaths outside the workhouses went unreported. People collapsed and died along the roadside, and whole families succumbed in their cottages, the stones of which were then tumbled over them to form a grave.

As the potato crop continued to fail, poverty and starvation increased. Landlords now had even more difficulty collecting their rents and paying the increased poor law taxes. In the summer of 1847, Sir William Gregory, the British minister of Parliament for the city of Dublin, offered a solution. The poor law rates were bankrupting some landlords, but Gregory was primarily concerned that undeserving persons were obtaining relief. He offered an amendment that anyone existing on more than a quarter acre would need to relinquish their excess land to qualify for outdoor relief or entry to the workhouse. The amendment passed. The Gregory Clause forced tenants to turn over nearly all their land. Some landlords refused surrender of the portion above the quarter acre and were thus able to force the tenant to yield their entire holding.

Workhouse admissions continued grossly over capacity, and work projects were oversubscribed or nonexistent. Many tenants simply starved to death rather than give up their homes with no guarantee of any kind of relief. Landlords were required to pay a tax to London on their tenants' holdings, and for many it became cost effective to evict their tenants and destroy their homes. Others offered assisted emigration to their tenants. The Gregory Clause was mercilessly efficient and effective. By death or emigration, the land was gradually cleared.

It was the third year of the famine. Patrick was eleven years old. There were three more years to go, and the starkest were yet to come.

Soup kitchens opened in March 1847, and by August they were feeding three million a day. The great irony of that dark year was that very few potatoes had been planted because hardly anyone had seed potatoes, but the few that had been sown were healthy. Bolstered by the expectation that 1848 would produce a good crop, soup kitchens were closed. In London, Trevelyan declared that the famine was over.

It was not. In 1848 the entire crop failed again. And just as tenants such as the Farrellys and their neighbors in their mud and thatch cottages felt the increasing effects of the blight, so did the landlords who sat at the top of the feudal hierarchical ladder. The end was coming for them, too.

In 1849 the British government passed the Encumbered Estates Act. It allowed for the sale of Irish estates that had been mortgaged and whose owners could no longer meet their obligations. An estate could be put up for sale by the owner or by a person who had a claim on it. Many of the aristocrats had lived on credit for years before the famine struck, and as the owners of their debts came to collect, they could no longer keep up the pretense of solvency. The buyers were often speculators and could turn out tenants at will. Five million acres went on the auction block. Ten years after the famine began, three thousand estates, the "big houses" of Ireland, had been sold under the act.

Lurgan Lodge, the grand house near the Farrellys', was one of them. The sale property included three townlands, Curraghmore among them. All tenants were auctioned along with the property. At the time, Miss Eliza Nixon was listed as the estate's owner. Her tenants could not pay their rent in these dark times, and like many estate owners across the island, she was bankrupt.

Searching the genealogy site Find My Past, I found a newspaper advertisement for the auction of Lurgan Lodge:

In the Court of Commoners for Sale of Encumbered Estates in Ireland: Sale on Thursday, the 18th day of March, 1852, County of Cavan. In the matter of the estate of Eliza Nixon, of Lurgan Lodge in the County of Cavan, Spinster, Owner; Exparte James Hunter and William Shaw, petitioners. Rental of the lands of Lurgan, Curraghmore and Currakeel, situate in the barony of Castleraghan, and part of the lands of Drung in the barony of Tullaghgarvey, all situate in the county of Cavan. To be sold by the Commissioners at their Court Henrietta Street, Dublin, on Thursday, 18th day of March, at the hour of twelve o'clock at noon.

The document includes a list of Nixon's tenants with the amount of rent that could be collected from them. The sale was petitioned by James Hunter, the same agent who had collected rent from the Farrellys. I read down the list of tenants, looking for Patrick's family, but they were not there. Sometime between 1838, when Patrick's younger brother, Andrew, was born, and this sale in 1852, the family had disappeared from the land that had been their home for generations. The Farrellys had lived in Curraghmore long before 1821. Patrick and his siblings were all born and baptized there. But after Andrew's baptism there is no record of them in the parish. Father Tom said, "They fell off the books." But where did they fall? And why?

Did they leave during the famine or before it struck? Some of their neighbors from the 1821 census were still on the tenant list in 1852, but other names were new. Other tenants may have taken over land that others had left willingly or unwillingly. Patrick's grandfather, the patriarch of the family, had been living on nine acres of land in Curraghmore, growing flax to spin and sell and potatoes to feed his family. They were decently secure. But all of that changed.

CHAPTER TWELVE

Maps

A FEW DAYS AFTER my productive research in the archives, Bob arrived on the red-eye Aer Lingus flight from Chicago. After he took a short recovery nap in our hotel, we went out for breakfast and a walk around town to help him get over the jet lag.

As we walked across Stephen's Green the sun was shining—not a cloud in the sky. It was a glorious morning. But by the time we finished our coffee at Bewley's, the clouds had moved in. We foolish Americans had not thought to bring an umbrella. Out the door, dodging raindrops and picking up the pace, we turned off Grafton onto Duke Street. The rain changed from gentle Irish mist to serious downpour.

"Let's duck into Ulysses," I said. "We can dry off while we look at books." Ulysses Rare Books is a unique family-owned bookstore in Dublin. It's tiny, cramped, and full of literary treasures. Somewhere between a small museum and an actual commercial enterprise, it's an institution on Duke Street. Locals, tourists, writers, collectors—all are welcome. Customers are left alone to browse; no one offers help unless asked. First and signed editions of Joyce, Wilde, Yeats, and Heaney are their stock-in-trade, along with used and rare books on Irish history and—my favorite thing—maps.

It was crowded on the first floor. We weren't the only ones seeking refuge, so I suggested we go to the map room. Narrow stairs lead down to a basement room even smaller than the space upstairs. Low shelves along the wall hold lithographs of Ireland from the nineteenth and twentieth centuries and large maps of the whole country. We were about to go back upstairs when I remembered the pocket Ordnance Survey maps that are kept on a shelf below the counter. I love these old maps. The original "Ord maps" were the product of a huge survey and mapping project undertaken by the British between 1825 and 1846 and printed in the 1830s and 1840s. They are finely detailed and include buildings and other sites that the surveyor deemed significant: bridges, chapels, holy wells, ancient forts, and cottage sites marked by little dots. In 1899, small versions of the larger maps were printed on card stock and folded into eighths, sized to fit in a jacket pocket for tourists and locals alike. The original purpose of the survey was to enable taxation and land valuation, but the small pocket maps became useful guides for nineteenth-century tourists. The government still prints up-to-date large Ord maps, which are found in tourist offices and especially useful for hikers, history lovers, and anyone wanting to explore off the beaten path, but if you have a soft spot for maps, as I do, the originals are both beautiful and fascinating.

Ulysses picks up old Ord maps at estate sales or from collectors, and every time I visit, I check to see if they have any that include sections of Cavan or Meath. I hadn't had any luck thus far, but I asked Bob to wait a minute while I browsed the ten or twelve sitting on the shelf. Dublin, more Dublin, Donegal, Cork, Galway, Leitrim, Roscommon . . . wait—Cavan! On the outside fold was the British crown and a date: 1903. I wondered what section of Cavan this covered. Not daring to hope, I carefully unfolded the stiff paper and caught my breath. The first thing I saw was a large splash of blue—Lough Ramor! And there's the village of Virginia, and down the road, the townland of Curraghmore where Patrick was born. It was incredibly detailed, marking St. Patrick's holy well, Lurgan Lodge, the flax mill, and the abbey. I couldn't believe it. Looking closer, I saw that the map covered a slice of Meath, too. Could it possibly be? I followed the roads, tiny red lines on a tan background, and there it was: Moynalty, the village where Patrick and Bridget were married. And not far from the church (noted as "RC chapel") was the townland of Skearke where Bridget was from and where Margaret lives. I was gobsmacked, as they say.

An inch to a mile. The entire real estate of my Irish ancestors' lives. I grabbed Bob's arm and said, "We're buying this no matter what it costs." It was a bargain at twenty euros.

Outside, the rain had stopped as quickly as it had started. We paid the shopkeeper and went for a walk. I kept thinking, *If it hadn't rained, if we hadn't turned down Duke Street, if we'd gone for coffee somewhere else . . .*

There are times when you know you are not alone on a journey. Some experiences are just hard to explain—well, that's the point. It's as if someone dropped a signpost, left a secret message, communicated in some unmistakable yet unexplainable way. I'm not a tarot-card-and-crystal-loving new-age kind of person. But I had to ask myself: Did some kind of force lead me toward something so small as an old map? Was Patrick guiding me? I don't know. But I can say with certainty that some events in our lives are more than coincidence. Someone might say, "Well, these things happen." But when they happen to you, you can sense that it's not business as usual. *Thin places* is the Irish phrase for experiences, times, or places in which the line between the living and the dead, the present and the past, becomes porous. Things can happen.

What was going on? At the National Archives I had found that fragment of the 1821 census record, a one-day snapshot of the Farrelly family and the townland of Curraghmore. Then I had held in my hand letters from Virginia and Moynalty, written on specific days during the famine, with descriptions of disaster and voices pleading for help. And now I'd found this map.

I didn't know what to make of it, but I can tell you that when I've had experiences like this—and I've had a few—it's as if a voice is saying, "You're on the right path. Just keep going."

The next day, the day after the Great Map Find, Bob and I drove out to Moynalty. We had two more weeks in Ireland, and we would begin them, as always, with several days at the Flanagan farm.

Warmly greeted by Margaret with fresh brown bread and copious cups of tea, we settled in and told her about our time in Dublin. I proudly displayed my prized Ord map. Because of her knowledge of local history, people contact her while searching their family roots in the area. She likes hunting down their histories, too. We made plans for an exploration drive the next morning.

After a good night's sleep and hearty breakfast we set out, armed with two maps: the old one from the bookstore, and a current version I picked up in Dublin. The updated version covers a larger area, but it was possible to line up my century-old find with the current one and work our way backward through time. We would drive through Curraghkeel, Curraghmore, and Cleggan. These three Lurgan parish townlands sit next to one another, their names like a children's rhyme. In the car, following along the old map and census, we tried to picture what the area was like at the start of the famine. It was a sort of historical treasure hunt.

We had driven these roads numerous times, but it's still easy to miss a turnoff. Ireland's numerous rural roads are rarely marked, and there are many ways to get to the same place. Locals each have their favorite way, but if you're not a local, it can be like driving through a maze. Even with directions from Margaret, who doesn't drive but has lived near here all her life, we got temporarily lost. We pulled over, stopped a farmer on a tractor, and asked, "Can you help us? We're lost."

He replied, "You're not lost—you're right here!"

He directed us to a turn ahead, and we got back to where we needed to be. We passed open fields, a smattering of smaller, older homes, and then the ruins of the Lurgan abbey and cemetery. There was the narrow stone bridge that had stood there since the 1700s, arching over the running stream that feeds St. Patrick's holy well. The same bridge, the same stream, and the same holy well that Patrick knew as a boy.

There is an atmosphere of mystery around Curraghmore. I've never passed another car on the road. The bridge that you cross to enter the townland always makes me think of *Brigadoon*, the Lerner and Loewe musical about a Scottish village that was placed under a spell. In the story, the spell caused Brigadoon to disappear except for one day every hundred years, when it emerges from the mist. Sometimes when I stand on that bridge, I want to cast a spell to make the past reemerge before me. But I had to be satisfied and grateful to be here in the twenty-first century in Bob's and Margaret's good company.

As we crossed the bridge, the trees and hedges grew closer, and the road narrowed and rose up a hill. A lane off to one side approached only empty fields and hedgerows; no old cottages remained. Straight up the hill were a few homes and some sheep grazing in the fields. Far back in the woods to the right, impossible to see from the road, was what remained of Lurgan Lodge, the former Nixon estate. Further up the road, one vacant cottage sat alone. Margaret said it looked like it had been built around the time that Ireland gained its independence in 1920, when people had increased access to the land. On the opposite side and further up the road was a restored stone cottage opposite a working dairy farm. And that was it—we had reached the end of Curraghmore and entered Cleggan without realizing it. We stopped at the dairy farm to ask if they knew of any Farrellys who had lived around here. There had been a Ned Farrelly, they said, in that 1920s house down the road, but he was gone years ago.

We turned the car around and headed back down the hill. Right after we crossed the bridge, we turned left and followed what the old map labeled "the flax road," which ran parallel to the stream that drove the wheel for the mill up ahead. The land here wasn't great for growing much of anything beyond brambles and rushes, but it was suited for growing flax and, of course, potatoes. The Farrelly family and their neighbors had been integrally involved in the flax industry.

I had brought along my copy of the 1821 census to show Margaret, hoping she could tell me more about it. On the day the census taker visited, the people in the Farrelly household were Thomas and Rose; their children Rose and Patrick (my Patrick's father); and two young granddaughters. Pat and Catherine Smyth and their daughter lived there too. This census had taken me back six generations, to Thomas and Rose, my fourth great-grandparents!

From the size of their land, even sharing their acres with another family, Margaret thought the Farrellys looked modestly secure in 1821. But their stability was tied precariously to a plant we barely think about anymore: flax. *Linum usitatissimum.* I asked her how flax farming worked. She made a face and said, "It's a very smelly business. And very hard work." Sometimes called linseed, the plant has tall, slender stems and delicate blue or white flowers. The stems contain fibers that are stronger than cotton and have been used to make linen cloth for thousands of years. Irish linen was in high demand in England, and Cavan was part of the flax belt that produced it. The Farrellys' townland of Curraghmore had all the prerequisites for flax growing, including a swift stream to turn the mill wheel. After harvest, the flax was put into a shallow pool to soak. This was called retting— the messy, smelly business that made Margaret wrinkle her nose. With their rigid outer layers partially rotted, the inner fibers could then be separated and worked into bundles by hand to be spun and eventually woven to create linen. The mill eliminated some of the hand work; it "scutched" the fibers, beating fragments of the outer stem off the fine inner fibers to prepare them for spinning.

We pulled up beside the shuttered mill, still standing, but so heavily overgrown with vines it was hard to see. Once it was a thing of glory, humming with life, its huge wheel turning by the force of the cold, clear water. We could barely see the wheel inside, but it was still there. I imagined people walking down this lane, shouts and noise rising from this brick edifice of a once-new technology, the pride of the community.

But, like much technology, the mill met its end. The industrial age gained speed, and the demand for linen in England and North America increased until small mills couldn't keep up. Larger mill complexes with spinning machines were built in the big cities of Belfast, Dublin, and Cork, near ports for shipping. Home spinning could no longer manage the demand. Many young women left home and moved to the cities to work on the machines that replaced hand spinning and weaving. The spinning wheels their mothers, sisters, and grandmothers had operated at the doors of their cottages slowed and then stopped altogether.

While the large industrial mills in the cities created more and more linen, the fabric of small communities began to tear. In townlands such as Curraghmore, living conditions for the small farmer and laborer began to deteriorate without income from the linen trade. Families who had enjoyed the cash buffer from spun flax that allowed them to purchase oats, butter, and flour now subsisted on potatoes alone. But the nutritious potato allowed the population to continue to expand, and tenants continued to subdivide their plots, each family living on smaller and smaller acreage. The stage was being set for the calamity to come. By the time Patrick was born in 1836, the economy of the Midlands of Ireland was already in a precipitous decline.

This situation in Cavan and across Ireland was similar to what happened in the United States when the car industry nearly crashed in Detroit or when the mines shut down in West Virginia. Suddenly, everything changes. When factories close, small shops and restaurants shut down, banks close, and the economies of small towns collapse seemingly overnight as homes lose their value and people lose their jobs.

Thomas Farrelly, Patrick's grandfather, died in January 1825, according to the parish records. But we know his family was still in Curraghmore when Patrick's brother Andrew was born and baptized in the parish in 1838. And then they were all gone.

Maybe the sale of Lurgan Lodge was a clue. Were they evicted? I may never know what happened to the rest of them, but I do know what happened to Patrick.

CHAPTER THIRTEEN

Paying Respect

HE WAS SIXTEEN when he left his home for North America. Was his mother still alive? His older brother and sister? I don't know. I know that his father was still alive when Patrick returned to Ireland in 1863, but what about the rest of the family? The 1851 census records might have helped, but only a fragment of them survives and it doesn't include Cavan. And Cavan lost 43 percent of its population to death and emigration during the famine. Two-thirds of that loss was from emigration and one-third from starvation and disease.

I've often wondered where Patrick's parents, grandparents, and other family are buried in Ireland. I don't expect there are markers with their names. I'm wiser now about graveyards. When I talk to friends who are looking for their own ancestors in Ireland, I tell them to visit the National Archives and the National Library. Find the parish, look for census records, talk to the parish priest, and find out the history of the area. Find the people in the village who still hold the stories, as Margaret has done for us. Be thankful for the internet, but don't neglect actual shoe-leather work. Use records and technology as a guide, but drive out on the small roads, get out of the car, talk to people. As our friend in Dublin's library said, "Walk the roads they walked."

I've done those things over the years, and I've discovered a lot, but I've never found where my family—those who stayed in Ireland, the ones who didn't emigrate—are buried, or when or how they died. But because I am part of the Irish diaspora, a descendant of famine-era emigrants, I don't feel that I can be a guest on this island where my ancestors lived through it without paying my respects to those who stayed and died. The fact is, I'm living in America today because someone from my family made it out. Four generations later, I can buy a plane ticket, rent a car, and drive through the land that they left. I can pay my respects.

Buchenwald, Wounded Knee, Charleston's slave port, Skibbereen. Those names carry a heavy weight. How can we begin to understand the suffering of others if we don't understand what our own people may have suffered? And if our personal history includes ancestors who were complicit in the suffering of others, then the need to know is even greater.

An Irish friend told me that famine dead were often buried along the sides of a cemetery, sometimes at night, sometimes in secret. Concern about disease, poverty, and the practical necessity of the moment—or, in the case of unbaptized infants, harsh religious constraints—put them there. Whatever the reason, they were placed away from the more respectable dead. On the edge.

In the village of Mullagh, just up the road from Lurgan parish, there's an old church and cemetery called Teampall Cheallaigh. At the back is a large stone placed there in 1997 for the 150-year commemoration of the famine. On the stone is a plaque that reads, "In memory of the three hundred and twenty sons and daughters of the parish of Mullagh who died during the Great Famine." This was Patrick's mother's parish. There are old McKenna graves there, too. It's likely family of mine are here under the ground.

Another cemetery not far from Patrick's townland is Moybologue. Set high on a hill circled by a stone wall, it holds the ruins of an ancient monastery built on top of a more ancient settlement. Layers upon layers, like all things Irish. Inside the wall is a fenced-off section with a plaque: "Those who died in the famine in 1847 are buried here." That simple statement hides a grim fact documented in the April 23, 1847, edition of *Anglo-Celt*, the local newspaper: "On average, eight bodies are <u>daily interred</u> in the burying grounds of Moy Bologue. The deaths in the workhouse amount to more than twenty a week."

Were any of my ancestors carried up the road in carts and buried here? I just don't know. Sixteen-year-old Patrick got out in the last years of the famine. Did it claim his mother? His sister? Aunts, uncles, cousins? All I know is that his family disappeared from Curraghmore in the midst of it.

I can't visit the certain resting places of my ancestors here, and because of that, I feel a need to stop at famine graveyards when I come across them in Ireland. It's an incomplete visitation, but it's something. And those under the ground are somebody's people. If I can't find my own, I can stand there for others.

Once, while driving through Kilkenny, Bob and I stopped at the village of Callan. I'd read about the Callan workhouse and cemetery in Lonely Planet's guidebook. In Callan, as in many other towns, workhouses bore the brunt of the worst years of hunger. Originally built to provide temporary relief for the poor, they were stretched to multiple times their allowed accommodation. The Callan workhouse was designed to hold 600 men, women, and children. By 1851 it held more than 2,000. At the height of the worst years of the famine, a total of 3,515 deaths were reported in this workhouse and the fever sheds that were built alongside it.

The unusual thing about Callan is that the workhouse is still standing. It's an active place once again, now occupied by artists, community groups, and researchers. Rather than tear it down, the town let it stand as a reminder. The building was closed when we pulled up, but we thought we'd try to find the cemetery while we were there. We stopped at a SPAR convenience store and asked the girl at the front counter for directions to the workhouse cemetery. As we left, she added a warning: "Don't drive down the boreen to the cemetery unless you want to get stuck in the muck. Leave the car at the turnoff and walk the rest of the way."

We followed her directions down a narrow road from the town center, past the workhouse, to a small white sign with black print that said, simply, "Famine cemetery." Heeding her warning, we left the car and started down the path—the boreen, she'd called it—on foot. It was very narrow and deeply rutted, a muddy road with overgrown hedges along both sides. From time to time a break in the hedge allowed a glimpse of a cow in a field. It was cloudy and had rained during the past week, so we had to look hard for a solid piece of ground to place our feet. Wise words about the muck. Only a tourist would be walking this path without wellies. It was mainly a cow path, so there was that evidence to watch out for as well. Just as we began to doubt that we were on the right path, we saw two stone pillars with an iron gate ahead of us, off to the right.

I lifted the heavy latch, and we entered. Inside were two large fields of grass separated by a low hedge and bordered by small trees bearing yellow cherrylike fruit. The guide book called it Cherryfield. This land had been given for a pauper cemetery by Lord Clifden, Callan's absentee landlord. Between 1846 and 1850, more than three thousand people who died in the Callan workhouse or fever sheds were buried here.

It was quiet and strangely peaceful. Bob and I sat down on a stone wall near the gate to take it all in. There was not another soul in sight. We had stepped into a world that seemed very far away from Callan town and the dark, muddy path we had walked to get here. The sun came out suddenly, the way it does in this country, sweeping across the wide swaths of green grass. Birds began to sing on cue. Bob tapped my shoulder and pointed out an old sign on the gate that we had missed when we entered. Written in both English and Irish, it read, "In memory of the uncounted victims of famine and poverty who died here in Callan Workhouse."

I remembered the urgency in the famine relief committee letters that I'd read in the National Archives, the way they tried to explain how bad it was, how they begged for assistance from the British Parliament. The bumbling, bureaucratic responses they received came wrapped in the guise of economic theory and specious claims of God's will. The lives of the people in this cemetery and others like it were silenced, unremembered. They ended up here because of the decisions made by politicians sitting at a comfortable distance.

Along the stone wall, next to the old sign, was a newer one. Speaking for Ireland and other nations, its words are a plea for justice: "Famine is the closing scene of a drama whose most important and decisive acts have been played out behind closed doors."

The unremembered have a voice.

CHAPTER FOURTEEN

Skibbereen

OUR STOP AT CALLAN, Kilkenny, was along our drive to Cork, where Bob and I were going to spend a week in what Ireland refers to as its sunny south. It does boast the mildest weather on the island, thanks to the Gulf Stream and the warm wind it brings from the sea. In fact, some of the landscaping we saw looked oddly out of place in Ireland. During the Victorian age, it was popular for landlords and gentry to plant exotic palm trees on their garden estates and in the towns. They survive, but to my eye they look a little lost and confused.

There is a lot for a tourist to see and do in County Cork. Cork City itself is vibrant, a little more gritty and less cosmopolitan than Dublin. With a history of uprisings, Cork is proud of its moniker, the Rebel County. The countryside around it is dotted with ancient history: Neolithic passage tombs, stone circles, and ogham stones inscribed with the most ancient form of writing found in Ireland.

One morning we drove out to the Drombeg stone circle, a frequently visited megalith in the county. On a hill, seventeen tall upright stones and one large horizontal stone are aligned to the winter solstice. A sign near the parking lot explained that the cremated remains of a teenager had been buried in the center of the circle some three thousand years ago. We walked the circumference and looked out on the rolling green hills, wondering about the people who raised these stones and the lone teenager who was important enough to be buried here.

From Drombeg we drove on to the town of Skibbereen, a place I'd wanted to visit since I began to learn about the Great Hunger. Skibbereen gained its notoriety from the traditional song of the same name. The lyrics are a dialogue between a son and his father. The son asks, "If Ireland is so beautiful, why did you leave?" and the father gives his poignant response:

My son, I loved my native land with energy and pride
'Til a blight came over all my crops, my sheep and cattle died.
The rent and taxes were to pay, I could not them redeem,
And that's the cruel reason why I left old Skibbereen.

Oh, it's well I do remember that bleak December day
The landlord and the sheriff came to drive us all away.
They set my roof on fire with their cursed English spleen,
And that's another reason why I left old Skibbereen.

Your mother too, God rest her soul, fell on the snowy ground.
She fainted in her anguish, seeing the desolation 'round.
She never rose but passed away from life to mortal dream.
She found a quiet grave, my boy, in the abbey near Skibbereen.

And you were only two years old, and feeble was your frame.
I could not leave you with your friends. You bore your father's name.
I wrapped you in my cota mór in the dead of night unseen.
I heaved a sigh and bade goodbye to dear old Skibbereen

The lyricist was Patrick Carpenter, a Skibbereen native who emigrated to the United States after the Great Hunger. Most likely written in the United States after the end of the famine, the song spread throughout Ireland during the postfamine years. It remains a powerful lament, recorded by many traditional singers.

Before the Great Hunger, Skibbereen was a busy market town. But once the potato failed and starvation set in, the thriving market was of little help to the poor. Major Parker, the Board of Relief inspector, reported on December 21, 1846:

> On Saturday the market was supplied with meat, bread and fish. This contradiction is occurring all over Ireland. Trevelyan insists that the resources of the country should be drawn out, failing to realize that those resources are utterly inaccessible to the wretches dying in the street and by the roadsides. The starving in such places as Skibbereen, perish not because there is no food, but because they have no money with which to buy it (quoted in Woodham-Smith, *The Great Hunger*, 156).

One year later, Parker himself would be dead, having caught famine fever on his inspections throughout the country. During the onset of the famine, Irish newspapers carried terrifying accounts of starvation and death in the town. Some in government who could not or would not believe the accounts chose to travel there themselves. Their witness confirmed that the reports, if anything, had underestimated the situation, and the name *Skibbereen* quickly became synonymous with famine and fatalities. In the December 21, 1846 issue, the *Cork Examiner* reported, "Disease and death in every quarter—the once-hardy population worn away to emaciated skeletons—fever, dropsy, diarrhea and famine rioting in every homeland sweeping away whole families. . . . Seventy-five tenants ejected here, and a whole village in the last stages of destitution there. . . . Dead bodies of children flung into holes hastily scratched in the earth without shroud or coffin— wives traveling ten miles to beg the charity of a coffin for a dead husband and bearing it back that weary distance. . . . Every field a grave and the land a wilderness."

Today, Skibbereen is a busy, vibrant place, with shops, restaurants, and colorful flower baskets lining the streets. The town works hard to straddle its dark history and its vibrant present. A brochure from the Cork Visitors Center advertises, "The thriving town of Skibbereen is the capital of West Cork, center of all agricultural, industrial and tourist activities of a wide region. . . . twenty-six pubs in town, and award-winning restaurants."

Bob and I found our way to the local heritage center, which has exhibits and information on the history of the Great Hunger. A tourist map pointed out local sites to see. I asked the woman at the desk for directions to the famine cemetery called Abbeystrowry, and she said we couldn't miss it. "It's just off the main road after you cross the bridge," she said. "You'll see the sign."

Driving out of town, across the bridge and onto the busy road, we almost missed the sign she'd mentioned. Abbeystrowry shows up in every Ireland travel guide as an important famine burial ground. The cemetery was built up around a medieval abbey on a hill above the river. There's an incongruence to its location just off the busy N71 that runs along the River Ilen and away from Skibbereen. I had expected it to be off on a small, isolated road in the countryside— quiet, private. But no, it's right outside town. And, in retrospect, that made sense.

Pulling the car off the road, we parked on a gravelly space between the cemetery and the N71. The iron gate was painted white and covered with a small roof, making the entrance look oddly like a little house. As we entered, I could see that the graveyard was terraced; it rose up a steep hill with dirt and gravel paths leading to the top. It was much larger than I'd expected. Gravestones covered the terraces all the way to the top, where the stone ruins of the old abbey stood.

Just inside the gate and to my right was a large, level stretch of thick, lush grass, an almost perfect rectangle about the size of a soccer field. It had no stones or markers. Since it was near the gate, I assumed this was a newer part of the cemetery. And then a glint from a small, low stone of bright white granite caught my eye. I walked along the path to where it stood and bent down to read the inscription: "In memory of the victims of the famine whose coffin-less bodies were buried in this plot."

This was a famine pit. I don't know what I had expected—but it was not this, so naked and visible, not hidden away down a long road like the Callan workhouse cemetery. It took my breath away. It was so large, so stark. Dense green grass blanketed the eight to ten thousand bodies that filled this ground. I cannot visualize eight or ten thousand bodies. But they are there, nameless, lying on top of one another under this grass. Men, women, and children from the town and nearby countryside, victims of starvation and disease. Horses drew carts piled with bodies down the road we'd just driven on; they passed through these gates every day during the worst years of the Great Hunger. At times a hundred bodies a week were brought for burial. No coffin, no funeral, no last prayers. Spilled into the pit and quickly covered with a thin layer of soil and lime by exhausted gravediggers because more were on the way. Their names forgotten. Their lives reduced to this brutal, cold, unceremonious end.

At first, the bodies of famine victims were buried unmarked around the old abbey ruins up on the hill. But as the deaths began to come too fast, a pit was dug conveniently near the road. Then it was expanded, and expanded again. By 1847 starving people from the countryside had fled to the town, looking for work, for relief, for food. Some crawled on their hands and knees, begging to enter the grossly over-crowded workhouse. They would go anywhere and do anything for food for themselves, for their families. Some died along the roadside, their mouths stained green from eating grass. Those who were carried to this cemetery were but a fraction of the twenty-eight thousand from the town of Skibbereen who had died of hunger and disease by the end of the famine.

Back near the gate I found another small monument: a row of four white marble stones with words engraved in both Irish and English: "Pause—and you can almost hear the sounds echo down the ages; the creak of the burial cart, the rattle of the hinged-coffin door, the sigh of spade on earth. Now and again, all day long."

Over my shoulder I could hear the cars on the N17 still speeding by. Beside the highway, the river flowed on as it had every day through those terrible years, bearing quiet witness.

CHAPTER FIFTEEN

I Heaved a Sigh
and Said Goodbye

LEAVING WAS THE ONLY RECOURSE for millions. I don't know
the day or month when Patrick left, or what ship he boarded or what
port he entered after making landfall in America. In 1851 he would
have been one of 11,500 from County Cavan who said goodbye to
parents, siblings, villages, and fields—to everything they knew. Everything that meant home.

In the last years of the famine, the death toll was still rising; for
survivors, the only sensible thing left was to go, or at least to send the
children out. They must have wondered whether this was truly the
end. Had the worst of it passed?

By 1850, the famine Irish who had survived the journey to North
America were sending an astounding annual average of £1.2 million
back to help their families escape. This sum came not from families
of wealth, but rather from those who were struggling themselves.
What came to be called "the American letter" would arrive by post
to family back in Ireland, bearing stories often filled with hope and,
more importantly, currency. In 1851 alone, that currency would help
250,000 Irish men, women, and children make the Atlantic crossing.

The darkest years of the Great Hunger, 1846 to 1849, were dom-
inated by desperation: landlord clearances, evictions, starvation, and
fever. The headlong rush to leave must have felt like the death throes

THE *JEANIE JOHNSTON*, CUSTOM HOUSE QUAY,
DUBLIN, IRELAND

of the country. When Patrick left, evictions, disease, and death were still taking their toll. Communities were decimated, the fabric of the culture torn to shreds. This accumulated sense that things had been irreparably changed drove laborers, small farmers, whole families, and single women to the docks. Families who couldn't save enough money for fare for all would choose one person, the strongest and most likely to survive the passage and succeed overseas, hoping that they would send for those who remained. It was an accepted fact that the best hope of a future lay on the other side of the ocean.

How did Patrick get out? Did someone in America pay for his passage? There is a good chance that one or more of his relatives had gone ahead to America and could provide help and a place to land. Emigrants generally go where they know someone.

By the time Lurgan Lodge was sold, the Farrellys were gone from Curraghmore; they are not listed among the tenants in the sale. Did the landlord turf them out, or did they leave of their own choice? The land they'd lived on may have been absorbed by one of the remaining tenants or by new ones. Their cottage may have been tumbled or become another family's home. Their ties to Curraghmore, this small bit of familiar land where generations of the family had lived and died, were severed.

Where did they all go? I know Patrick came to the United States, of course. His younger brother, Andrew, followed many years later. I don't know what happened to his older twin siblings, Thomas and Rose, or their mother. But in 1856, Patrick's father shows up in a new townland. Griffith's Valuation was a record of land value used to enable British taxation. Enumerators went house to house in each townland, determining the value of homes, from mud cottages to massive estates. The process took years. In the absence of lost census records, it's one of the most valuable resources for people trying to locate their family in postfamine Ireland.

In Griffith's, a record shows Patrick's father living about five miles away from his old home in Curraghmore. Now he's in the townland of Lisnabantry, part of a different parish with a different landlord. His life had changed radically. Born on a small family farm of nine Irish acres, now he was living in a corner of a one-acre field in a dwelling worth just five shillings. He shared the field with three other families. What could have caused that dramatic downsizing? Eviction? Patrick's departure for America seems to have coincided with the family's move from Curraghmore.

I've tried to imagine what the leaving was like for my great-grandfather. Was he alone or traveling with a cousin, an uncle, an aunt? Did he walk the fifty miles to the nearest port, at Dublin? Maybe he caught a ride on a cart with others heading toward the docks. It would have taken several days to walk. He may have passed people looking for food or work. The countryside would have revealed its fresh, raw wounds: deserted cottages, fallow fields, and the faint, lingering smell of potatoes rotted deep in the earth. An uneasy quiet.

Dublin was a loud, crowded, and dirty place. Unlike the countryside, where population declined during the famine, city and town populations had swollen with people desperate for work and food. Temporary lodgings—most of them just large, crowded rooms with straw on the floor to sleep on and, if you had the money, a pittance of a breakfast—had sprung up to deal with the emigrant surge and the influx of people. How did Patrick find a safe place to stay?

He was just sixteen. Did he have shoes? Did they hurt? He wouldn't have worn them at home. His clothes would have been simple: linen shirt, pants, a jacket, and cap. Perhaps in his pocket a bit of soil or a small stone, a reminder of this life to carry to the other side. Did his ma send a bit of food for the journey—was she even alive? Any cash and his ticket would have been sewn into the lining of his coat or pants, maybe with the address of a relative in Philadelphia or New York.

He must have had mixed feelings—the excitement of a sixteen-year-old boy for this new thing, the grand adventure of a great ship on the ocean. But also the slight catch in his throat at saying goodbye. A handshake with his da, Andrew looking on at just fourteen, wondering when he, too, would go. I envision Patrick walking away from his hearth, his cottage, his homeland. In a moment he would catch sight of the main road ahead, the turn away from all this and toward whatever mysteries were to come. He couldn't possibly have imagined what lay ahead. Soon he couldn't see the house or his family and friends waving goodbye. Did he look back, or did he try to keep his eyes straight ahead?

These departures were so common that there was a ritual for them: the American wake. Most parents knew it was coming at some point, even in the best of times, and this was the worst of times. Parents who had seen their children survive all kinds of peril now said goodbye to them forever, as if they had died. Tried to memorize a face, the sound of a voice, a laugh. Knowing that this child was unlikely to ever return, they prayed for a safe journey, for a reassuring letter to come.

In a culture where extended family was the organizing center of life, the continual rupture of mass emigration was an open wound. Solace came from community. In rural Ireland, there was always a person—the priest, the publican, the teacher—who could read out the American letter and translate it for Irish speakers. When it came with money for passage, this person might hold on to it until the ticket was purchased, knowing that it meant survival for another neighbor or friend. These communal anchors knew other families going through the same thing. They knew that comfort could be found in knowing you weren't alone in your loss. The leaving was endemic: a great, silent wail drifting up like the ghost of the turf smoke from the now-cold hearths in empty cottages.

The emigrant carried this loss with them too, painful emotions tangled with hopes. I want to believe Patrick wasn't alone on the crossing, that someone he knew made the trip with him. I want to believe he had someone to watch out for him.

There was a tradition that the last person to leave a cottage would bring a few smoldering sods of their turf fire to a neighbor's hearth, to "keep the fire burning" until their return. But rarely did they return. It was a bold act of hope that revealed how hard it was to go. The idea that you would *choose* to leave your country, your land, your people, forever was an alien concept. In fact, the Irish language has no proper equivalent for the English word *emigrant*. Kerby Miller explains in *Emigrants and Exiles*, "Rather the Irish word primarily used to describe one who left Ireland has been *deorai*, the literal meaning of which is exile" (105).

I can see the teenaged Patrick in the faces of today's refugees and migrants on the evening news. A young man, dark hair and tired eyes, stepping over the edge of a rubber raft that somehow managed to reach solid ground. Daily they still come, refugees from war, hundreds a day crossing the Mediterranean Sea to land on the Greek islands. Fleeing homes in Syria, Iraq, Somalia, Afghanistan. I see him in the eyes of the teenage boy fleeing gangs in Honduras or El Salvador, brought to the border by smugglers who took the money his family couldn't spare and left him to cross on his own. Exhausted from walking hundreds of miles, sick and thirsty, fleeing violence and poverty. Heedless of the dangers, doing whatever it takes to survive. He knows his family is counting on him to be the one who escapes, the one who holds their hope for the future.

It's a piercing echo of the famine Irish who arrived on our shores. I find it dispiriting that anyone of Irish descent in a position of power can have the moral amnesia to not make this obvious connection, to ignore their own family's history. It's all there, what their own people experienced: the physical risks, the hustlers making money on the misfortune of others and caring little for their survival. The emigrant's tenuous hold on life and their few precious belongings; the emotional and physical weight of hunger and fear and loss; all caught in the politics of the nation on the receiving end.

What was it like for Patrick? I have none of his own words about his passage, and I haven't been able to find a record of his ship. But I can generalize from information in historical reports. Between 1845 and 1855, two million people left Ireland's shores, primarily for North America, some for Australia, and some 750,000 for England. It was the largest movement of people in the nineteenth century. For perspective, imagine all the inhabitants of Chicago vanishing over a ten-year period. This was Ireland's loss from emigration alone. Starvation and disease took another million—nearly the equivalent of Dallas's population in 2020. Some left Irish ports directly for their destination, but most took the ferry to the Liverpool docks, where their ships were waiting. Those headed for Canada disembarked in Quebec at Grosse Isle; those headed for the United States, like my ancestors, found ports along the East Coast, primarily New York, Philadelphia, and Boston. The best time to cross was in the late spring and through the summer, but as things got worse, ships left in all seasons. In the winter, the port of New Orleans offered an alternative to the iced-up waterways of New England. Five thousand ships made the Atlantic crossing during the Great Hunger in a steady stream.

Crossing the Atlantic during the years of the Great Hunger was an enormous risk. Dependent on wind and weather, the crossing could take one to two months or longer. In 1847 alone there were 17,465 documented deaths during the ocean passage, largely from fever and disease, but also from fire or shipwreck caused by icebergs. Bodies were wrapped in a sheet and dropped overboard. Sharks followed the wake of the ships. Unknown but likely high numbers of deaths went undocumented, and many of those who made it across died soon after disembarking or while they waited in quarantine stations.

As the demand increased, passenger ships were joined by freighters. Cargo ships would dock in Liverpool with lumber or grain from

North America, unload the cargo, and refit the hulls with six-by-six-foot berths, double- and triple-decked for the emigrant trade. Each berth accommodated four to six persons. A child was not considered a full person, so six or eight might share the space. There was little regulation of British ships, and what existed was frequently ignored. American ships were more regulated and could therefore command a slightly higher price. The cost of passage to New York on a ship under US control was four to seven pounds, but a British ship to Canada was cheaper. Those were the infamous coffin ships, so overcrowded that hundreds died during passage. Landlords who offered assisted emigration to their tenants typically chose the cheaper British ships. When it was up to a ship's captain to limit or ignore his ship's capacity, greed drove the overloading of ships and increased mortality.

The first slow trickle of departures grew to a chaotic crescendo by 1847. Ships bound for Canada carried more of the poorest people, who were often the sickest. On arrival, they had to pass through the quarantine station at Grosse Isle in the St. Lawrence River before going on to Quebec or Montreal. In June 1847 one report documented forty ships that dropped anchor in a line stretching over two miles, waiting for permission to land at Grosse Isle to unload their starved, ragged, and diseased passengers. While they waited, typhus, cholera and dysentery continued to pick off those still on board. By midsummer the line had grown longer. More than five thousand people are buried in a mass grave on Grosse Isle, some who died on board and many more who died in fever sheds after they disembarked. Thousands of those bound for Canada had died at sea. Even on the better-regulated US ships to Boston, Philadelphia, and New York, tens of thousands died before they reached shore.

When I try to imagine Patrick's journey, it's the departure of his ship from the dock in Liverpool that fills my mind. He waits in a long line of his fellow countrymen and women, his hand clenched tight on the rope along the side of the plank as he follows them up to the deck. His other hand holds tight to his small bag of belongings. He tries to keep his eyes away from the dark water below. His ship is one among hundreds of tall ships that line the dockside, their masts like tall, leafless trees in a giant forest. He's trying to be brave. He is excited and terrified all at once.

The last of the passengers steps on board. Then, suddenly, the captain shouts and the crew pulls up the plank, closes the gate, and lifts anchor. Patrick holds on to the rail to steady himself and get a better look. Everyone jostles for space along the rail. The ship creaks on its way out into the middle of the watery lane, her sails still down but ready to be lifted to the wind. The people back on the dock grow smaller. His heart is beating hard and fast. The sails billow as the ship moves out into open water. A short while later, someone cries out that they see the Irish coast. Patrick is aware that the ship will go past it, will not turn back even if, for a moment, his heart might wish it to do so. It will go farther and farther away from Ireland and toward this idea of America.

PART THREE

America

CHAPTER SIXTEEN

Philadelphia

WE HUMANS HAVE BEEN migrating since we emerged on Earth—following food sources, exploring the next horizon, escaping wars, famine, climate crisis, persecution, and oppression, some of us captured, enslaved, and sold, some of us simply searching for a better life for ourselves and our children.

Sitting down with my coffee one morning, I opened the front page of the *New York Times* to a photograph of a father and his young child, her arm wrapped around his neck, washed up along the banks of the Rio Grande. Desperate to cross the border, they had risked the river and lost. The child's mother, on the other side, had watched them drown. It echoed another front-page photo several years earlier: a small Syrian boy in a red T-shirt and blue shorts, lying facedown in the sand, his rubber raft washed up on the beach of a resort town in Turkey. Both photos testify to the fact that people will do whatever it takes to survive, even when the odds are mightily stacked against them.

During the Great Hunger, the coffin ships left a chain of Irish bones at the bottom of the ocean. There were no photojournalists to document those deaths. All that survives are a smattering of diary entries and numbers from ship logs. But throughout those eight years of famine emigration, the vast majority did make it to the other side, and those who survived left their mark. Today, approximately thirty-three million people living in the United States claim Irish ancestry. In the United Kingdom the number is about six million. In Australia, two million.

In Mexico it is somewhere between seven hundred thousand and one million. For a small island in a big world, those are impressive numbers.

During the Great Famine exodus, there was no Statue of Liberty holding her torch aloft to welcome the tired, poor, and huddled Irish masses. An immigrant herself from France, she wouldn't arrive until 1885. Ellis Island didn't exist as an immigration depot until 1892. Although ship crews were required to keep a list of passengers, many didn't, and many of the records that were made have been lost. The desperate passengers, each with their own unique story, were now simply part of the "famine Irish," their new common identity.

Approaching New York, most ships entered the East River through the Narrows, the deepest part of the eastern seaways. Once within sight of the Manhattan docks, a ship might wait for weeks to be inspected for typhus or cholera before passengers could leave. Those deemed sick were deposited in the quarantine hospital on Staten Island until they could be released, adding as much as a month to their ordeal. Passengers cleared to enter the country were released without any guidance. Hundreds of immigrants would flood into the city in a single day looking for shelter, food, and work. With no easy way to communicate, families could be separated for an extended period. Newspapers printed advertisements such as these, from the *Boston Pilot* section called "Information Wanted" in, respectively, the October 23 and December 18, 1847, editions:

> Of JOHN QUILMAN, late of the parish of Inch, Co. Tipperary, who sailed from Waterford with his family last April. His daughter, Mary Harrington, wishes him to know that her husband, James Harrington, died on their passage to this country; also her two children since. She is now in Troy and wishes to know where her father is. Any information respecting him will be thankfully received by Mary Harrington, care of S. Duffy, or Mrs. Daly, Fifth street, Troy, N. Y.

> Of BRIDGET CARROLL, a native of Killacooly, parish of Drumcliff, Co. Sligo, who was taken into Grosse Isle hospital,

below Quebec, in June last, and has not been heard from since. Any information respecting her will be thankfully received by her brother, Patrick Carroll, care of Mr. Samuel Downer, Second street, South Boston, Ma.

It was an impossible situation of urgent, immediate need. The rush of poor immigrants was overwhelming. So much depended on ordinary people. Generous amounts of famine relief had crossed the ocean through Quaker relief committees and the Philadelphia Irish Relief Committee. To Patrick, contemplating his emigration from Ireland, Philadelphia may have seemed like a more welcoming place than New York, not as large, a sanctuary of sorts for the famine emigrant. It is where the first records of Patrick in America appear. I wondered what kind of welcome he received.

Ships to Philadelphia entered the wide mouth of Delaware Bay and proceeded up the river channel toward the city's docks. When the larger ships were unable to pass through the channel, smaller boats would take their passengers ahead to a point where they could dock.

Philadelphia might have been an easier place than New York to start a new life, but the City of Brotherly Love was also tainted by the nativism that was spreading rapidly throughout the eastern coast of the United States. Secret societies coalesced into a movement that gave birth to the Native American Party, later renamed the American Party. It was not a short-lived movement. By 1854 nativists controlled the entire Massachusetts legislature. They were anti-immigrant, anti-Catholic, and convinced of conspiracy theories of a papal takeover of the US government. Adherents were called the Know-Nothings because in answer to questions about the movement they would say, "I know nothing."

The city had been dealing with this violent strain of politics even before the famine opened the floodgates of Irish immigrants. In 1844 nativist riots broke out in Kensington and Southwark, areas just outside Philadelphia that housed a growing Irish population. Germans shared these areas too, but it was Irish Catholic churches that were the primary targets of violence.

Fueled by false rumors that Irish Catholics were planning to remove Bibles from the local schools, nativists called on all Americans to "defend themselves from the bloody hand of the pope." Riots broke out at a public gathering in May. Both sides were armed, and two or three nativists died in shootings. Nativists attacked Catholic homes and the convent of the Irish Sisters of Charity. Because Kensington and Southwark were outside the city proper, Philadelphia policing did not extend to them. Local constables tried to tamp things down, but then a nativist mob descended on the Irish parish of St. Augustine in Philadelphia itself and set fire to the church. Rioters broke into cheers as the steeple fell. A nearby German Catholic church was unharmed. A grand jury found the responsibility for the riots lay with "a portion of the community trying to exclude the Bible from schools."

Things got worse. The Irish parish of St. Philip Neri asked the governor of Pennsylvania for a volunteer company to guard them from nativists bent on destruction. The governor provided armaments to the church. Outside, crowds gathered. The anti-Catholic faction dragged a cannon up from the wharf and fired it at the church. Government soldiers fired back with muskets and cannons. For five days, the nativists hurled stones, broken bottles, and nails at the soldiers, who replied with bullets and cannon fire. In the end, fifteen people died and fifty were injured, including both soldiers and rioters. A grand jury again blamed the Irish Catholics.

In New York, Archbishop John Hughes was so worried about the spread of anti-Catholic violence that he organized defenders of New York Catholic churches. Philadelphia elected a nativist mayor four years after the riots and again in 1854. The welcome mat was not exactly out for Irish Catholic immigrants. But they kept coming anyway.

Five years before the Great Famine, Philadelphia was a city of only 93,665 souls. By the time Patrick's ship docked, the population had quadrupled. Ships crowded the Philly docks. In one week in April 1847, five ships deposited 1,200 Irish on the docks of Philadelphia's waterfront (Gallman, *Receiving Erin's Children*, 32). It doesn't take much to imagine how housing and jobs were strained as the Irish refugees poured in. Compassionate citizens trying to meet the basic needs of these new and needy arrivals were overwhelmed.

Patrick, age sixteen, arrived in the middle of this. To navigate his new world, he needed the help and wisdom of the Irish who had come before him to learn how to present himself in this new country: how to speak, what was considered proper behavior, how to understand what was valued and what was not. He had to learn a second cultural language. The good news was that there was work to be had for a strong and willing laborer. But the nationwide hostility did not begin to ease until Irish immigrants fought alongside native-born citizens in the US Civil War.

It's easy to forget how young the country was when all these desperate Irish arrived. The great democratic experiment of the United States was only seventy-six years old in 1850, and population growth and territorial expansion increased tensions. In a population of over twenty-three million, more than three million people were enslaved. New territories had been gained in the war with Mexico. Would they be slave states or free? That was the burning question consuming Congress. The issue that had been avoided at the country's birth was growing into a cancer that would not go away.

Only a few years after Patrick set foot on American soil, a tall, ungainly politician and former circuit lawyer was offered a seat in the Illinois state senate. He had bigger ambitions and declined the position, hoping instead to be elected as a senator from Illinois. His gamble didn't work; he didn't win the post he desired. But Abraham Lincoln's ideas wouldn't wait. They developed into a new political party that proposed to limit the growth of slavery in the United States. He had strong thoughts about the Know-Nothings, too. On August 24, 1855, he wrote privately in a letter to his friend Joshua F. Speed,

> I am not a Know-Nothing—that is certain. How could I be? How can anyone who abhors the oppression of negroes, be in favor of degrading classes of white people? Our progress in degeneracy appears to me to be pretty rapid. As a nation, we

began by declaring that "all men are created equal." We now practically read it "all men are created equal, except negroes." When the Know-Nothings get control, it will read "all men are created equal, except negroes and foreigners and Catholics." When it comes to that I should prefer emigrating to some country where they make no pretense of loving liberty—to Russia, for instance, where despotism can be taken pure, and without the base alloy of hypocrisy.

Chapter Seventeen

Panic

By 1851 Philadelphia was the second-largest city in the United States and growing fast. It was the primary leader in industry and finance, a fast-paced place in need of unskilled labor to drive the country's expansion west through railroads, canals, coal, and textiles. A perfect place and time for new immigrants to find work.

The look of the city was changing too. Unlike New York, Philadelphia had been laid out on an orderly grid, with wide streets and parks on each square. But the rush of new and generally impoverished immigrants strained the infrastructure. Buildings became crowded, streets dirty. Wealthy Philadelphians began to move out of their large homes near the city's center to what they perceived as safer ground. The poor—mostly immigrants—moved in, dividing what had once been grand family homes into tenements housing multiple families.

The new arrivals were predominately Irish and German. The Irish composed the largest group and by far the poorest. Those who survived the Atlantic trip had already run a gauntlet of swindlers, unseaworthy ships, and disease—cholera, dysentery, and typhoid, sometimes called "Irish fever." Some had grown hard and learned to be wary of strangers, to stay close to those they knew. The message was "Don't trust anyone, and keep your head down. Keep moving forward; be grateful for kindness and pass it on to your own people as they arrive, for they will surely need it." The fortunate ones arrived with a name and address, someone waiting for them with a place to stay, at least for a while. And perhaps a name on a slip of paper: "Go see this man for a job."

Was someone there to greet the teenaged Patrick when he got off the boat in 1851 or 1852, his legs a bit wobbly on shore, carrying all his earthly possessions under his arm? Did he stare at the crowds of people, buildings taller than any he'd ever seen, indecipherable shouts from the stevedores, long shadows thrown by the tall masts of the scores of ships docked along the wharf? He may as well have landed on the moon.

I'd like to think he had a name and an address when he arrived. I wondered if his ship had arrived directly in Philadelphia or if he disembarked first in New York and then took a steamer up the Delaware River. Maybe he knew of relations or neighbors already in Philadelphia. I've had no luck finding him in ship records or city directories—the name *Patrick Farrelly* is just too common. His surviving letters make no mention of Philadelphia. I wish I knew how he spent those early years in his new country. The one thing I do know is that he joined the army on June 5, 1858. What happened between the day he walked off the boat and the day he enlisted?

Most Irish who arrived on our shores during the Great Famine came from rural areas. They had farmed or worked as itinerant laborers. Many had never seen a large city, much less lived in one. Their universe included their neighbors, their parish, the local priest, the schoolteacher, and the publican. The largest group of people they encountered would have been at the local fair, where cattle, pigs, and sheep were sold. Finding work in a new country offered a number of challenges, but they were willing to do hard work, the jobs that few others would do. The prospect for women was primarily servant work. For men, plenty of hard manual labor was available: digging canals, building railroads, laboring in foundries, and making bricks. Is that what Patrick did for those first years?

Trying to answer my questions, I looked into the history of Philadelphia and found another possibility that might have driven him and many others to the recruiter's office. In September 1857 a financial panic, sudden and unexpected, upended the financial security of the entire country. The first to fail was the Bank of Philadelphia. Others quickly followed. From Pennsylvania to Maryland, Rhode Island, and Virginia, banks closed their doors. Individuals, large companies, and small businesses couldn't access their savings or their funds. The panic reached New York in October and spread like a virus across the Atlantic to England. It was the first time an economic crisis had spread worldwide. There was nothing in place to sound a warning.

The explanation of the Panic of 1857 sounds like the global recession of 2008: "In this country the banking system approached the anarchic in its lack of uniformity or regulation, with 'wild cat' banking and note issue especially rife in the west. A rapid rise in prices of both securities and commodities brought general derangement of values, with extravagant living standards and importation of luxuries from abroad, accompanied, as during the late lamented era, by reckless borrowing, foolish investment and speculation, and general belief in unparalleled and permanent prosperity" (Hutchinson, "Philadelphia and the Panic of 1857," 184).

There was no precedent for a financial disaster this large and no backstop. The panic came at a time when eastern American cities felt the squeeze from rapid population growth due to mass immigration. Anti-immigrant feelings surged as businesses went bankrupt. Now it was harder than ever to find a job. Overreach and the absence of any regulation had immediate and real effects on families and individuals, especially along the densely populated East Coast. Banks collapsed, homes lost their value, jobs dried up, and debt increased as prices for basic commodities rose. Those on the lowest rung of the economic ladder found it hard to afford the very basics of life: bread, milk, rent.

The newly arrived Irish must have felt that the world was working against them. First the famine, and now the economy of their new country was falling apart. It called forth all their inner strength to put their heads down and do what they needed to do to survive. But as in any economic crisis, there were beneficiaries as well. In 1858, the year after the panic, the biggest beneficiary was the US Army.

At the same time, political parties were preparing for elections to come, and Lincoln's ideas were reaching far beyond Springfield,

Illinois, all the way to soldiers posted at the forts on the western frontier. On July 20, 1858, only a month after Patrick signed his enlistment papers, a reporter from the *Chicago Tribune* wrote:

> Great crises demand great men. And there is some wise overruling Power that sends the man for the occasion and prepares the heart of the people for her reception. In the hour of her peril, England had her Alfred—Scotland her Wallace—Switzerland her Tell—France her Bonaparte—Columbia her Bolivar—America her Washington—and there seems something not less over-ruling in the miraculous unanimity with which the people of Illinois have risen up in favor of Abraham Lincoln, as the fit man to heal the wounds inflicted by the "ruthless hand" that repealed the Missouri Compromise.
>
> Today we raise the name of Abraham Lincoln to the head of our State Ticket. We go for MEN as well as measures—for men who embody PRINCIPLES—and that name shall stand till victory perches upon our banners.

I don't know that Patrick was aware of it when he enlisted, but his new country was in the middle of a great crisis and heading toward a war. It may be that he was simply in need of a job and glad for an escape from the city. Or perhaps he was aware of this self-taught man from the rural heartland, Lincoln, who would become president and his commander-in-chief in only two years. Perhaps Patrick simply saw the army as something dependable and exciting at the same time, a chance to see the wider world. He would get all that and more.

Chapter Eighteen

Enlistment

Declaration of Recruit:

I, <u>Patrick Farrelly</u>, desiring to ENLIST in the Army of the United States for the period of FIVE YEARS, Do declare, That I am twenty-two years and three months of age; that I have neither wife nor child; that I have never been discharged from the United States service on account of disability or by sentence of a court-martial, or by order before the expiration of a term of enlistment; and I know of no impediment to my serving honestly and faithfully as a soldier for five years.

Given at <u>Philadelphia, P.</u> The <u>4</u> day of <u>June 1858</u>

Witness: <u>Charles Bauer</u>

The document is faded and hard to read. I ordered this copy of Patrick's pension and military records from the Library of Congress. The army was glad to enlist immigrants, no citizenship required. The first step for a recruit was his declaration of intent and his statement that he would faithfully serve.

Patrick had to return the next day for the rest: a surgeon's exam, an officer's inspection, and finally his swearing-in. The officer and surgeon filled out their portions of the form after the recruitment office's part, and Patrick signed too, off to the side in a different style and with a different pen. I like his handwriting. It's strong.

The second step was the surgeon's exam:

I CERTIFY ON HONOR, that I have carefully examined the above named Recruit, agreeably to the General Regulations of the Army, and that in my opinion he is free from all bodily defects and mental infirmary, which would, in any way disqualify him from performing the duties of a soldier.

    C. A. Finley, Examining Surgeon

Third step, the inspection by the recruiting officer:

I, CERTIFY ON HONOR, That I have minutely inspected the Recruit Patrick Farrelly previously to his enlistment, and that he was entirely sober when enlisted; that to the best of my judgement and belief, he is of lawful age; and that, in accepting him as duly qualified to perform the duties of an able-bodied soldier, I have strictly observed the Regulations which govern the recruiting service. This soldier has hazel eyes, dr. brown hair, dark complexions, is five feet seven 1/4 inches high.

    D .L. Floyd-Jones, Capt. 4th Inf. Recruiting Officer

Officer D. L. Floyd-Jones could have been physically describing my father, Patrick's grandson, exactly, to the inch. And finally, the last step, the swearing-in:

State of Pennsylvania, Town of Philadelphia.
I, Patrick Farrelly, born in County Cavan in the State of Ireland aged twenty-two years and by occupation a laborer Do Hereby Acknowledge to have voluntarily enlisted this fifth day of June, 1858 as a soldier in the Army of the United States of America, to serve for the period of Five Years, unless sooner discharged by proper authority; Do also agree to accept such bounty, pay, rations and closing, as are, or may be, established by law. And I, Patrick Farrelly do solemnly swear that I will bear faith and allegiance to the United States of America, and that I will serve

them honestly and faithfully against all their enemies or opposers whomsoever; and that I will observe and obey the orders of the President of the United States, and the officers appointed over me, according to the Rules and Articles of War.

Sworn and subscribed to, at <u>Philadelphia, Pa.</u> This <u>5</u> day of June 18<u>58</u> before <u>Chas. F. Helffnecht.</u>

Now he was a US soldier, locked in for the next five years. He was in good company. Immigrants such as Patrick made up the majority of army recruits, primarily Irish and German and a few English. Many had been affected by the Panic of 1857 and showed up in the one place where they could be assured of a job—the army. The benefits were many: steady work, food, shelter, clothes, and a chance to see the great untamed West of their new country. It wasn't easy money, but for most enlistees it was a step up. And for immigrants, it was a way to show that they, the newcomers, were part of this nation now and ready to defend it.

US Army recruit Patrick would say goodbye to those he knew in Philadelphia, pack a few personal belongings, and get back on a boat, this time for New York. His destination was the muster center on Governor's Island, a small island between Manhattan and Brooklyn that had been used by the military since the War of Independence. There he would find himself among hundreds of other young men, most of them immigrants like himself. They would receive their infantry assignments, uniforms, and equipment, and live in barracks on the island until other new recruits were ready to join up with the rest. When Patrick's group had been fully assembled and processed, they would leave Governor's Island by boat and begin the journey to join Company C of the Second Infantry in Minnesota. It would be a long trip by train, riverboat, and foot, with a lot of time to think about this new position. Even as an army private, Patrick was part of the government now, his role no less than the defense of the United States of America against "all their enemies or opposers whomsoever."

He had come from a country without self-rule. It would be decades before the Irish could reclaim their own land, make their own laws, and govern their own people. Now Patrick was in the United States, a country created around the idea that people should be self-governing, that all men are entitled to life, liberty, and the pursuit of happiness— the great experiment of democracy.

The soaring rhetoric of the Declaration of Independence, the Constitution, and the Bill of Rights stand as the ideals we strive for— the very ideas that drove Patrick and millions of other emigrants like him to seek refuge and a better life here. We are an imperfect union, but we keep reaching for those ideals. We fail and fail and fail the test, two steps forward, one step back—sometimes two. When Patrick landed here in the middle of the nineteenth century, it was the most tumultuous of times for the young republic. Massive immigration, financial strain, and ideological division between the agrarian South and industrial North—rooted in the unsettled issue of slavery, the country's original sin—swirled in a violent brew. If you could have flown over the country, you would have seen small eruptions in all sections of the United States and its territories. West of the Mississippi, nonnative populations were pushing out onto land that had been tribal territory for millennia. Texas, until recently a part of Mexico, had separated and become its own country, precipitating war. In the Southeast, the Seminole people were trying valiantly but unsuccessfully to defend their lands, and Native American tribes everywhere were fighting to save a remnant of their homeland via treaties that the government broke as fast as they were made. Midwestern states were grappling directly with the question of the expansion of slavery, and Kansas and Missouri were imploding into bloody chaos. Could the Union hold, or would it split apart?

After the American War of Independence, concern lingered about the United States maintaining a big army in the European mold. It was a healthy skepticism about having a standing army versus a citizen militia, held by a new country that did not want a reminder of colonialism. So, when the war with Mexico ended in 1848, the army was reduced to only twelve thousand men. But with disruptions increasing, the idea of keeping the standing army small lost popularity. The government ramped up army personnel to sixteen thousand, still a very small military for a country with a population of nearly thirty million. Soldiers were scattered among forts on the western frontier. When Patrick joined the army, that frontier began at the Mississippi River.

Those early forts were simple affairs. They housed soldiers, officers, and sometimes white civilians who requested support. Simple housing was built by the soldiers themselves, and the materials provided did not always match the climate because decisions were made back in Washington, without any real experience of the location. Soldiers in the Dakotas and Nebraska nearly froze to death in uninsulated dwellings with insufficient heat during the brutal winters. In summer, uniforms designed on the East Coast didn't take into account long marches in the hot Southwest. But still, for a recruit, such problems were manageable in exchange for adventure and a regular job, food, and shelter.

Patrick's company was assigned to Fort Ripley, along the Mississippi, on land that the Ojibwe and Eastern Dakota both claimed, and where the Ho-Chunk had recently been relocated from their ancestral land in northeastern Iowa. The territory that held these native peoples was now part of the new state of Minnesota.

For soldiers, Fort Ripley was a remote and harsh outpost. Officers were given a bonus for serving there. The long winters were brutal, and whiteout blizzards increased the feeling of utter isolation. In the summer, mosquitoes were the primary enemy. And, beyond the elements and wildlife, there wasn't much going on. Patrick and his fellow recruits learned soldier life: discipline, the order of command, the way to make your bed, how to care for your military clothes, how to keep your equipment shined and in working order. They played cards and sports and sang songs to pass the time. They learned each other's names and stories. They made friends. And, slowly, they became a unit, a company of regular soldiers.

Chapter Nineteen

US Archives

After reading through Patrick's enlistment papers, I was curious to learn more about his time in the army. When Bob had a conference scheduled in DC, I jumped at the opportunity to come along, figuring I could get some time at the National Archives while he was in meetings. My main goal was to unearth what I could of Patrick's army life in the lead-up to the Civil War. I'd done a lot of research in Ireland, but this was a chance to learn something about his early years in the United States.

The National Archives are housed in an impressive neoclassical building reminiscent of a Greek temple. The architect, John Russell Pope, envisioned a monument to the nation's history. Ground was broken in 1931—an audacious feat in the depths of the Great Depression. Up until this building was complete, the country's historic record and artifacts had been moved from place to place for 150 years, risking damage and destruction. It's a miracle that major historical documents weren't lost.

Researchers enter through a small, inconspicuous door at the back of the building. Driving past the front, I saw a line of people waiting on the steps outside to tour the main viewing room, the rotunda. This is where people come to see America's crown jewels, the Charters of Freedom, which include the Declaration of Independence, the Constitution, and the Bill of Rights. Another display holds the Emancipation Proclamation, Washington's first inaugural address, the Treaty of Paris, and an original copy of the Magna Carta. It's a powerful thing to see them all in one place, the building blocks of American democracy. It's easy to sense the historic importance of Washington; despite whatever political shenanigans are going on at the time, the city itself exudes a gravitas that is hard to ignore. You feel the weight of history here.

But I was not there for the big documents. I had come to look for small traces of one immigrant soldier. For family historians, military pension records can be the key to important information. Patrick's pension records had already unlocked important doors for me in Ireland because when asked where he was from, rather than simply writing "Ireland," he had listed his actual parish, Lurgan. Imagine how much easier it would be to find someone from "St. Sabina's parish, Chicago, Illinois," rather than just "the United States." Place was clearly important in his identity.

I only had a day and a half to look for records of his army unit. I knew he joined up in June 1858 in Philadelphia, reported to New York, and was assigned to the Second Infantry, Company C, Regular Army. His company of one hundred men was sent to Minnesota. In no way could they have foreseen the war that loomed in their future.

I thanked the Uber driver and walked down the slight slope to the back door of the massive building. You could miss this entrance if you were driving or walking by. Once inside, it was all business. Security reminded me of traveling through a major airport: coats, bags, jackets, and laptops all went through the screening machine. Once I got clearance I was sent to a desk where I signed up for a card and wrote my name and time in the day book. After a body scan with a metal detector, I was allowed to enter. Laptops are allowed, but no bags, pens, or paper—a world of difference from the National Archives in Dublin. I stored my things in a locker and headed toward the research room.

I was hoping to find actual archival material, not just microfilm, related to Patrick's time at Fort Ripley. I found a few items that looked promising and filled out request sheets. I wouldn't get access to those until the next morning, so I moved on to microfilm. Each army unit officer was required to keep a daily record of what was going on under their command, and these reports have all been microfilmed. Reading microfilm is the most tedious part of research. Sitting in a dark room, scrolling endlessly, it's hard to keep your mind focused on the one name you're looking for. Reading on the machines is notoriously difficult; they are temperamental at best and out to sabotage your work at worst. But until everything is digitized, film remains the only way to access material that for years was stashed in boxes, gathering dust on shelves in assorted government buildings.

A research consultant pointed me to the correct films, and off I went to my cubicle. It was so dark and cool in there that I had an immediate strong urge to take a nap. Alas, no coffee allowed. I dug out a peppermint candy from my pocket, hoping sugar would help, took a deep breath, and flipped the machine's switch. There could be rewards if I persevered, so I attached the roll and began scrolling through, peering at the tiny handwriting from over 150 years ago. Scrolling, scrolling, nothing, nothing, nothing.

And then . . . bingo! There he was, on a list of enlistees recently arrived at Fort Ripley, really and truly there, my Patrick! Twenty-two, one young enlistee among many immigrant soldiers on a long list. It was proof that my great-grandfather had existed in this specific time and place. I wanted to shout, "Hey, Patrick, it's me! I've been looking for you!" I had managed to crawl back in time to see this line of new recruits about to engage in the country's most painful and devastating war. Of course, they didn't know that, which made reading through their names all the more poignant.

The men on the list—four hundred of them—were all privates, freshly arrived from the depot. Their officers were graduates of West Point or had earned their rank in the war with Mexico or even as far back as the war of 1812. Reading through the officer reports, I learned that Patrick had volunteered for sentry duty several times. I also found reports of deserters, men who couldn't take the isolation anymore, including one who left one night in a snowstorm and was found frozen to death the next morning. The prospect of spending five years here in comparative isolation with little or no military action was clearly hard for some to bear.

Minnesota had just become the thirty-second state. The United States of America was only eighty-two years old, a mere child in the family of nations. The Constitution had been ratified only seventy years before Patrick put his name on a list to defend it. But unfinished business from the very founding of the country reared its head. Compromises had been made to get all thirteen original states on board to ratify the Constitution. In 1776 the issue of slavery had been put on the back shelf. Thomas Jefferson, who himself held more than a hundred enslaved men and women, wrote that the practice of slavery was a "blot on America." At one point late in life, he worried in a prescient letter to a friend that the practice of slavery might split the new country that they had worked so hard to create. George Washington, another owner of hundreds of enslaved people, called the practice "repugnant." Patrick "Give me liberty or give me death" Henry held enslaved persons from the time he turned eighteen, eventually keeping eighty people from liberty at one time. He wrote in support of abolition and worked to abolish the slave trade and yet never freed those he held. How did they live with these contradictions? The country had banned slavery in the Northwest Ordinance under Jefferson's presidency, but that just seemed to legitimize the practice in the southern states. And so it went on. The abolitionist movement in the north grew louder and the tension in the country increased. A festering wound that would not heal, it brought the country to a crisis.

Chapter Twenty

Civil War

My dad was interested in the Civil War for as long as I can remember. He was proud to share his birthday with Lincoln and proud of the fact that his grandfather Patrick had fought for the Union. He had several books on Lincoln and a whole series on the war. I remember visiting some battlefield with him when I was young, although I have little memory of where we were or what the battle was. Growing up in Iowa, my dad had only visited his grandfather in Nebraska once, when he was ten. Whatever he learned about Patrick's experience of the war must have come from what his father told him and later from records that his sister, my aunt Ruth, had uncovered.

History mattered to my dad. On road trips, he pulled our car over at every roadside historical marker, no matter how seemingly insignificant. It was my dad who discovered that Bob and I shared a unique Civil War connection. On a visit to my parents in St. Louis, Bob had mentioned that his great-grandfather Abel Shuford had fought in the Civil War. The Shufords are all from North Carolina, and Bob's ancestor had fought for the Confederacy. Intrigued, my dad wrote a letter to Bob's grandfather, and they discovered that these two men—the native son of North Carolina and the Irish immigrant—had fought on opposite sides in several of the same battles. Bob and I started calling ourselves the reconciliation couple.

I wanted to know Patrick's experience of the war. What was it like for immigrants to go into battle for a country they barely had time to get to know? I had the reports from his time in Minnesota and a list of the battles that he fought in, but my own understanding of the war had been relegated to dry high school history classes that focused on dates and generals and battles. Bull Run, Gaines' Mill, Malvern Hill, Fredericksburg, Chancellorsville—before I researched Patrick's life, they were just names. For me, they carried none of the weight of war. But did those names bring the taste of war back to Patrick's mouth? The memory of swamps and thick woods, wheat and cornfields filled with the dead, cannons booming in the distance and shells whistling above his head? Soldiers on his right and left falling, screaming, limbs blown off? Did those names evoke the complex scent of sweat, mud-encrusted boots and uniforms, the closeness of thousands of men marching, exhausted beyond imagining? I imagined him among them, stopping briefly to sleep where he fell and then having to get up in the dark and march for miles again. Burned coffee, dry hardtack in his pocket. Drinking water from a stagnant creek, and so thirsty it hardly mattered. Just drink, don't look at it.

Soldiers accumulated small superstitions about survival. If they lived through this battle, was their chance of surviving the next less or greater? Fatigue became a kind of mercy in which they were unable to think of what they had just experienced or imagine what was ahead.

Patrick had been at Fort Ripley two and a half years when the war started. He'd had time to get used to the discipline, the boredom, the camaraderie of fellow soldiers. But before Southerners fired on Fort Sumter, Patrick's division must have heard news of disturbances in the South. Newspapers took a long time to reach forts on the frontier. But as they arrived, more and more words were spent on the unrest in Kansas and the heightened national disagreements over the "peculiar institution" (a euphemism for slavery used by white Southerners) that fueled the engine of the South and, some would argue, the entire US economy. It was a painful irony that the same nation that opened its doors to those escaping famine and oppression was also the captor and subjugator of millions of people from Africa and their descendants.

In spring 1858, while James Buchanan, a states' rights advocate, was president, five free-state men were massacred in Kansas by proslavery men. It was a prelude of things to come. Eleven days after Patrick enlisted, Lincoln declaimed at the Illinois Statehouse, "A house divided against itself cannot stand. I believe this government cannot endure, permanently half slave and half free. I do not expect the Union to be dissolved—I do not expect the house to fall—but I do expect it will cease to be divided. It will become *all* one thing or *all* the other."

Lincoln had hoped to be elected to the US Senate but lost to Stephen Douglas. Some blamed his radical speech, but it struck a chord with enough people, and only two years later he was elected president of the United States. The inauguration was held later then than it is now. On his way to the inauguration, Lincoln toured several states by train, stopping in Indiana, Ohio, Pennsylvania, and New York to greet the crowds that lined the tracks. But there were rumors of an assassination attempt, and rather than inviting the public to welcome him to Washington, DC, his train car arrived unannounced in the middle of the night. On March 4, 1861, after a cold and cloudy morning, the sun broke out a little after 1:00 p.m., and Abraham Lincoln was introduced as the sixteenth US president. He removed his hat and spoke for only thirty minutes, closing with bold words of hope that belied the situation in which the country found itself: "The mystic cords of memory, stretching from every battlefield and every patriot grave, to every living heart and hearthstone, all over this broad land, will yet swell the chorus of the Union, when again touched, as surely as they will be, by the better angels of our nature."

What had been simmering now unfolded quickly. Even before Lincoln arrived in Washington, secessions began to snowball. South Carolina left the Union in December 1860, and Florida, Alabama, Georgia, Louisiana, Mississippi, and Texas rapidly followed. Tensions were high in Washington, and the inauguration ceremony took place amid a heavy guard of cavalry and infantry.

On April 12, six weeks after the inauguration, Fort Sumter was fired upon. Lincoln knew that war was imminent, and at this first sign of Southern aggression, he called for seventy-five thousand volunteers from state militias. After the fall of Sumter, four more states—Virginia, North Carolina, Tennessee, and Arkansas—broke away and joined the newly formed Confederate States of America. Now the nation's capital was at risk. Lincoln called a special session of Congress and addressed the challenge ahead: "This is a People's contest. On the side of the Union, it is a struggle for maintaining in the world, that form and substance of government whose leading object is to elevate the condition of men."

Patrick's life was about to change. In June, two companies of men from the Second Infantry at Fort Ripley—Patrick's Company C and Company K—were called to Washington. The soldiers packed up their equipment, bid goodbye to the fort, and headed east. In the 1860s railroads were concentrated in the east; beyond them, rivers functioned as the interstates of the day. So the men boarded a riverboat and traveled down the Mississippi with a stop to resupply at Camp Defiance in Cairo, Illinois, where the Mississippi and Ohio Rivers meet. Then they journeyed east up the Ohio River. At Pittsburgh they finally disembarked, stretched their legs, and began the 150-mile march to the campground near Washington, where new volunteer recruits awaited them. There, army units were reassembled and moved close to the capital. There was a genuine and immediate concern that Washington would be invaded. Patrick's company camped in Arlington, Virginia, on what had been the property of Robert E. Lee before he left to join the Confederacy. The US Regular Army soldiers and officers had two tasks: bring discipline to the new volunteers and be prepared to defend Washington. They set up camp, drilled, and worked to bring the volunteers up to proper army standards.

Washington, DC, as they found it in 1861 would be unrecognizable today. What had begun as a small town built along the Potomac and the Anacostia grew into a major city in five years. There, in the sweltering heat of mid-July, after weeks of training new volunteers, Patrick and the rest of Company C were now an integral part of the growing army whose purpose was nothing less than to save the Union. They got their orders, broke camp, and began to march, this time south toward Virginia and the army of the Confederacy. The two armies would meet at a sleepy river called Bull Run.

CHAPTER TWENTY-ONE

The Regular Army

I WISH I HAD PATRICK'S VOICE during the war to tell me his thoughts and experiences. He must have written letters to friends or perhaps family in Philadelphia or even back in Ireland, to let them know that he was okay. There was a lot of downtime in camp, waiting for the next battle, the next marching order. Perhaps he kept a journal, as some soldiers did, but if he did, it has vanished. Without that, where would I start to sketch a picture of this time in his life? The American Civil War is a deep rabbit hole of history, with thousands of books and films dedicated to it. I've tried to learn what I could. But I wanted to know what it was like *for Patrick*, for this one single soldier. One man's war.

One day, trying to move from the general to the particular, I did a quick internet search for "2nd Infantry, Company C, US Civil War." I knew that because he was in the Regular Army and not a volunteer, there might be less information. When most people think of Civil War soldiers, they think of the volunteers and not the thousands of regular soldiers who were in the thick of it too. The volunteer units got far more notice because they were representing their states, and that created local news. But searching for information about the regulars, I hit the jackpot where I would have least expected it.

The first thing that popped up on my search was the American Civil War Society in the United Kingdom. Seriously. A historical society in England that has meetings and puts on battle reenactments. It seemed bizarre. I clicked on their site and found a contact for a guy who represented "the federals," meaning the Union forces. I sent off an email explaining that I was trying to find information about my great-grandfather's unit, and I received a quick and gracious reply including the name of a man in the United States who, I was told, would know everything. Timothy Reese, himself a former reenactor in the United States, had written an entire book on Patrick's division, called "Sykes' Regulars" after their commander, George Sykes. *Sykes' Regular Infantry Division, 1861–1864* is a deeply researched and highly detailed history of a group that most Civil War historians have ignored.

I emailed Mr. Reese and told him my story (Patrick's story, really) and asked if he could help me learn more. He was not only helpful but offered that "it would be my honor" to show the great-grand-daughter of one of Sykes's men around the battlefields of Antietam and Gettysburg if I ever happened to be in the area. This was one of those more-than-coincidence things, especially via the odd route through an English historical society. It felt like one more reassurance that I was supposed to be following Patrick's path, another signpost on "the path that fate marked out for me," as Patrick had written. Now I had a roadmap for this new part. Over my lunch break I found Reese's book, bound in Union blue, in the library at Northwestern. I pulled it off the shelf, sat on the floor between the tall stacks, and began to read.

The basics: The Regular Army was made up of professional soldiers, highly trained and disciplined, the core of the US Army. When the war broke out, those serving in the nearest western forts, including Patrick, were called in to protect the capital. Although the Regular Army soldiers were the standard by which the new volunteers would be measured, they earned less than the volunteers, who had received incentives to enlist and additional support from their states. At the beginning of the war, it was easy to tell the regulars from the volunteers because regulars wore standard blue wool uniforms in contrast to the flashy volunteer New York Zouaves or the kilt-wearing Cameron Highlanders. The regulars were exactly that: Regular. Dependable. Their units made up only 3 percent of soldiers at the height of the

MATTHEWS HILL, BULL RUN BATTLEFIELD,
MANASSAS, VIRGINIA

Civil War. Although small in number, they were a critical nucleus, the backbone of the whole army.

The first battle of the Civil War, Bull Run, was supposed to be the only battle. Of course the Union soldiers would win. All of Washington was convinced of it. But the volunteer soldiers were new, and many were untrained. It went badly. At first, the North seemed to have the upper hand, but the huge Union army of thirty-five thousand moved slowly, and only a portion made it into the battle. By then, Lee's army had brought in ten thousand fresh troops by train, expanding the Confederate forces to twenty thousand. Now with numbers slightly larger than the engaged Union forces, they saw that they had a chance, and the course of the battle changed. Some of the Union volunteer units panicked and fled, and any semblance of order began to crumble. The regulars covered the retreat, standing their ground to protect the retreating Northern forces. Forming a square, they moved like a kind of armed creature, firing from three sides, replacing the fallen with the next row in the square. As they approached the bridge over the creek called Bull Run, they formed two columns, Patrick among them, firing at Confederate snipers to give cover as the last of the Union soldiers crossed the creek and headed north to safety.

It was humbling and humiliating. Citizens who had driven their carriages out from Washington to get near enough to hear sounds of the great Union victory came home in shock. Hearing the news, President Lincoln sank into a state of depression and frustration, reading the accounts of the battle over and over. Washington's citizens, stunned, began searching for someone to blame.

Losses totaled 2,896 Union soldiers killed, wounded, or missing. The Confederacy's casualties numbered 1,982. General Irvin McDowell of the Union had managed to get less than half of his men into the fight, feeding them piecemeal into battle rather than sending a full assault that might have pushed the Confederates back before their fresh reinforcements arrived. McDowell entered the war with no large-scale combat experience and had underestimated the difficulty of moving a huge body of mostly inexperienced men and officers. Still, no one had thought this battle would be anything but an easy Union victory. Lincoln immediately sent McDowell west and turned the army over to a new general, George McClellan.

Back in Washington, everyone from senators to chambermaids began to take stock of the new reality. It was evident now that this would not be a short war. Newspapers reported casualty lists and offered their own assessments of what had happened on the battlefield. Uneasiness spread. The nation's capital was only a river crossing away from the Confederate army. Its population had swelled overnight as thousands of soldiers joined politicians, freed and enslaved Black people, spies, grocers, tailors, innkeepers, teachers, and preachers. At first, the soldiers slept anywhere they could: the Capitol's hallways and conference rooms, and even in the House and Senate chambers. Army tents surrounded the city to a three-mile radius. Cavalry horses grazed on the mall. When Lincoln first arrived at the White House, he could look out the window and see a Confederate flag flying just across the river. The infrastructure of the town was hardly able to handle all of this. Pennsylvania Avenue was mired in mud so deep that carriages got stuck and pedestrians had to walk extra blocks just to find a clear way across. Pigs, goats, and the occasional chicken rambled down streets, looking for scraps. The sewage system was overwhelmed, and diseases including dysentery, cholera, typhoid, and even smallpox could run rampant at times. It smelled bad. What would later become Constitution Avenue was still a canal. The whole place had the feel of being patched together. The Capitol, where the Senate and House meet, was unfinished, with wooden scaffolding covering what would eventually become its shining dome. A visitor commented, "Everything worth looking at seemed unfinished; everything finished looked like it should have been destroyed."

But the players were assembling on this rough stage in history. Mathew Brady, the successful portrait photographer, came to town before the battle at Bull Run to record the war in images—something new and somewhat radical. After some negotiating, Lincoln gave permission, with the understanding that Brady was on his own in this endeavor and the government would not pay him for his work. Brady went off to document this first, and what he assumed would be the only, battle for the preservation of the Union. Just after the battle, poet Walt Whitman arrived and would return again and again, looking for his brother in army hospitals and giving what comfort he could to soldiers broken in body and spirit. Whitman saw the war coming before others did and viewed it as purgative—an event that needed to happen in order to deal with the unfinished business of the country's beginnings—its "feudal elements," as he called them.

In this milieu of the famous and the ordinary, the native and the foreign born, Patrick Farrelly and his fellow Second Infantry Regulars returned to camp, exhausted from the disaster at Bull Run. Major Sykes had command of five companies of regulars, including Patrick's, and they had successfully defended the only escape route while the frantic and rapidly disintegrating volunteer army fled to safety. When the president came to review the troops in the difficult aftermath, Sykes introduced his small battalion to Lincoln, saying, "Mr. President, these are the men that saved your army."

The army and navy headquarters and camps were within walking distance of the White House, and Lincoln liked to walk over to visit his officers and talk strategy and lift morale among the soldiers. McClellan spent the next months training and unifying the army; the sounds and sights of soldiers drilling were constant. Discipline was a top priority; passes were needed to leave and enter the army camps. Sykes' Regulars were stationed around the city as guards to rein in any untrained troops who ran amok, to give a needed example of army discipline. They guarded bridges, reinforced defenses, and wondered, like everyone else, what was coming. Civilians and soldiers alike lived day to day with an unsettling tension. The Confederacy, buoyed by its success at Bull Run, saw taking Washington as the way to a quick and total victory. With the Southern forces just across the river, there was a genuine threat to Lincoln's life and the capital itself.

The Union army was becoming professionalized. But for some of the volunteers, who had signed up in a rush of patriotism and hopes of personal glory, it was also a time of disillusionment and grumbling. Many were filled with frustration over the Bull Run defeat, the boredom of army routine, and the life-and-death reality of what it meant to be a soldier.

Most days were routine, but from time to time the frustrations came to a head. Once, a large contingent of the Seventy-Ninth New York volunteers (originally called the Cameron Highlanders, kilts and all) decided to desert. Sykes' Regulars, Patrick among them, were called in. They surrounded the errant group, raised their rifles, and made it clear that joining this army was a serious commitment and deserters would be shot. The offending soldiers surrendered; their colors were taken away, the regiment was marched off to a new camp located near the Government Hospital for the Insane, and the ringleaders went to prison. After a few months and appropriate remorse and embarrassment, they were reunited with their more compliant compatriots and their regimental colors returned.

Things settled down after that episode. The city itself had transformed into an armed camp. One young officer, John Henry Page, described the scene he encountered when he arrived at the nation's capital: "Here was a city of canvas sheltering over a hundred thousand patriotic soldiers. The splendid parks of Artillery, the thousands of army wagons, the never-ending procession of ambulances, the number of forts being constructed, were a never ceasing wonder to me" (Reese, *Sykes' Regular Infantry Division*, 66).

As part of its reorganization, the army on the eastern front would now be called the Army of the Potomac. While its leaders focused on enlarging numbers and training new volunteers, the war progressed on the western front, led by Ulysses Grant's Army of the Tennessee. The eastern front had been quiet since Bull Run, but that was soon to change.

In March 1862, Patrick and the rest of Sykes' Regulars moved out from Washington, heading south with the Army of the Potomac. Volunteers and regulars had become one unified army. They carried with them a mix of excitement and anxiety; they knew better now what fighting meant.

Many years later, John Henry Page described the moment:

The band struck up a merry tune, the regiment broke into columns of platoons; when in view of the Ebbitt and Willard Hotels we could see the windows were a mass of waving handkerchiefs, fans and parasols; when near enough a shower of bouquets greeted us; here and there a messenger boy darted between the ranks, handed a youth a parting flower and billet doux containing words of affection and God-speed. . . . When the columns reached Long Bridge, the music was hushed. As Sykes' command came back to us to route step, break step, march, I became an atom of that grand and glorious, patriotic, patient and preserving Army of the Potomac, that through no fault of its own, left its dead on half of its battlefields to be buried by our southern brothers (Reese, *Sykes' Regular Infantry Division*, 69).

The Army of the Potomac was mobilizing for the Peninsula Campaign, the drive to Richmond, the capital and heart of the Confederacy. The plan was to conquer Lee and shut down the war once and for all.

CHAPTER TWENTY-TWO

Peninsula Campaign

IT'S HARD TO IMAGINE the complicated mechanics of moving a giant army across land with only foot power, rail, and ships. Not just soldiers, but also their equipment had to move: clothing, a wagon store with dry goods for cooking, and coffee, flour, and livestock to keep them fed along the way. No cell phones, no trucks, no jeeps. Just horses, who also needed to be fed, and wagons that got stuck in mud and had wheels that needed repair and replacing, which meant blacksmiths invaluable in keeping horses shod and broken tools mended. A few women marched as well, as laundresses and later as nurses. When an army went on the move, it brought along its own city.

In the fall of 2008, Bob and I took a long road trip. I'd just retired from my position at Northwestern University, and we had some time for a real vacation. We planned to visit our kids in New York, then swing down to North Carolina where Bob's cousins lived. On the way south, we decided to visit a couple of Civil War sites. We needed no horses, wagons, or laundresses—just an old, reliable Subaru.

Welcome to Virginia signs sprang up on the highway, greeting us with the state's slogan: "Virginia is for lovers!" Funny slogan for the state that was the location of more battles than any other in the country. But let's hear it for Virginia's tourism office, focusing on love not war. And no argument, Virginia is a beautiful state, with much more than battlefields to inspire any visitor. As we drove along I thought about Patrick and whether soldiers ever appreciated the beauty of the land they were marching through. I wondered if these rolling green hills reminded him of the small hills of Cavan.

In Mechanicsville, just outside Richmond, Bob and I stopped at the National Park Service Information Center for the Gaines' Mill battlefield. Both of our great-grandfathers had fought there (on opposite sides) during the summer of 1862; we didn't know much more than that. The visitor center is small, located on an out-of-the-way road, and doesn't get a lot of visitors. Our car was one of two in the parking lot, and the other belonged to the park rangers. Since we had their full attention, we told them our story. They were so excited that we had shown up with our unique family histories that they called the main NPS office in Richmond to tell them. The rangers directed us to the nearby battlefield park, which was relatively small—an example of how development continues to encroach on many Civil War battlefields. The rangers gave us a map and told us where we should each stand on the battlefield to experience the general location of our great-grandfathers. We did as instructed, lifted our imaginary rifles, and yelled, "Fire!"

It was early September, and for a while we were the only visitors there. Wooden fences ran along a thickly wooded swampy area opposite a few cannons and a replica of a farmhouse from the time of the battle. Over another line of split-rail fences was a large wheat field, golden in the fall sunlight, sloping down to the narrow, lazy Chickahominy River. The field was planted in corn at the time of the war. I had to strain to imagine fire and fury in this quiet, pastoral scene.

The battle took place over a much larger section of land, including the field, several wooded areas, a swamp, and the area around the small farmhouse. Gaines' Mill is not one of the more famous Civil War battles; I had never heard of it before looking through Patrick's records. But it was a truly terrible encounter, part of a series of engagements called the Seven Days' Battles that raged from June 25 to July 1, 1862. The Union Army of the Potomac had made camp at Fort Monroe and then moved up the James River toward the Confederate capital of Richmond. General McClellan was loved by his soldiers because he focused on preparedness—sometimes to a fault. Lincoln was losing

GAINES' MILL BATTLEFIELD, MECHANICSVILLE, VIRGINIA

patience with him. McClellan was overly cautious and continually believed he was outnumbered by the Confederates. Gaines' Mill turned out to be the one time he was right.

I tried to picture what had happened here. From what the park rangers told us, I knew that McClellan had divided his army into two sections, one on either side of the Chickahominy, to protect the railroad, an essential link for supplying his army. Patrick's division was ordered to hold the Confederates back. The morning of June 27 broke warm and humid. It had rained the week before, and what roads existed through the dark pine forest were broken by meandering brooks. Union soldiers must have been miserably hot in their wool uniforms as they moved into position.

At first, it seemed that Patrick's division would prevail. They had the better position on a small hill in front of the swampy woods, firing into the approaching Confederate troops. But by late afternoon, Lee learned that only half of McClellan's army was in the field and showed up with reinforcements. Suddenly the Confederates outnumbered the Union forces almost two to one. The men of the Second Infantry were stationed on a vulnerable open space, but they held their ground for the better part of the day while Confederate fire poured out of the woods. Eventually Bob's great-grandfather's North Carolina regiment managed to plow through the woods into the open space, yelling their piercing rebel cry as they finally broke through the line. As dark approached, Lee's reinforcements arrived. At 7:00 p.m. he unleashed thirty-two thousand men in one furious assault on the smaller Union forces. It was the largest single assault of the entire war—twice the size of Pickett's charge at Gettysburg. Patrick fled with the Union soldiers across the Chickahominy as the rebels pursued, leaving their dead and wounded on the field. Thousands were killed, wounded, or missing on both sides. Gaines' Mill was a hard-fought battle in a relatively small area. Much of the fighting was close, the kind of struggle where soldiers look one another in the eye, hear their cries, feel the terror of it. By the end of the day, there were 15,500 combined Union and Confederate casualties, including 894 Union soldiers dead.

I stood looking out at the field, at the woods, at the little farmhouse. All that had happened right here, in this quiet place. The farmhouse stood empty; it had served as a hospital in the heat of battle. This land was a simple family farm near a mill until it became the ground fought over by two great armies. Now it was memorialized as a national park. Old photographs and maps told the story on park signs. Over there, I saw a row of picket fences; over here, a row of cannons pointing toward a wood. Only the ghosts remain among the few visitors and their imaginations.

CHAPTER TWENTY-THREE

Standing on Battlefields

SOME YEARS LATER—the same year I visited the National Archives in Washington—I took Timothy Reese up on his offer to accompany me to the battlefields. Bob and I drove from DC up along the Potomac, roughly following the path of the Union army as they marched north from their camp at Washington. In the parking lot of a small restaurant in Gettysburg, a tall, lanky, mustached guy stepped out of his red Jeep to greet us. "Just call me Tim," he said.

We went into the restaurant to get acquainted over lunch. A multi-talented person, Tim had worked at the Smithsonian as a graphic exhibits specialist for eighteen years before writing his book. His research involved long days in the National Archives, which is evident from the detail in his writing. After lunch, we took off for a personal tour of two of the most significant battlefields of the war, Gettysburg and Antietam. Tim knew them the way a farmer knows every inch of his acreage, every hill and valley.

Bob's great-grandfather, a Confederate officer, had been captured at Gettysburg, the later battle of the two, fought July 1 to 3, 1863, and that may have accounted for his survival. He was later released in a prisoner swap. Tim showed us the exact place where that probably happened. Patrick, too, was likely saved by circumstances: his five-year commitment had elapsed one month before Gettysburg began, and he did not reenlist. The fact that he enlisted in June and not

July may have saved his life. Something so arbitrary—a capture, the month of enlistment—saved those two men, and thereby Bob's and my existence.

We moved on to the battlefield that the Confederates called Sharpsburg and the Union called Antietam. Patrick did fight here with Company C of the Second Infantry on the day of the battle, September 17, 1862. Tim parked the car, and we walked up a low hill of farm fields. We were the only people around. If it had been summer, the place would have been filled with tour buses and visitors.

A cold, sleet-like rain was falling. It was late March, but there was no evidence of spring. We stood on a narrow road that sliced across a large field with split-rail fences bordering each side. Corn and wheat grew here. This was Sherrick's Lane, just off the Boonsboro Pike in Maryland. Tim pointed out a plaque that commemorated the Second Infantry; they had stood exactly where we were standing. A foggy mist rose from the snowmelt, lifting off the field on my right. It was utterly quiet, the birds having the sense to stay somewhere dry. Tim told us that the locals here tell a story: that on that September day, the sound of cannons and gunfire and shouting and screaming was so deafening that all the birds left and didn't return for a year.

This was Antietam—the bloodiest single day in the history of the United States. Out of 23,000 total casualties, 3,650 people were dead.

Up to this point, the Union army had no victories to claim in the east. President Lincoln needed a win to support his release of the Emancipation Proclamation. A triumph now would give Congress the confidence that the war could be won. Lincoln knew that the proclamation would decimate the economy of the South, which would draw the country closer to the end of the war. The Confederates, on the other hand, saw their army gaining the upper hand in battle, and Lee had decided to make a bold move to cross into the North. It was paramount for the Union forces to keep him from closing in on Washington. Outside the town of Sharpsburg the armies engaged early in the morning, and fighting increased throughout the day to spread over fields, woods, and Antietam Creek. The fighting was close and horrific. But by late afternoon, it appeared that Lee's army was weakening.

Union officers believed that if he was pursued, the Confederate army could be smashed once and for all.

Patrick's company had been held in reserve, resting and waiting, about five miles away. When they were called up, they crossed the bridge over Antietam Creek, moving forward under heavy fire toward the point along the road where we were standing. Now they took their position on the east side of the lane, lined up behind the rail fence. Their direct commanders sensed that an assault on Lee's shrunken and fatigued army could be a fatal blow. They waited for orders from higher up. They wanted this; they were primed and ready. Confederate forces waited just over the crest of a hill. Suddenly a short burst of fire from the hill sent part of the Second Infantry pushing over the fence toward them, like a false start in a race, ready to charge through the field and up the small rise. But word came to stand down. McClellan had hesitated, afraid he would be sacrificing the regulars, whom he held in respect almost like Napoleon's royal guard. The men wanted to attack, and this time the numbers were on their side. But soldiers aren't allowed to make the call; it had to come from their generals. Frustration must have been high.

As it turned out, this part of Sherrick's Lane would not be as bloody as the rest of the Antietam battlefield, where so many had died earlier in the day. Arguments have been made about how an assault at this point could have been a turning point, could have vanquished Lee. What *didn't* happen is one of those what-if moments that, according to some historians, might have changed the course of the war—shortened it, or maybe even ended it, right here.

Tim's words hung in the air alongside the soldier ghosts. Maybe it was the misty weather, or the fact that the three of us were alone here, but it was impossible not to feel a presence in this place. Looking over the fence behind me to the frozen field, dotted with patches of snowmelt, I wondered where Patrick had stood. Was I close? He had been somewhere nearby, maybe right here in this spot. I saw the same view his eyes had taken in.

How many Americans, of North or South, have stood like this on Civil War battlefields, trying to imagine a scene from the past?

I fantasize about having a time-machine camera app. You would frame a scene with your smartphone camera, click on the app, and set the dial to a specific year, day, and time. Suddenly your screen would show the scene exactly as it was then: sights and sounds, maybe even smells. But alas, imagination is all I've got.

For some, the intrigue of the American Civil War is the military maneuvering, the game of what-ifs and whys of generals on both sides. War games. But for others it's the desire to stand in the places where our soldier ancestors stood and fought. They were players in the most traumatic event in our national family story. What was going on in their heads? Their days veered wildly between the mind-numbing boredom of camp life and never-ending marches and the adrenaline-pumping heightened awareness of battle.

Recent research estimates that more than 750,000 soldiers died in the war from 1861 to 1865. It's a number greater than all the combined American combatant losses in all wars since then. The Civil War tore apart families and ripped through the land, littering it with the bodies of soldiers, civilians, and horses. Farming families had their fields trampled, their herds confiscated, their homes taken over for officer quarters or hospitals. Secure homeowners became refugees overnight. In Gettysburg, twenty-year-old Jennie Wade was baking bread when a bullet pierced her kitchen window, killing her instantly. In Chancellorsville, Sue Chancellor's piano was turned into an operating table. The town of Martinsburg, Virginia (now part of West Virginia), changed hands between the Union and the Confederacy thirty-seven times during the war. Families gave refuge to escaped slaves and army deserters or caught them and turned them in. Entire towns were destroyed by shelling or fire, and homes and stores were looted. People and animals alike were terrified. Townspeople watched as armies moved through their world, destroying roads and any sense of normalcy or convention. And death, always death, occupied the land, the newspapers, and the mind.

When I was growing up, the war was consigned to American history classes, a long-ago and abstract moment in America. Causes and generals and slavery and Lincoln were reduced to academic discussions and questions on a quiz. Teachers didn't talk about what living through it must have been like. But they should, because the American Civil War was unlike any other event on our nation's soil. It was a brutal eruption of the country's early and unfinished business, decisions postponed for political expediency. All men are created equal, but seldom are all treated equally. Sooner or later the gap between words and reality had to be dealt with, and that cost fell on the ordinary soldier, the local shopkeeper, the small farmer, the nurse, the widow, the orphan.

I wonder what it's like today to live in towns named Manassas, Fredericksburg, Gettysburg. Do people get used to separating their twenty-first-century life from history? Do they drive past signs marking Antietam Creek oblivious of the trauma that happened there? How do people come to grips with the lasting effect of events at this specific place in history, both personal and national? It must be strange to be constantly surrounded by all these reminders. I was grateful for Tim's knowledge and willingness to show us sites we wouldn't have otherwise known about. Grateful to have this picture in my mind, and to fill in some of the gaps of Patrick's path during the war.

Places hold the past as well as the present, and some places retain more evidence of their history than others. On a road trip, you might find yourself passing a sign for a battlefield, perhaps on a road in Virginia where there are so many of them. Take a minute and stop. Get out of the car and stand along the road, beside the fence, the stone wall, the field, and give those places the honor they're due. This is not about glorifying war. It's about remembering and honoring those whose lives were caught up in it, including those whose DNA we share. For a moment, just stop and listen. And if you're near Antietam, listen for the birds and be grateful they've returned.

CHAPTER TWENTY-FOUR

Fredericksburg

AFTER THE BATTLE OF ANTIETAM, which ended in a draw between the two forces, President Lincoln made two decisive moves. He replaced the slow-moving McClellan, who had hesitated to bring the full force of his army upon Lee's retreating forces. And he called that retreat a victory, which gave him enough cover to announce the Emancipation Proclamation. He had been holding on to it since that summer after being advised to wait for a victory. The proclamation gave Confederate states one hundred days—until January 1, 1863—to rejoin the Union or all enslaved persons would be declared "thenceforward or forever free." As much as Lincoln believed in ending slavery, he also knew this act would devastate the economy of the Confederacy. It was as much a practical move as a moral one.

It's hard to know what most Union soldiers thought about it. If you'd asked what they were fighting for, they would probably have answered, "The survival of the Union." For many, and perhaps especially for immigrants, slavery was a side issue. Some even voiced concern about whether freed slaves would be competing for their jobs once the war was over. We want to believe that those who start out on the bottom rungs of the social and economic ladder will be supportive of one another, but that is often not the case. More often they are competing, climbing over one another to get to the top. I have no way of knowing what Patrick thought about slavery, as there's nothing in his letters to give any hint of how he viewed his adopted country's "peculiar institution." I want to believe that he thought, as Lincoln once said, "If slavery is not wrong, nothing is wrong."

When the proclamation was signed on September 22, 1862, Patrick's regiment was headed south again, more miles of marching until they learned their next move. The plan was to camp at Falmouth, outside Richmond, where they would meet up with Lee's army. Some dared to hope that the end of the war was near. The proclamation was indeed a turning point, but two more years would pass and much more blood would be shed throughout the country before it ended.

In the war years, the population of many cities in the South and the border states was a mixture of locals, soldiers, and enslaved and formerly enslaved people. By this point, most of those who were enslaved had heard of the Emancipation Proclamation and had walked or run away from their plantations or owners. Some who worked in town simply left their positions and followed the Union army, seeing it as a refuge as they sought help to get further north. Many found work with the army as cooks, blacksmiths, and spies. They helped build fortifications and bury the dead. When the army moved, they moved with it.

Fredericksburg and nearby Falmouth were no different. Mixed populations and mixed ideologies simmered there on the edge of war, and yet day-to-day life continued. Goods were delivered, letters written, children schooled, and sermons preached. People got married, doctors cared for the sick, and life carried on as best it could under the circumstances. Each town hoped it would be spared the direct clash of armies. Fredericksburg might have escaped too, except for a bungled bureaucratic request.

For a time, the Union army seemed to be cursed with ineffective generals. Many of the elite West Point graduates were residents of Virginia and had sided with the Confederacy as soon as Virginia seceded. The major battles in Virginia had been catastrophic losses for the Union. When Lincoln replaced McClellan, many loyal soldiers were unhappy to see him go, while others were frustrated with his slowness to act. McClellan's second-in-command, Ambrose Burnside, was reluctant to take command of the Army of the Potomac but accepted the position.

What Burnside knew for sure was that, after McClellan's inaction, his one goal must be to engage Lee in battle.

Burnside had a good plan, but plans and execution don't always match up. He intended to march his army south of Fredericksburg and cross the Rappahannock River in November on pontoon bridges, then hurry to Richmond ahead of Lee. The pontoon boats were critical because the Confederates had blown up the bridges to protect the town from northerners. Burnside's army of 123,000 men reached Falmouth in mid-November, slowed by rain and muddy roads. But the pontoons were not waiting there. Burnside's order had been delayed and mishandled, leading to a terrible result. By the time the pontoons arrived in December, Lee knew what Burnside was planning and had moved his army to block the crossing. Now Burnside had a problem. He was stuck directly across from the town, and Lee knew that the Union forces were sitting across the river with no way to cross. Lee sent in additional Confederate regiments and prepared for an attack.

Fredericksburg's residents began to leave, aware of the coming battle. The roads out of town were crowded with carts and wagons filled with satchels, pots and pans, furniture, and personal belongings. Residents of means rode in carriages, and those without went on foot, everyone moving to whatever safety they could find.

Across the river, Patrick and his fellow soldiers waited in camp, nervous and unsure what was ahead. They played cards, cooked their meals, polished their rifles and bayonets. They were restless to engage the enemy but unsure what would happen with a town directly in the way. Battles were supposed to be fought on fields or in woods or on the sea, not in towns.

When pontoon boats finally arrived, Burnside's choices were limited. Should he abandon his plan and advance directly through Fredericksburg? Aware of Lincoln's dismissal of McClellan for inaction, he decided to attack. He ordered his officers to begin sending their men across in the early morning of December 11, while the fog rising off the river would give them some cover. But as soldiers put the pontoons together in the dark to create a bridge, bullets rained down on them; snipers were firing from the attics of Fredericksburg's houses across the river. Eventually giving up on the pontoon bridges, soldiers rowed small boats across, dodging bullets, and scrambled up the riverbanks to move into the streets of the town. The first troops to reach the city were angry and frustrated and lost all measure of discipline. Hand-to-hand combat broke out as Union soldiers tried to evict the remaining Confederates. As they tried to rout the snipers, they looted homes and businesses, destroying property and confiscating what they could carry. Officers struggled to regain control of their troops. They eventually restored order, but not before homes had been ransacked and some burned. It was one of the first instances of urban warfare in the United States.

By the time the Second Infantry and the remainder of the Union troops had crossed the river, the vandalism and looting had ceased. Soldiers formed orderly narrow columns and filed through the now-deserted streets of the ravaged town to the battlefield: a flat, open space outside the town. As they approached, they crossed a shallow canal parallel to a stone wall where Confederate soldiers were waiting for them at the bottom of a bluff called Marye's Heights. Lee had posted artillery on top of the bluff directed down at the field. Burnside planned to advance lines of soldiers wave after wave and, by sheer force of numbers, overtake Lee's army. But Lee had plenty of time and a prime position. Behind the low stone wall, forces from Georgia were lined up three rows deep, their rifles aimed at the advancing blue lines of the Union. When the Confederate rifles on the front line got too hot, a fresh rifle would be passed up the line. There would be no break in the firing.

Fredericksburg was one of the most disastrous battles of the entire war. The Union suffered thirteen thousand casualties. Patrick would likely have been among them but for sheer luck. On the night of December 13, he and what remained of Company C took up position, lying flat in a low ditch with cold standing water, eighty yards from the stone wall, waiting to be called up. They watched and listened as the Georgia Twenty-Fourth sent volleys of bullets toward the open field, mowing down each approaching Union line. An eyewitness, possibly General Darius N. Couch, said, "I had never seen fighting like that before, nothing approaching it in terrible uproar and destruction. It is only murder now."

They hunkered down, making themselves as flat as possible against the cold, wet ground. For twelve hours the Confederates fired down on them. They were unable to raise their heads or snipers would pick them off. The temperature dropped to thirty-four degrees overnight, and yet they lay there, stock-still among the dead and wounded, waiting for dawn and instructions.

I imagine Patrick lying there with his fellow soldiers, his feet growing numb, telling himself, *Breathe, keep breathing, don't move.* Packed like sardines as, somewhere near, a soldier tries to muffle sobs. Above his head bullets fly, the sound of them a sung note that hangs in the air, off-key. The low moan of pain and the sharp cry as someone lifts his head and is hit. All of them, frozen in a cocoon of fear, still as coffined bodies. He thinks about his tent across the river, his folded blanket, breakfast, the smell of coffee, anything to remove his mind from this mass of bodies living and dead or dying. *Don't let yourself move, just freeze.*

His line was to be the next sent up for slaughter; fourteen Union charges had gone before only to be mowed down. Only New York's Fighting Sixty-Ninth, Brigadier General Thomas F. Meagher's famous Irish Brigade, wearing sprigs of green boxwood in their caps, had advanced to within thirty yards of the wall. In that assault, the Irish Brigade lost half of their men and all but one officer. The Confederate Georgia division that mowed them down also included many Irish immigrants. It made little difference in this war, far from their homeland. The courage of Meagher's Irish Brigade so impressed the Georgians that their fellow Irishmen cheered them for their bravery, even as they melted into the ground. It was that kind of war.

Patrick lay there in the damp and cold all through the night and into the next day. Across the river, Burnside's subordinate officers had been pleading with him all night to stop the pointless attacks. As morning broke, they finally convinced him that there was no hope in continuing this madness. Burnside had been holding on to his belief that one of the lines would break through and they could rout Lee's army. He seemingly could not grasp how the terrain made it impossible for his army to advance. He worried that if he wasn't aggressive enough, McClellan's fate would be his own. But this defeat by Lee was far worse than the draw at Antietam. Dead and wounded lay tangled together on the field. In some places Union men had stacked up the dead bodies of their fellow soldiers to create a barrier against the Confederate firepower. Patrick's regiment, still stranded in the ditch, eighty yards from the wall, waited. Finally, in the afternoon of December 14, a truce was called to allow him and the other survivors to crawl back to safety. When darkness fell, they removed as many of their wounded as they were able and buried some of their dead as best they could. Through the night they moved quietly in retreat through the war-torn town and toward the Potomac. Behind them, twelve hundred Union dead littered the frozen ground. Nearly one thousand more were wounded and seventeen hundred missing or captured.

It would be another day before all the survivors of the slaughter finally reached safety. But that night, those who had reached the river climbed into the rowboats that waited on the river's shore and rowed back across the Potomac, back to the safety of the campground they had left only a few days before. Exhausted, dejected, they pushed their oars soundlessly through the water. Then, suddenly, the dark sky lit up with bright streaks of colored light—the aurora borealis. Those in the boats, the wounded still on the field, the soldiers digging shallow graves—all looked up, frightened and confused. It seemed like an omen, or a parting of the curtains of heaven. The northern lights are rarely seen that far south, but there they were, undeniable, ranging across the sky. As the evening deepened, the waves of blue, red, and yellow light grew brighter, like shards of brilliant colored glass against the darkness. They rose higher and higher, their vivid swirling colors shining over the soldiers in their small boats and down upon the battleground where the dead lay mute.

CHAPTER TWENTY-FIVE

Return

WHEN LINCOLN RECEIVED the news of Fredericksburg he fell into a state of deep depression. "If there is a worse place than hell," he said, "I am in it."

Patrick and his fellow survivors buried their dead, tended to their wounded, and wrestled with this mismanaged defeat. In the face of fifteen thousand casualties, it's hard to imagine what went through the minds of these soldiers and officers as they waited in camp. How do you go on after that? Orders came down on January 20. They broke camp and marched toward Richmond, the Confederate capital, on Burnside's futile hope that he might have another chance to subdue Lee. But, as cold and freezing as it had been in December, January was wet and stormy. Men slogged for days through rain and mud that rose above their boots in what became known as the Mud March. At times they were barely able to move at all. Wagons got stuck, horses were injured, cannons were unmovable, and the entire plan collapsed. By January 26, soldiers were exhausted and officers enraged, and they had gained nothing. Lincoln replaced Burnside.

This time the president put the army under the control of Major General Joseph Hooker. He inherited an unenviable situation. Desertions had multiplied, and those soldiers who remained were demoralized. But Hooker was good at discipline and organization, and by spring he had managed to improve the morale of his soldiers. They spent several months resting and recouping in camp at Falmouth, across the river from Fredericksburg and all those bad memories. The armies did not engage again until May 1, near the town of Chancellorsville, Virginia, just ten miles from Fredericksburg. Here it looked like the Union would finally have the upper hand. And, at first, it did. But once again, thanks to a combination of miscommunication, ineptitude, and lack of confidence on Hooker's part, things went from bad to worse. They should have won, but after three days of fighting, despite Hooker's forces vastly outnumbering Lee's army, they were forced to retreat.

Patrick was confined to the infirmary while the battle was going on. He may have contracted malaria in Fredericksburg or on the Mud March. As the troops began limping back to camp, he would have learned the dismal news that the Confederates had beaten them again. The Army of the Potomac was devastated. The North had hit its lowest point in the war.

Because we all know how the war eventually ended, it's hard to imagine the state of mind of the country in the spring of 1863, and certainly that of any individual soldier. But it could not have been good. Foremost in Patrick's mind must have been the fact that his five-year term of service in the US Army would be over in one short month, on June 5. The war was going badly, and there was no guarantee of victory. If the Union didn't survive, what then? His new country, in which he had placed his hope for a better life, was struggling for its own survival.

He might have heard the rumors that Lee was planning an invasion of the North, moving toward the capital, possibly into Maryland or Pennsylvania. In the early hours of June 4, word came down that the rumors were true. On the fifth, officers woke their troops early and instructed them to pack up; they would begin the move north to counter Lee's invasion. The armies would meet near the small town of Gettysburg.

But when Patrick woke up on the warm summer morning of Friday, June 5, 1863, his war was over. Two weeks before the battle of Fredericksburg, he had been promoted to first sergeant. He would have surely been encouraged to reenlist. The army badly needed good soldiers and dependable officers, and he was probably offered a reenlistment bonus. Instead, he signed his honorable discharge papers at Falmouth, Virginia, where he had camped with his regiment before and after the battles of Fredericksburg and Chancellorsville. He left his soldier's life with a recommendation letter from his supervising officer, something to help him get started in life after the army. It is one of Patrick's few personal items that survives in our family. He kept it all his life; it was that important to him. The letter reads,

> This is to certify that I have known for several years, the bearer Patrick Farrelly, 1st. Sergeant, C company, 2nd U.S. and can bear testimony to his sobriety, intelligence and efficiency as a soldier and to his moral character as a man. Sergeant Farrelly's enlistment expires tomorrow and I strongly recommend him as entirely trustworthy and his past service and conduct justly entitled to elicit employment and I hope he may secure in some capacity in the Government. He has served faithfully through the present war from the first Bull Run.
> N. H. Davitz
> Lt. Co., Assistant General
> Army of the Potomac

PATRICK'S RECOMMENDATION LETTER,
FARLEY FAMILY

While his fellow soldiers were breaking camp and preparing to move north, Patrick tucked his letter in his jacket pocket along with his final army pay and headed toward Washington, where he could board a train back to Philadelphia. The Confederates controlled the railroad in Virginia, so he may have taken an army transport ship up the Potomac, a familiar mode of travel for Union soldiers. Perhaps he visited familiar sights and memories from when he and his company first arrived in Washington from Fort Ripley in the spring of 1861. He would have passed new volunteers training on the parade grounds, the makeshift hospitals treating the injured, the shining new government buildings so far removed from the battlefield. Each step took him away from the militarized city, away from the army camps and training grounds and the injured survivors, away from the seat of government and toward what qualified—for now, at least—as home, in Philadelphia.

Once at the station, the simple act of stepping onto a civilian train car must have been heavy with emotion after three years of war. He would take his seat in a car full of civilians and perhaps a few soldiers like himself, also heading home. He was leaving army life behind while others, his friends, were back in camp, still in uniform, polishing their rifles or marching onward to face the fear and adrenaline rush of battle. Up until now, the Army of the Potomac had found no success in the east. Only General Ulysses Grant on the western front was winning battles, and he was currently in the thick of the siege of Vicksburg. But whatever the future held for the Union army, Patrick was done fighting.

He had seen close up what war could do to the body and the mind. He had seen fields trampled and sown with bodies instead of corn and wheat. Seen little homes and farms, built with care by people like him, destroyed and ruined. As the train moved north, he could see through the window the battle wounds across the countryside. He had lost friends. I wondered if he was losing faith in his new country. The Union army was still fighting for the idea and promise of America that he had held in his mind when his ship left Ireland so many years before. Victory was precarious, a hope not a promise. The Confederacy was not subdued. What if the country split apart forever?

What was he thinking as the train rolled on? What did he see in the eyes of his fellow passengers? The world he'd left five years ago, when he had walked into the recruiter's office in Philadelphia, was drastically different now. Perhaps he had received letters that told him how things were going back home, but letters can't paint the whole picture.

All wars are fought on two fronts: the battlefield and the home front. But in the US Civil War, the home front was often the battlefield as well. No one was untouched by this "citizens contest," as Lincoln had called it. Although there is no way to precisely measure it, historian James McPherson estimates that fifty thousand nonsoldier civilians were killed or died of disease directly as a result of the war. Every home, North and South, waited for the casualty lists that were tacked up daily at the local post office. Neighbors shared newspapers and pored over battle reports. Were the armies headed your way? Did the postman have a letter from your son? Did he know anything, have any news? There were shortages of food and other basic needs. Almost half of the Union army's soldiers were farmers; their farms were now being run by their wives and daughters and any sons too young to go off to fight. In the South, cities and towns that stood in the path of the Union army were destroyed, homes and businesses ruined. Inhabitants fled from battles, and refugees filled the roads, looking for shelter until it was safe to return.

It was supposed to be a brief war. Both sides had expected victory in a matter of months, but it stretched on with no end in sight, year after year. Wounded men wandered the streets, many no longer able to work due to amputations or permanent injury.

The Civil War was the last time that great armies faced each other on US soil. What would it be like if you found your city or countryside in the middle of a battle or in the path of an army on the march? How would you feel, how would you cope, if the landscape you had known for your entire lifetime was ravaged or destroyed? Recent immigrants to the United States understand that kind of fear and loss, and even if your family has been living here for generations, there's a good chance that you have ancestors who lived through it, too. Maybe they were soldiers, farmers, bankers, or gunsmiths. Maybe they were immigrants like Patrick, caught up in a war in their new country. Maybe they were enslaved; maybe they enslaved others. But the thing is, they were involved. Directly or indirectly, they experienced the trauma that tore apart our nation.

It would be two more years before Lee and Grant would meet at a farmhouse in Appomattox and the fighting would finally come to an end. But Patrick's war was over. Did he have a plan when he left Falmouth? Did he look for government employment as his superior had hoped? I don't know. But I do know this: after only a month in Philadelphia, as Patrick later reported in his pension record, he went back to Ireland.

He left the same way he arrived. I can see him back on the crowded, noisy Philadelphia or New York docks, the air filled with the smell of the sea, the commingled sounds of squawking gulls and yelling dockhands. Tall ships lined up in close ranks, the dark waters lapping below. Passengers crowded together, waiting to board, carrying their bags and bundles. It must have felt familiar and strange all at once, heading east, not west. Newsboys hawked the latest edition of their broadsheets, and men and women sold food from carts among the waiting passengers. Before Patrick boarded the ship, he might have purchased a copy of the July 3 edition of the *Philadelphia Inquirer*. On the front page, the headline echoed what the newsboys were shouting: "The Great Battle near Gettysburg! Gallant Fighting of the Army of the Potomac! Meade Victorious! Repulse of the Rebels!"

Once aboard the ship, he could set down his bag and open the paper. Following the reporter's account, he would have read, "The Second Division went into the fight at eleven o'clock and there remained all the time, subject to a grilling fire, without support or reinforcements, until five o'clock." That's where he would have been: under withering fire for six hours, perhaps more, in the Wheatfield and in the woods near Little Round Top. His mind would fill with faces of the men he had served alongside, and he would wonder if they had survived. He had time to think now as his ship drew up anchor and pulled out of the harbor. Back out on the open ocean, with the city fading away and the wind blowing sweet and clear, the sounds and smells of battle were now only words on paper.

By the time he reached the Dublin docks, Gettysburg, the name that would eventually become synonymous with the Civil War, was long past. After weeks on the ocean and a world away, his feet would be back on Irish soil. It had been twelve long years since he said goodbye. A teenager when he left, he was now a war-tested man of twenty-seven. The Dublin dockside, much smaller than the one he had left in New York, carried the voices of women with baskets of bread or fish to sell and newsboys hawking their papers in an old familiar accent. As he walked away from the ship, he might have crossed the Carlisle Bridge (later renamed for Daniel O'Connell) on his way to find a pint or a bite to eat after weeks on the ocean.

He might have picked up the latest *Dublin Evening Mail.* The August 11 edition ran an eyewitness story from a New York journalist who wrote,

> I have just returned from Gettysburg. The estimated number there [in hospital] on July 7, was 20,000 Union and rebel soldiers. . . . About half are under canvas in the various corps hospitals, the rest in churches, barns and private houses in and around Gettysburg. . . . Medical stores and food could not be at hand. The neighboring country had been stripped bare, first by the rebels, then by our own. . . . Only one-third of the surgeons, ambulances and wagons could be left with each corps to care for their wounded and no detail of well men to nurse them. . . .
>
> The roads were thronged with wounded men, here on canes and there on crutches, not seldom with amputated arms and heads still bleeding, making their way on foot, from the corps hospitals, two, three and four miles, to the depot. At the hospitals, the spectacle was intensely wretched. Men with both legs shot off, shot in the eye, the mouth, both hands gone, or one arm lost were lying in rows that seemed pitiably long, and in patience, fortitude and patriotic pride facing their suffering.

Many in Ireland would have been following the news of the war. Many had family who, like Patrick, had boarded ships for America during the famine and found themselves caught up in the conflict. Brothers and sons had joined the fight. Sisters and daughters had been left at home as breadwinners after their husbands had been injured or killed. By the time Patrick returned to Ireland, little remained of his regiment. Companies were consolidated as their numbers shrank. Of Company C, the men he had known back in Fort Ripley, Minnesota—those with whom he had laughed, complained about the winters and the mosquitoes, and learned how to be a soldier—many hadn't survived. But he had.

Why did Patrick return to Ireland? When he was discharged, the survival of the Union was not guaranteed. Maybe it was better to return to Ireland, where at least people weren't killing each other. Whatever the reason, twelve years after he'd survived the famine, would he recognize the land he had left?

CHAPTER TWENTY-SIX

Strange Land

IN MY MIND'S EYE, I see him in crowded Dublin, carrying a small bag of belongings over his shoulder, maybe a newspaper tucked under his arm. The morning fog is beginning to lift off the river as he walks along the dockside, listening to seagulls fighting over scraps of food from the ships. He turns up Sackville Street, away from the Liffey, stopping to buy a loaf of brown bread from a woman with a cart near the bridge. He finds a bench beside the General Post Office, glad to put his bag down for a moment, and breaks off a piece of bread. It's been a long time since he's tasted the rich, nutty flavor of real Irish brown bread. Across from his bench is the imposing pillar topped with the statue of British Lord Horatio Nelson, a reminder to the Irish of who is in charge here. After a short rest he walks up the cobblestone street, avoiding puddles and horse manure, looking for a place to stay the night before setting out for home—something cheap but safe. The further up the street he goes, the more evidence he sees that Dublin has sunk even further into poverty than when he left. Many of the impressive Georgian homes of the wealthy have now been reduced to tenements. Some of the worst slums in all of Europe are here. He avoids the area around Henrietta Street. What he needs is a good simple meal and a decent night's sleep.

In the morning he would leave Dublin and head west, home to Cavan. The distance from the crowded, noisy, and relentlessly grey city to the countryside would be further in mood than in miles. He had choices for transportation; the standard coach run would take him directly to Virginia, the village nearest his former home. Coaches had been operating out of Dublin since the 1700s, and the roads were better now. It would take less than a day. Or he could walk. Was he in a hurry, anxious to see his family? Or was the distance a helpful transition, a way to reconnect? He was a hardened soldier who had traveled much greater distances on crowded trains, on rivers by flatboat, on roads by foot. Would people think he was putting on airs if he arrived by coach or train? I doubt that his bag was a heavy load: a change of clothes, some food for the journey, a newspaper to read. The heavier load was what he carried in his mind. Maybe he laughed at the irony of how much time he had spent in the other Virginia during the Civil War.

Patrick was the exception to the rule. Very few famine Irish ever returned home. It held little promise. They reached across the Atlantic by sending money so relatives could join them, but they rarely got on ships themselves to go back. They were more likely to settle in Philadelphia, Boston, New York, Chicago, or other cities; some tried their luck moving west. Although famine emigrants were predominantly rural people, they tended to cluster together in urban settings for survival and security once they arrived in North America. Cities offered more opportunity for work and the comfort of being among other Irish. A small number ventured west to California, following the lure of gold and cheap land. But Patrick had gone home.

I can only speculate why he went back to Ireland. Did he try to find work in Philadelphia and come up empty? Did he get a letter from home because someone was sick or dying? Or had Ireland—even devastated Ireland—now become a place of refuge after the carnage of Bull Run, Gaines' Mill, Antietam, and Fredericksburg?

Whatever the reason, he was now out in the countryside. Whether by foot or by carriage, as he approached the village of Virginia from the Dublin Road, he would have gone right past the turnoff to the road that sloped down to the old, abandoned abbey in Lurgan parish, down to the small stone bridge that led to Curraghmore. There was no reason to go down that road. So much had changed. No one in his family lived there now. His father was in another cottage in another townland. The new place, Lisnabantry, was only a mile and a half away from Virginia. There he would find his father, his own namesake, in a small cottage in the corner of a small field shared with two other cottages. A tiny spit of a place.

What was the greeting like when he came through the door into his dad's home, dark and smoky from the turf fire? His father was sixty-seven now, his younger brother, Andrew, an adult at twenty-five. Was his mother still alive? His older sister and brother? Had they left Ireland too?

The same year that I found the old map of Cavan and Meath, Bob and I and Margaret went in search of this field where Patrick's father lived after the famine, the place where Patrick would return to find him. On Patrick's civil marriage record, his father was listed as living in the townland of Lisnabantry. I found the rough location of his actual cottage in Griffith's Valuation. *Follow the money* applies in family history too, and tracking down those land records had involved a hunt on foot through a few government offices in Dublin. Reaching the actual place in the country required a car and a bit of sleuthing. We were lucky to have my old Ord map and a current one to guide us.

Lisnabantry is on a higher plain than Curraghmore, but it's just as remote. Its name means "place of the ring fort," an ancient circular dwelling, the remains of which showed up on the old map. We ventured forth, passing no cars or people on the road, just sheep and cattle in the nearby fields. By following a few landmarks, we spotted a crossroad that matched on both maps. It was clear that this was the place. We stopped the car and got out for a closer look. The field where Patrick's father's cottage would have stood was empty, just a few trees along a fence and a small, sunken stream hidden by a row of hedges. A barbed-wire fence with a locked gate at the corner separated the field from the road. No one seemed to be around, so I gingerly climbed over the fence to explore while Bob and Margaret kept a lookout.

The ground sloped down toward a line of low trees. Two mounds of overgrown brambles and stones sat in the field, one in the middle, one toward the back. I'd seen this sort of thing before. They were likely tumbled cottages—messy mounds that were once someone's home. In the field behind Margaret's house were four such mounds, all that remained of deserted cottages, and they looked just like this. Perhaps one had been Patrick's father's cottage. Had Patrick returned and walked through a door here after his absence of twelve years? Was there a hearth somewhere under all this mess? Most Irish farmers have a superstition about the tumbled cottages in their fields, preferring to let them remain and sink back into the ground. Whether it's out of respect or because they don't want to trifle with the spirits of the past, the cattle and sheep don't care and birds and small creatures find a safe home in the brambles. Margaret told me about an old woman who always kept a pot of geraniums beside the ruins in the field behind her home as a small gesture of remembrance.

After standing there for a while, I climbed back over the fence, carefully avoiding the wire barbs, and knocked the dirt from my boots. We decided to head across the road toward a lane where the old map indicated a big house with surrounding grounds had stood. It was probably the home of the landlord's agent. And there we found it, abandoned sometime in the last few decades. We walked down a long lane lined with old trees and overgrown rhododendrons to get a closer look. It was much smaller than the Nixon estate, just a sturdy, grey, two-story house, built in the late eighteenth or early nineteenth century. It may have belonged to the Bell family, Protestants of some means who owned the surrounding area, including the field where Patrick's father once lived. It had a lonely, empty feel, and none of us wanted to stay long. We headed home to Margaret's for tea.

In the United States there are few places that are left in this kind of historic limbo—not the past, not quite the present. But in Ireland there are so many. The present is only a thin membrane covering the residue of the past. I'm grateful for that, for these chances to glimpse another time, to stand on the same soil where my ancestors stood and to try to grasp even a partial understanding of their lives.

CHAPTER TWENTY-SEVEN

What Did You Find?

THE POSTFAMINE COUNTRYSIDE that Patrick found when he returned was familiar and strange all at once. As someone interviewed by the Irish Folklore Commission cryptically summed it up, "There were fewer people around." The air was full of absence. If an emigrant did return, they would meet old friends and exchange some small talk, and then the rush of questions began: who had gone, where had they gone, who survived, and how did they manage? Who took over whose land?

There were fewer people indeed, but more cattle—although the cattle didn't appear to be doing very well. For those who survived the famine, the years immediately following had been good ones, relatively speaking. Large landholders had consolidated their fields, and cows and sheep now filled fields that had previously held tenants' cottages and farms. But, beginning in 1859, while Patrick was learning to manage the extremes of Minnesota summers and winters, Ireland was wracked with several years of extreme weather. In the spring and summer of 1859, a major drought left little grass for the cattle to feed on. The drought was followed by three years of heavy rains that fell on hardened soil, inundating fields and ruining grain and potatoes. Rivers overflowed their banks and drenched the grazing land. The bogs became impassable, and it was hard to store enough dry turf to burn through the winter.

In town, shopkeepers tried to help as they were able, extending credit to farmers and laborers and expanding the availability to

households of "Indian corn"—imported maize, called yellow meal—
to alleviate the situation. By far not as terrible as the years of famine,
those five years of bad weather and agricultural depression had taken
a toll on the land and the people by the time Patrick returned home.

There was also an uptick in unrest driven by local "ribbon men,"
loosely organized groups of tenants who struck out against landlords
for charging too much rent or evicting families with no cause. It was
nothing new, but there was more of it. And now there were whis-
pers about Fenian men who had a much bigger goal: a free and independent Ireland. Patrick would have been familiar with the Fenian
Brotherhood—a secret society driven by those who held the British
government responsible for centuries of Irish oppression and for the
famine itself—from his time in the army. Radical Irishmen on both
sides of the Civil War planned to bring their military training back to
Ireland and use it to liberate their own country by armed rebellion.
He would have been aware of US campaigns to raise money to send
to Ireland to support a major uprising. He may have known men who
had joined this organized and serious brotherhood. Did Patrick con-
sider joining? He might have, or perhaps he agreed with their cause
but not with their means—I have no way of knowing. But whatever
he felt, the desire for an independent Ireland might have been a topic
of whispered conversation with his family and friends.

What he thought about his future before he returned home and
what he thought after he got there is impossible to know. He left no
journal, no letters to give a hint. If he had come home hoping to stay,
his friends and family may have discouraged him. It remained difficult
to make a living there, and unrest was increasing. He must have felt
the comfort of being in the old places, with old customs, the familiar-
ity of just being with his people after over a decade in a foreign land.
But I wonder if he could see his future there.

He stayed in Ireland until sometime in the spring—just nine
months, such a short time. But when he left again for the United
States, he wasn't alone. On February 8, 1864, Patrick married Bridget
McKenna in the church in Moynalty. I asked Father Joe, the current parish priest, what a wedding would have been like back then.

Both groom and bride came from tenant farmer families: Patrick from Cavan and Bridget from Meath, just across the border from each other. The marriage record lists Patrick as a laborer and Bridget as a spinster, the designation for all unmarried women regardless of age. Another couple was married on the same day, their names listed after one another in the book. Father Joe explained that in the 1800s, Catholic weddings were a simple sacrament, short and serious, nothing like today. No walks down the aisle, no bridesmaids, no music or flowers. The couple would meet the priest in the sacristy, a small room off the sanctuary. They were joined by their sponsors, one for the bride and one for the groom, who might be friends or family or neighbors who acted as witnesses. The priest would ask the couple the sacramental questions, and they would answer; then he would bless them and pronounce them man and wife. The priest would record their names and those of their sponsors below the date in the parish record book.

Back in the rectory, Father Joe brought out the book where their names were recorded, and we pulled up chairs beside the long dining room table to take a look. It was a tall record book with a marbled-paper cover, dating back to the 1700s. Inside was the writing of Father Patrick Ginty, the priest in 1864, preserving this moment with the people of his

MARRIAGE RECORD OF PATRICK FARRELLY AND BRIDGET McKENNA, CHURCH OF THE ASSUMPTION, MOYNALTY, MEATH parish. Father Joe said that after the sacrament of marriage, both couples would leave the sacristy, walk around to the church door, and enter for Mass. That was it. There might be a gathering in the bride's home afterward. I had to brush away my twenty-first-century images.

Who was this Bridget, and how did Patrick meet her? Had someone arranged the marriage—is that why he came back? It's hard to believe that they had known each other twelve years earlier and waited all those years. And they hadn't lived close enough for that to make any sense. She was Patrick's age, twenty-seven; although early marriages were less and less the norm after the famine, that was somewhat late in life for a marriageable Irish woman to be single.

From what we inferred from the marriage records, Bridget was living with her sister and brother-in-law in the Skearke townland when she married Patrick. Maybe this had been arranged by someone in her family, or maybe she met Patrick at the town fair and they fell in love. As much as I would like to believe that, I have no way to know. He didn't have land or money to offer, but he *was* a soldier, someone who had made his way in America, and that carried some prestige. Whatever brought them together, contract or attraction and desire, they became husband and wife just seven months after his return home.

And then, only two months later, they would both say goodbye to their little villages in Cavan and Meath, to their families and their friends, and to Ireland, this time for good. Spring and summer meant good sailing weather. The ship would be better equipped, the journey easier than during the famine years. It was the second departure for Patrick, but the first for Bridget.

CHAPTER TWENTY-EIGHT

New Haven

I WONDERED HOW THEY made the decision to go to America and how they came up with the fare. The marriage record says Patrick was a laborer. Maybe he worked at one of the big estates, perhaps Lake View, not far from where he grew up. It had been home to the Mortimer family since the 1600s. The Mortimers were respected landlords in the area, considered kind to their laborers and tenants. Perhaps that was where he learned to be a gardener.

Back at Margaret's after exploring Lisnabantry, we warmed up with tea and a slice of brown bread slathered with delicious homemade plum jam. I asked about the Mortimers. Margaret had told us that she has a connection to the family; her parents had worked for them when she was a young child. A descendant of the family still lives there, and Margaret made a call to the house that evening to see if we could come by while we were still in town.

The next morning, we drove along the winding roads until we came to a shady tree-lined drive that brought us to the house, which lies about halfway between Moynalty and Virginia. Margaret's mother had been a dressmaker for the elderly Mrs. Mortimer. "We have an old iron pot back home from the famine times that came from here. Mrs. Mortimer gave it to us," she said. "They fed people from it during the famine."

We turned up the drive, past the guardhouse and onto lands that had been given to the Mortimers by Charles II in 1660. We parked beside a large country house that had been standing long before Patrick was born. An expansive and perfectly manicured lawn reached down to the edge of Mullagh Lake. Looking far across it, I could see the old church and cemetery where the ancient graves of the McKennas lay.

A descendant of the Mortimers welcomed us and asked if we'd like to walk through the gardens. We followed a gravel path along the house to a gate that opened to the estate gardens. They were bursting with color in the morning light. As we followed down the garden paths, I thought again about the possibility that Patrick might have worked here. Perhaps he might have laid the bricks I was walking on. I asked the Mortimer niece who gave us a tour of the gardens if there were any old accounting records that might mention the names of gardeners from years past. She didn't know of any, at least not there on the property.

Back at the Flanagans' that evening, I thought about Bridget and what it would have been like for her when she left. What did she know of the world outside Moynalty? She had likely been no further than the villages of Kells and Virginia. Certainly not to Dublin or Liverpool, not to the big cities full of unfamiliar sounds and people she didn't know. Bridget's Ireland was quiet. She knew the sounds of nature: cows needing milking, donkeys braying, birds singing, pigs squealing, the wind through the trees. She knew the families in her parish, owners of the shops in the village, the Rathbornes in the Big House and Father Ginty at the church. And that was about it. Living with her sister Catherine and her brother-in-law, Bridget would be a help with the children, but she was also one more mouth to feed. It was a full household in a small place. And her sister was pregnant again. She delivered her fifth baby just one month after Patrick and Bridget said their vows in the church.

The cottage in Skearke had no indoor lighting or plumbing. Water for drinking, washing, and cooking came from the stream down the hill. Light came through the two windows and the half door during the day and, at night, from thin rushes dipped in wax and lit from the fire. One black pot would have hung over the turf fire for cooking potatoes. A straw tick for a bed would be rolled up each morning. Walking was the primary form of transportation on narrow and rutted dirt roads. Rural Irish women dressed as they had for as long as anyone could remember: a long linen shift, which functioned as a combination blouse and slip, worn under a long wool skirt, usually red or black or grey, sometimes with an apron over the front. Every woman had a shawl, which they wore around their shoulders, crossed over in front and tucked into their skirt. The shawl was needed for warmth. Few women or children living in the countryside wore shoes, though they might have a pair saved for going to Mass or into the village. Margaret told us that even in her childhood, people would walk to Mass barefoot and then put on their shoes when they got close to the church door. Bridget would have needed new clothes for America. She wouldn't want to look like a "shawlie," so she may have sewn a dress of homespun linen for herself. She knew what the landlords' wives wore—big skirts and dresses of silk trimmed with lace and buttons—but it wouldn't be like that for regular women in America. And shoes. She would need shoes.

She'd never lived in a house with wood floors and real glass in the windows or water that didn't come from a well. Carpets. Real beds. Sidewalks. Streetlights. Such changes in physical surroundings in the abrupt move from a remote rural setting to an urban one were a shock for most Irish immigrants in the nineteenth century, but for women the difference was magnified because their world was centered around home. Bridget's ideas of what she would encounter on the ship and beyond would have come from stories or letters from those who had gone before her. Patrick may have done his best to give her a picture—albeit a man's picture—but there was no way of truly translating that in her mind until it was a reality.

When she and Patrick left, most Irish emigrants to North America traveled from Dublin or Cobh or Belfast to Liverpool and then, by steam or sail, across the ocean. By 1864, ships were better provisioned than the famine ships had been and not as crowded or rife with disease. But that did not make it an easy trip. It would have taken weeks to a month to cross the Atlantic.

Once they arrived, Patrick would catch up on the news and Bridget would listen, sorting it out. Adjusting to a new country is a challenge.

I wonder what she felt. She might have kept her eyes alert to how women dressed, how they greeted each other, how they spoke. Other Irish women may have pulled her aside and told her, "This is fine, but this needs to change; just ask me if you are wondering." It's the same today among immigrants. The speed and bustle of the big cities was hard to adapt to. Seeing people pass on the streets not greet each other must have felt strange and cold. It would have been a relief to her to be among her own, other Irishwomen, immigrants like herself sharing stories of how it was for them at first, laughing at mistakes they made, commiserating. Language wasn't an issue, as most Irish people spoke English, even if they retained their own native tongue, but local expressions were different and confusing. Everything was confusing.

Few people had or needed passports in 1864. Those who could afford passage simply landed and got off the boat. If Patrick and Bridget landed first in New York, they would have gone through the processing station at Castle Clinton. It opened in 1855 as the first processing point for immigrants coming to New York from Europe. Ellis Island wouldn't be open for business until 1892. I've searched but have yet to find a record of their passage. When Ellis opened, Castle Clinton closed its doors and its records went to the new station, but many were destroyed in a fire in 1897.

The newly arrived couple probably traveled next to Philadelphia and stayed for a while. It had been home to Patrick before and briefly after the war; he may have had family there. But one year after they landed, they were living in New Haven, Connecticut. The war was winding down but was still the daily preoccupation of the country.

The war had upturned society, upturned the very idea of what it meant to be an American. Immigrants who fought for the Union were more accepted. Formerly enslaved people were now free, and some were fighting on the front lines for the Union. The war had sped up developments in technology and medicine. When Patrick's ship left Ireland in July 1863, the North was losing. Patrick had missed the brutal fighting at the battle of Gettysburg, where so many of his fellow soldiers lost their lives. He had missed the horrific New York draft riots just weeks after the battle, when his own Second Infantry had been called into New York to restore calm. He missed Lincoln's stirring Gettysburg Address and the appointment of Ulysses S. Grant as commanding general of the Union army. By the time he returned with Bridget, there was a growing sense that the tide was turning. Yet there was a year to go, one of victories and defeats and more loss of life on both sides of the divide. But there was a slowly growing hope that the country would once again become one nation, reunited.

Patrick arrived in New Haven in time to read about the massacre of Black soldiers at Fort Pillow, the Siege of Petersburg and its seventy thousand casualties, and, in the fall, Sherman's march to the sea. He was not yet a citizen and couldn't cast a vote that November for Lincoln's reelection, but he would have read Lincoln's second inaugural address in the newspapers: "With malice toward none, with charity toward all . . . to bind up the nation's wounds, to care for him who shall have borne the battle." Reading about Lee's surrender and the beginning of the end of the war that had torn it asunder, he would have known that he, and so many immigrants like him, had played a part in preserving the Union in order to "achieve a lasting peace among ourselves."

But five days later, news reports of the assassination of the president whose words had offered mercy and healing shocked the nation. The *Daily Morning Chronicle* of Washington, DC, announced on April 15, 1865, "ABRAHAM LINCOLN IS DEAD! If tears had audible language, a shriek would go up from these States which would startle the world from its propriety." The next day, the *New York Herald* reported, "We have read accounts of similar scenes in the history of other nations, but they were never before brought home to our doors. It is not, therefore to be wondered at that the people were almost dumbfounded as the startling intelligence spread over the city that the assassin had carried out his hellish plot upon the person of the President of the United States."

Word of Lincoln's death sped across the country and cast a dark pall over the euphoric celebrations of the end of war. Five days earlier, bells from churches throughout the North had rung out, signaling the end of five years of conflict. People had left their homes and run into the streets with shouts of joy. Now the bells tolled again, but this time it was the deep, mournful sound of the funeral bell. Lincoln was killed on Good Friday, 1865. Easter and Passover services took on new meaning.

There is still a debate on the ultimate death toll of the Civil War. The current accepted estimate from Professor J. David Hacker, at SUNY-Binghamton, is 750,000 soldiers killed. The number of civilian deaths is virtually impossible to know with any certainty, and the deaths from disease, poverty, and suicide indirectly linked to the war will never be known. But its effects were dramatic, especially in the South, in ways that still reverberate today. Patrick and Bridget must have felt the shock of it all. What would it mean? But they were here to stay. Their first child, Mary, was born a month later, on May 19, the Farleys' first natural-born American citizen. She added one more soul to the forty thousand living in New Haven. The city was a good place for a new start as a family. The Flanagan cousin from New Haven whom I'd met through 23andMe told me that Flanagans had been in New Haven for generations. Perhaps that's why Patrick chose to sink his roots there.

New Haven at this time was a vibrant town with new businesses popping up, thanks to the entrepreneurs and progressive ideas emerging from Yale, and plenty of jobs to be had. Politics was part of the mix too. The town had a forward-thinking energy that attracted people. Frederick Douglass had addressed new African American recruits there in January 1865 with a stirring speech. New Haven's most famous son, Eli Whitney, had invented the cotton gin back in the 1700s and, later, the concept of interchangeable parts in manufacturing. Ironically, Whitney's inventions had stoked the engine that drove the Civil War on both sides: the cotton gin increased the production of cotton in the South, which increased the demand for enslaved labor, and his advances in mass production accelerated the industrial engines of the North, producing firearms that supported its armies.

By the time Patrick and Bridget arrived, Irish immigrants made up a growing percentage of the population and anti-Irish sentiment was less overt, as the nation had witnessed immigrants fighting and dying for the Union. They had proved their usefulness digging canals, laying rail, and working in industry, taking on hard and dangerous work rejected by others. The Irish Catholic community of New Haven offered support to new arrivals and helped them find work and feel accepted. A man from Patrick's own County Cavan, Bernard Reilly, formed the first Hibernian Society and organized New Haven's first St. Patrick's Day parade in 1842. Reilly started out as a drayman (wagon driver) and eventually became a successful contractor who dedicated his life to promoting Irish causes. He gave funds for the first Catholic cemetery in New Haven, which was named in his honor as St. Bernard's.

In 2014 my cousin Michael hosted a Farley family reunion in Connecticut. My cousins and I met with an archivist at the New Haven Immigration Center, which held most of the Irish, Italian, and African American records. She gave us the background of the city and how it was influenced by its immigration history. Being there in New Haven brought my research to life; physical place always helps me understand the context. While we were all together, we drove out to St. Bernard's cemetery. Patrick and Bridget's daughter Mary was buried there in 1945, the year I was born. She shares the grave with her husband, James Gallagher, who had died several years earlier. They had no children, and he was the only one with a grave marker, which was almost overgrown. We got on our hands and knees and pulled back the grass and weeds and dug around the edges until it was legible once again. We may have been the only visitors to their grave for years.

The Immigration Center had a good collection of old directories, organized year by year. I looked through them and made copies of the pages where I found Patrick and Bridget. The family moved several times, but always within a few blocks, part of an area called East Rock, colloquially known as Grad Haven for its population of Yale graduate students. I found them living on Willow Street, on Nicholl and North Vernon (now renamed Eagle Street) and Anderson and Orange. After a drive-by search for each address, I stood on the corner of Eagle and looked down the street at a row of older two-story frame houses, some old enough to have been there in 1870. The archivist told me that address numbers were not dependable that far back, so I couldn't be certain. Still, I thought, *Patrick and Bridget lived here, somewhere on this street. This is where they began their family.*

Old census records are much more interesting than recent ones; they asked more questions and the information they contain tells you so much. You can see who lived on the street, what kind of work they did, where were they born, where their fathers and mothers were born, what language they spoke, and how many people lived in one dwelling. You can get a real picture of the neighborhood.

Patrick and Bridget had been living in New Haven for six years when the 1870 census was taken. This is the snapshot of the Farley family (their name already anglicized) that it gave: On June 1, Patrick and Bridget had three children: Mary, born a year after they arrived, Anne, born two years later, and a baby, Elizabeth, three months old. (My grandfather George would be born a year later, and eventually there would be two more girls.) In 1870 they lived in a section of New Haven's old Sixth Ward, not far from the Whitney factories. The census taker listed five dwellings and eleven families on that page. All the houses were multiple-family dwellings. Two families shared the house with Patrick and Bridget: the Currans and their two children, and the Muldoons, who shared their space with a young boarder named Kershan, apprenticed to a blacksmith. All the adults had been born in Ireland. Irish names and occupations filled the street: blacksmith, iron molder, carpenter, laborer, house painter, a couple of policemen, and one gardener: Patrick.

In 1870 the Sixth Ward was a jumbled mix of income levels—a few large single-family homes, many multiple-family dwellings, and small working men's housing. It was an interesting place to live in an interesting city. Nearby was a small, innovative boarding school, a Lancastrian School built on a progressive concept where older students teach the younger. The census listed seven "boarders" at the school between the ages of nine and seventeen.

The ward bordered Yale University to the south, the Whitney factory to the north, and the Quinnipiac River and port of New Haven just a few blocks to the east. At the time, New Haven had only two Catholic parishes to serve the whole city, St. John's and St. Patrick's.

But a big cathedral, St. Mary's, was being built, not in the poor Irish settlements, but right on prestigious Hillhouse Avenue. In one of his letters, Patrick asks if the priests are still collecting money for the new church. Years later, baby Mary would grow up, move back to New Haven, and be married in that new cathedral. Whether the older residents liked it or not, the Irish immigrant population of New Haven was growing and finding its place in society.

CHAPTER TWENTY-NINE

Migration

PERHAPS THERE IS SOMETHING about immigrating that gives a person a clean slate. Freed from life's previous expectations, a person might find that a new country opens up new possibilities: opportunities to better one's lot beg for someone to take the chance. One of those opportunities caused Patrick and Bridget to leave New Haven after living there only ten years.

Their migration path was New Haven, Connecticut; to Farmington, Connecticut; to Columbus, Nebraska. Most Irish who came to the United States during and after the famine tended to stay in cities, close to their people and to work. But Patrick moved his family from a city to a small town and eventually to the western plains. He'd seen a lot of the country before and during the war. Maybe it was the vast expanse of land in the west, which he'd had a taste of in the army, that called to him. Or maybe it was the simple but powerful idea that in this country, an Irishman could own his own land and be his own boss.

But first they left the busy, diverse city for the quiet, homogeneous small town of Farmington. Patrick's brother Andrew had arrived in America two years after Patrick and Bridget. He had settled in New Haven too, working at Eli Whitney Jr.'s company as a drayman. The brothers had each other and friends they'd made over the years. Leaving couldn't have been an easy decision. But the opportunity was unique. Miss Porter's School for Girls—then, as now, the most prominent establishment in Farmington—needed a gardener. It would be steady, dependable work, not leaving him at the whims of whoever needed a gardener's help.

This prestigious boarding school for young women of standing, founded in 1843, was run by Miss Sarah Porter, a remarkable woman who had pursued education in Farmington beyond what most girls were allowed. She had even studied with Yale professors, which was unusual for the time. The younger sister of Noah Porter, who later served as president of Yale, she had a vision of establishing a place where girls could get a real education, delving into science and the humanities, similar to what was offered in boys' boarding schools. Her students included Nellie Grant, the daughter of President Ulysses Grant.

Did Patrick hear about the opportunity while working for someone who knew someone at Yale? Perhaps one of his clients, in a town with many successful, wealthy families, liked him and wanted to give a hard worker a break. However it came up, regular work was an opportunity for more security, landscaping the grounds of an respected, attractive place rather than going from job to job. It may have meant better pay and better housing. Farmington was a small town; it might have been better for the children, a move up for the family. But I wondered if it was better for Bridget. She would be leaving women she'd gotten to know, women like herself. She'd only been in the country ten years. Patrick was already well assimilated. But how was the move for her? Was Farmington a place where she could feel at home?

The family would have packed up their children and their belongings, said their goodbyes, and boarded the train to Farmington to set off on this new adventure. The Hartford/New Haven line was a short ride forty miles north, but physical proximity belied the cultural distance between the two towns. New Haven was a vibrant city of sixty-two thousand people, loud, bustling, and full of other Irish immigrants. Farmington was a quintessential New England village with just under three thousand inhabitants, quiet, refined, and populated by families who could date their arrival back to the founding of the country.

On a trip east, Bob and I stopped by Farmington to see the town and school. I had contacted the school archivist and told her that my great-grandfather had been a gardener at Miss Porter's in 1874. I thought there might be accounting records with his name. She had nothing along those lines but said we were welcome to stop by the school and walk around the grounds. She sent along some materials and a little map with the location of "the gardener's house" circled.

Farmington is full of history and proud of it. Many of its citizens were active abolitionists before and during the Civil War, and their homes served as safe houses for people escaping slavery. The town was so active in the pursuit of freedom that Farmington was called Grand Central Station among enslaved persons and their guides. Local families had played a large role in the *Amistad* trial only two decades earlier, housing Mende captives who had successfully revolted against their slave ship's captain.

As we drove around, it simply felt like a small, attractive New England town. I had expected Miss Porter's to be big and fancy (perhaps because I'd heard that Jacqueline Kennedy was a student here), but the school itself was unpretentious in the way that old wealth doesn't have to announce itself. We parked in front of the main building, stopped in, and explained to a student at the front desk why we were there. She gave us some materials about the school and told us we were free to explore the campus.

We'd had a heavy rain the night before, and the morning was unusually humid for October. Before we'd left home, I had been in touch with an elderly cousin who mentioned that she had visited the school years ago when she was a child. She said that there was a fern garden on the grounds that Patrick had planted. We could find nothing that remained of a fern garden now, except possibly a small, recessed pool with a low wall around it. We took our time, strolling along the paths. We stopped at a grove of tall cedar trees and one very old hardwood, maybe an oak or a sycamore. One of its large branches, ancient and gnarled, was supported by a wire to keep it from breaking. No doubt this tree was as old as the school. Certainly, it was here when Patrick, Bridget, and the children arrived.

Using the little map, we found the gardener's house.

THE GARDENER'S HOUSE, MISS PORTER'S SCHOOL FOR GIRLS,
FARMINGTON, CONNECTICUT

It was old enough that Patrick and Bridget might have lived there. A simple two-story frame house with a double porch, it was painted New England white and set directly across the road from the main campus. An extension had been built on one side, so perhaps it held more than one family. A white picket fence surrounded the house, and a little arbor led to the front door. An American flag hung from the top porch. About fifty yards away to the back, overgrowth almost hid what had once been the greenhouse, now falling to ruin.

Sadly, I recently learned that the house and greenhouse have been demolished and replaced by a new gym and pool. At least I visited before they disappeared.

The job at Miss Porter's must have seemed perfect for Patrick and Bridget in many ways: a secure job in beautiful surroundings. Two years after they arrived in Farmington, Bridget gave birth to their sixth child. They named this new baby Elizabeth, reusing the name of their child who had died in infancy in New Haven. Now there were five children, four girls and one boy: George, my grandfather.

The school was doing well when the family arrived in 1874. Sarah Porter had enrolled one hundred girls. Gardeners had plenty of work keeping the grounds up for the students and prospective families. Perhaps Bridget worked for the school too, taking in laundry or working as a seamstress. It would have been a very different scene from New Haven, living in this idyllic place, seeing the privileged young girls in their fine clothes, strolling with their friends across the campus or departing in their parents' carriages for the holidays. Miss Porter herself was a force of nature, a woman who believed that women deserved an education equal to men. It was a mark of honor to be a student at Miss Porter's, and it was a prestigious place to work.

But Patrick stayed at Miss Porter's only four years before he moved the family again. This move was the big one, from the East Coast all the way west to the new state of Nebraska. Railroad companies were placing ads in the newspapers every day for cheap land that they owned. Maybe it was just too hard to resist. Out west, Patrick could have his own land, be his own boss and his own person. He wouldn't have been alone in that dream. In Boston and New Haven, cities full of Irish immigrants, Catholic churches held recruitment drives to encourage parishioners to move west and help build up the church in the new settlements. But it was not without risk.

I'd heard a family story that seemed odd: while the Farleys were in Nebraska, Miss Porter offered to adopt Mary. Why would she do that? Was that just a made-up story?

For as long as I'd been tracing this path of Patrick's, there had been a very big missing piece: Bridget. We were proud in our Irish family roots; there was always talk of Patrick coming from "the old country" at reunions and my dad's interest in his Civil War service, so why was there never any talk about Bridget? What happened to her? I have no memory of the question being raised by my dad and his siblings at family reunions. Why were there no photographs of her, when we have one of Patrick and their three surviving children? How did she die, and where was she buried? Until my cousins and I got interested as adults, she was absent, as if she'd been edited out of the family. How strange that a missing grandmother or great-grandmother was never discussed.

After the trip to Connecticut, I pulled out Patrick's army pension records again and noticed things I'd overlooked. It's curious how you can read something and think you've taken it all in, but on a second read new things pop out at you. On the form requesting his pension, dated 1915, he had to list his children, alive and dead. He lists three children alive: Mary, George, Lizzie. Three children dead: Annie, Elizabeth, and Katie.

I went back and reread his letters to Mary, sent after she left Columbus for New Haven. In a 1912 letter reflecting on his life, he wrote, "If I live till the first of April I will be 76 years old and that is not a bad age. Every person got to die. We do not get to Heaven in the flesh. I have three of my children before me who died in their youth and innocence and I hope to meet them in Heaven and if I do my happiness will be complete."

No mention of their mother. And what had happened to Annie and Katie, the other two girls who didn't survive? It seemed like someone should acknowledge their short lives. I didn't want them to be forgotten.

Though I knew eventually I'd have to make a trip to Columbus, Nebraska, I started at home, laying out on the dining room table all the documents I had: the census records, Patrick's army pension papers, his letters, and my maps. I read through my timeline of Patrick's life again, figuring out where the gaps were for Bridget and the two girls. I was determined to find them.

Most cities on the East Coast kept records of the births, marriages, and deaths of their populations, but not every city or county kept vital statistics that far back, and some don't make their records easily available. These records are slowly getting digitized, but there's still much that is only available on microfilm. Enter the Church of Latter-Day Saints (LDS). Anyone doing family research owes thanks to the Mormons for their vast library of genealogy records, which makes public information easy to access for family researchers. Fortunately, there is an LDS reference room not far from where I live.

Research at an LDS center is a bit of an involved process: First you must establish whether the records you need actually exist. Once you know that they do and have the microfilm numbers, then, for a small fee, you can order the rolls through their online repository. You wait for the message announcing that they have come in, and you hope they will contain what you're looking for. Once they're available, you have a few weeks to access them. The grunt work of scrolling through them will either yield success or leave the question hanging in the air unanswered, depending on the diligence of the authority whose job it was to register the birth, death, or marriage. You hope for legible handwriting, too. If you're patient and like mysteries and investigative work, so much the better.

As soon as I got notice that my order was in, I drove over to the research room, which is inconveniently open only two days a week. I settled into a dark cubicle with a microfilm reader, my precious rolls of film, reading glasses, and a notepad and pencil. To boost my chances of success, I'd prepared a rough time frame (in some cases, I was lucky enough to start off with an actual date) before scrolling through years and months of hundreds of names in the birth, marriage, and death records, looking for my family. Reading microfilm is a bit like working out on a treadmill—there's a reward eventually, but it's not much fun in the process.

After working like a detective for several days, I finally hit pay dirt. New Haven kept pretty good records, and the penmanship of the recorder was clear enough. In the roll of birth statistics I found the birthdates (and even the name of the midwife) for the first four children in Patrick and Bridget's family: Mary, Ann, Elizabeth, and George. I cross-verified the first three with the federal census in 1870. There they were: the emergence into the world of my Irish immigrant ancestors' native-born children. I thought about friends in our parish who had immigrated from Mexico and the pride they felt when their children were born on American soil.

But now I had a mystery to solve: when did Elizabeth die? The 1870 census said she was born in March, so she couldn't have been alive for long if my grandfather was born on the last day of June 1871.

Counting back nine months, I placed the start of Bridget's pregnancy with my grandfather in October 1870. It would be unusual for a woman to be pregnant while still nursing a young baby, so I guessed that Elizabeth might have died between March and October.

Next, I went through the microfilm roll of death records. In the nineteenth century, infant mortality was high. Geography was a factor in survival; infants born in rural settings had a much better chance at seeing their fifth birthday than those in urban areas. Poverty, overcrowding, and lack of sanitation were a deadly combination. New Haven's nineteenth-century death records are a litany of sorrow. Sometimes the cause of death was simply marked "unknown."

My estimate of March to October was correct. I found little Elizabeth's death recorded on September 4, 1870, at only six months old. The cause of death: convulsions, a catchall term referring to seizures. They may have been brought on by various things: a high fever from an undiagnosed illness, meningitis, or a bacterial infection, or the result of dehydration caused by some gastrointestinal illness. Born at home in a crowded living situation, she had numerous strikes against her: viral or bacterial infections or disease could spread quickly. The convulsions must have been terrifying to see, her little body suddenly taken over, her muscles rigid or shaking. What did Mary and Ann, just five and three, think as their baby sister, who was starting to crawl and laugh, was now lying silent and still in her bed? They may have been present when the doctor came to certify death, seen her placed in a tiny coffin, been present for the wake in their home, or perhaps attended the burial. It might have been their first encounter with death.

Soon after the baby's death, Bridget was pregnant again. This next child—a boy at last—would live, and then the family would add two more girls: Katie and the youngest child, named Elizabeth. Vital statistics and census records only give you the bare facts, no descriptors, no emotion. But there in the microfilm cubicle, all I could think about was Bridget, pregnant again when her grief for her child was still so fresh, her heart so tender.

And then Bridget is gone, vanished from the family picture. Back home, reading through Patrick's surviving letters again, I found no mention of Bridget. Not one word. Why the omission? If she had died, wouldn't he have mentioned her in his letter to Mary in that sentence about heaven, "three of my children *and my beloved wife*"? When Mary read that letter, did she whisper, "Don't forget my mother?" Or were letters that *did* mention her not kept? Patrick is buried in the Catholic cemetery in Columbus with the dates of his birth and death on his gravestone and a bronze star, *Civil War Veteran, Grand Army of the Republic,* beside it. He lies next to his youngest daughter, Lizzie, and her husband. So where is Bridget buried? Why don't we know? She had disappeared from the family picture. Unknown. Unspoken. Forgotten.

In the same army pension record where he lists the names of his children, dead and alive, Patrick reports his marriage status as widower and his wife's name as Bridget McKenna. In the space for the year of her death, numbers have been crossed out twice before the date of 1888 is legible. The numbers are in dark ink, as if it had been written over several times, as if the ink had weight to it. When I first saw this, I thought, *Surely that's a mistake. He must have remembered it wrong or written it wrong.* My dad had said once that Annie and Katie died in a diphtheria epidemic. I googled "diphtheria, Nebraska, 19th century" and found that there had been outbreaks in Columbus. If that was the cause, when did the girls die? How old were they? And there was still the nagging question: if Bridget died of diphtheria too, or some other illness, why doesn't Patrick mention her in that letter? Why isn't she buried beside him, her name on the grave marker?

As my cousins and I got older, we became intrigued with the mystery of Bridget. Maybe the passage of time makes questioning easier. But, unfortunately, by then our parents were dead and we had missed the chance to ask them about it. Still, we would ask each other, "What do you think happened to Bridget?" She was the invisible guest, always present at our cousin gatherings, though not yet a person in our minds, just a mystery to be solved.

In 1878, when the Farley family of seven left Farmington, they headed west, traveling 1,400 miles to a new town in a new state. They left behind friends and family and a tiny grave in New Haven that held their third child.

It was a safer time to go west. Small towns were strung like beads on a necklace, following the railroads, while others grew up near government forts that provided protection for white settlers. The Lakota War had come to a close. By 1878, when the Farleys went to Nebraska, Cochise, Sitting Bull, Red Cloud, Crazy Horse, and Chief Joseph—the great leaders of the Apache, the Lakota, the Ponca, and the Nez Percé—had been killed or conquered. The way was now opened for white settlers, many of them immigrants, to take over ancient tribal lands. Ironically, it was not unlike the early British seizure of the ancient lands of Irish clans.

The trip would take days. They would travel from Connecticut to New York and spend a night or two there, perhaps with friends or relatives. They must have seen the Brooklyn Bridge still under construction: it was an engineering marvel. Next they would board a series of trains to get to Chicago, where they would board the Union Pacific to Omaha and beyond. Mary was thirteen and Ann eleven, both old enough to help their mother with the young children: George, seven; Katie, five; and Elizabeth, not yet two. The train rattled along, day after day, passing through cities and then the small towns that sprang up along the tracks amid endless miles of tallgrass prairie. It must have been an exhausting journey, corralling five tired and excited children

UNION PACIFIC RAILS, COLUMBUS, NEBRASKA

and all the family gear through multiple transfers, making sure every-one was fed. This trail west was lined not with wagon ruts, but with rails laid down by fellow immigrants.

Eventually the big black Union Pacific engine, billowing smoke, squealed to a stop at their destination: Columbus, Nebraska. The town had sprung up beside the Platte River by the railroad tracks in the past twenty years. Everything was new. When the Farleys got off the train, they were greeted by the sounds of hammers and the smell of sawdust. The city was being built right before their eyes. Where would they live? Where would they sleep that first night?

They were far from Connecticut now. Was Columbus always the destination? Had Patrick bought a plot of land before they left, a place where they would build a home? There was a small Irish settlement, Shell Creek, nearby. Maybe he knew someone who had gone out before them. In any case, Columbus was growing and that meant there would be plenty of work.

New families there were starting from scratch, living in dugouts or rough-built log cabins. One small glimpse of their early home comes from a few lines of a poem my grandfather wrote many years later that he called "Nebraska Memories":

There's a loneliness comes o'er me
As memory brings before me
A little family home of long ago
There's a rustic old log cabin
with its little window panes
A roof of rough-hewn boards
and a crooked fence of rails
A pioneer's place of native wood
All weathered brown and gray
With wild flowers growing here and there
Along the grass grown trails.

Simple, idyllic, nostalgic. Was George thinking of the early days after they first arrived, a close-knit family of seven?

For Bridget, this move west may have felt almost as monumental as the Atlantic crossing. She was joining the ranks of immigrant women on the frontier who had made new homes only to leave them behind. As it was for Bridget, that first new home was usually in an eastern urban setting where multiple immigrant families, often from the same home country, were thrown together in tight living quarters. Those urban neighborhoods brought over a bit of the Old World, and close bonds formed. For women it was a sisterhood of survival.

We often see a rosy picture of strong pioneers in the West, fighting the elements and succeeding against all odds. But surviving in an environment in which these settlers had little experience was much more complex. Sometimes the hard edges of life make a person stronger, more resilient. Sometimes, struggles multiply and build up until the weight becomes too much to bear.

Bridget, like Patrick, had survived the famine, but she had lived into adulthood in its direct aftermath. Her community had come to grips with the loss of 30 to 40 percent of its population—family, friends, and neighbors gone forever in one way or another. The survivors lived with the loss of cultural cohesion and traditions, the decline and suppression of the Irish language, and varying degrees of survivor's guilt.

While Patrick was fighting to preserve the Union of States in America, Ireland was convulsed with continued evictions and land wars. Bridget spent those years in a changed landscape. Empty cottages sat in untended fields, their former inhabitants and caretakers, dead or emigrated, barely mentioned for the pain of it. How long did the sods carried from a soon-to-be-deserted hearth burn in a neighbor's cottage before that home fire, too, died out? Some tenants took over their missing neighbors' land, while others hung on to tiny plots by their fingernails. Survivors whispered stories of greed and misfortune. How much of this haunted world did Bridget carry with her?

All I knew was that there, on the remote grassy plains of the American West, Bridget and two of her children died. But where? Along with his scratched-out dates finally settling on 1888 for Bridget's death, Patrick recorded that she died in Norfolk, a town forty-six miles north of Columbus. That didn't make any sense.

Children in the Earth
by Karen Wingett

Lavender irises grow oddly wild
in the pioneer cemetery
south of Wayne
My friends exhume the antique bulbs
for reburial in their own garden plots

I don't dig . . .

fearing the mad mothers of the plains
forced to leave their babies and hearts
in this land with few flowers,
who wait through seasons of hot wind
and brittle leaves
and the crystal stillness of winter
for April
when their children spring from the good earth
briefly and colorfully alive,
blooming playfully by the chalky stones.

CHAPTER THIRTY

We Found Bridget

"WE FOUND BRIDGET." That was the email's subject line. It was almost eleven o'clock in the evening when I checked my email before going to bed. I was waiting for a music list for an upcoming wedding in which I was scheduled to sing, but this was from my cousin Steve's wife, Ruth Ann. I caught my breath, paused, and clicked to open it.

Attached to the body of the email were three digitally captured articles from old Nebraska newspapers, all from February 1886. The *Columbus Journal* reported, on February 3, "Mrs. Patrick Farley of this city attempted suicide by cutting her throat on the evening of Jan. 29th but was discovered in time to be saved from fatal results. Her mind from fright has been affected for several years."

Another column, a sort of editorial printed on the same day, stated, "It seems to me that Columbus needs a considerable number more aggressive humanitarians or Christians or both. There are subjects here that are deserving of attention from those of generous impulses who look after the wounded spirits languishing by the wayside of life. We are told the case of Mrs. Farley is one deserving immediate attention, for more than a few reasons."

The last one ran in the *Omaha Daily Bee* on February 4: "Mrs. Patrick Farley of Columbus, deranged by venturing out on the great Brooklyn Bridge during its construction years ago, attempted self-destruction on Saturday evening by gashing her throat with a case knife, but was discovered in time to prevent fatal results."

What? My head was spinning. First of all, Omaha? Omaha is eighty miles from Columbus, and this story made the news in the largest town in the whole state. I was trying to take all of it in, and my mind was not cooperating. Second, what was this thing about the Brooklyn Bridge? They would have gone to New York to take the train to Nebraska, but still. And finally, like a punch to the gut, the hard cold fact of it. *Oh my God, she tried to kill herself. Tried to slit her own throat with a knife. What does it take to come to that point? She must have been so desperate.* The article says "in the evening"; it was February and probably winter-dark. Was she in the kitchen when she grabbed the knife? Did one of the kids find her, or was it Patrick? Who ran to get help? What did they do?

I tried to slow down and think. I pictured the family by calculating their ages in 1886. Mary, the oldest child and the one who must have been holding the family together, would have been twenty years old; George was fourteen, and Lizzie just nine. How did they handle this? The newspapers had printed this horrible story about their mother. Everyone would be talking about it, whispering behind their backs. They had to go to school, to church, to the store while everyone they saw knew the graphic details. I didn't get much sleep that night.

I called Ruth Ann first thing the next morning. She had found Bridget through Chronicling America, a Library of Congress website of old newspapers, by keying in "Bridget" and "Farley" and an approximate range of years. My cousins and I had once speculated that Bridget might have been institutionalized. After all, if she'd died of disease, the family would have said so and she would have been buried in Columbus's Catholic cemetery with a marker next to Patrick's grave. Institutionalization would explain that, and also why our parents' generation didn't talk about her. Like a loose puzzle piece that I couldn't throw away, I had created a convenient fiction in my mind of a kind of soft, gauzy depression, the loss of her daughters too much to bear. I imagined her sitting in a chair, staring into space, unable to function. Apparently, I hadn't looked very hard for the truth.

"The wounded spirits languishing by the wayside of life." Shame is a powerful force. After talking to Ruth Ann, I hung up the phone, logged on to the computer, and dove into Chronicling America to see what more I could find. The story began to unspool.

A few years back, Bob and I had visited Columbus, Nebraska. It was the first time I'd been to this small town where Patrick and Bridget settled after leaving Connecticut in 1878. We planned to spend a week doing some family history sleuthing. I knew from Patrick's pension and the census records that two of their children must had died in Columbus. I wanted to find their graves, or at least learn how they died, and maybe—just maybe—find out what happened to Bridget.

Even with population growth, highways, and Walmarts everywhere, rural Nebraska still has a feeling of frontier, big-sky country. Beyond Lincoln, the land is uncompromisingly flat and the horizon goes on forever. We approached Columbus on Highway 30, which runs along the very Union Pacific railroad tracks that originally made it a town and brought seven Farleys here.

We found a bed-and-breakfast and checked in for a few days. The visitor website describes Columbus as "a community of 21,000 people, where the air is still fresh, and manners still matter." This was quickly confirmed when we stopped in the county courthouse to ask for help. Built in the 1920s, the granite-and-marble courthouse was impressive. Ionic columns out front and wide stone steps leading up from the sidewalk exuded security and stability. Inside, the staff was friendly, helpful, and genuinely interested, the blessings of a small town. The woman at the front desk suggested two resources we could investigate, both housed inside the building: school census records and old newspapers.

We headed up the staircase to the second floor where the school records were kept. The school census consisted of lists of local school-age children recorded each year in the spring. The town used them to determine how many classrooms and teachers would be needed for the next school year, which would tell them how much money to ask for in the coming year's budget. Perhaps the girls, Annie and Katie, would show up there. They weren't on the federal census of Nebraska in 1880; since the family had moved out here in 1878, the girls must have died during those first two years.

A clerk with a warm smile took us to a small room with a table and file cabinets along the wall. "They're in the metal file cabinet over there by the window. Top drawer. You can look through all of it; just don't get it out of order." Outside the window, the wide Nebraska sky stretched blue and clear. As I pulled the file drawer open, the musty smell of old paper rose up from its contents. I gingerly lifted out a file marked "School Census: 1870–1899" and began to read the reports. One sheet for each year. Someone's handwriting from over a hundred years ago dutifully listed children eligible for school and their ages, alphabetically by family. I carefully turned each page over until I reached 1878. No Farley children. They must have moved to Nebraska in the summer after the census was taken.

But on the next page, in 1879, there they were. On an April day in 1879, under a sky perhaps as blue as today's, the county official had captured in fading ink: *Mary, 13, Annie, 11, Katie, 6, and George, 5.* George's age is wrong—born in June 1871, he would have been seven that April. They must have mixed up George and Katie's ages. Lizzie would be next, but she was just two and a half, too young for school. In the spring of 1879, Annie and Katie were still alive a year after leaving their friends and relatives back east. But the next year they don't show up in the school records. They barely had time to experience life out here on the plains. From 1880 on, only Mary, George, and eventually Lizzie are recorded on the school census reports, until they are no longer school age.

The clerk stepped back into the room. "How are you doing? Do you want copies of anything?"

"Yes, yes, doing good, thank you—I'd like copies of all of these—the pages from 1878 to 1890. All the pages with the Farley children."

"I'll do it for you—we don't let people use the copier themselves. The paper is so old, you know."

She returned in a few minutes and gave me the copies, still warm from the machine. It felt good to hold them, to carry proof of these children, my grandfather's sisters, to acknowledge their existence. They were little girls who got up in the morning, dressed, combed their hair, waved goodbye to their mom, and went off to school with their friends. Little girls who greeted their teachers and sat down at their desks with schoolbooks open. Who never suspected their lives would end so soon.

Tucking my copies in a folder, we headed out into the hall, down the stairs, and out into the bright sunshine. Our next stop was St. Bonaventure's Catholic Church. I knew Patrick was buried in the cemetery there; we'd visited his grave earlier that morning. But where were the girls buried? Speaking to the church secretary, we learned the parish burial records didn't go back as far as 1879. The original church had been just a small frame building, built in 1877. The large, brick "new" church we were standing in had been built in 1884. The early records were spotty, and she said many of the very old gravesites didn't have markers. They might only have had a wooden cross, which would have disappeared long ago. She suggested we try the funeral home in town, which had been run by the same family since 1871. They might have something.

The Gass Haney Funeral Home is a family business that started in 1870, making furniture and coffins. As the population grew, the need for coffins increased and eventually the funeral needs took priority. We parked in the lot behind a small red-brick building with decorative white shutters on the windows and attractive planters beside the doors, neat and clean and proper in that funeral-home way.

We explained to the receptionist why we'd come. She brought us to an office in the back and pulled out two chairs at a small, round table before stepping out again. She soon came back with a stack of old red and green accounting books. At first I didn't understand, but she explained that the funeral home didn't keep burial records, but we could go through the monthly accounting books for 1879 and 1880 and see what we could find. I ran my hand across the cloth cover of the first book, opened it, and read what amounted to an accountant's history of death in a small town. So many children: boy, girl, infant. A litany of pain. I turned page after page, and then, suddenly, I found it in the very last days of December 1879: "Orders for two caskets. December 28, coffin for Mr. Farley, $4. December 31, coffin for Mr. Farley, $5." There they were, Katie and Annie.

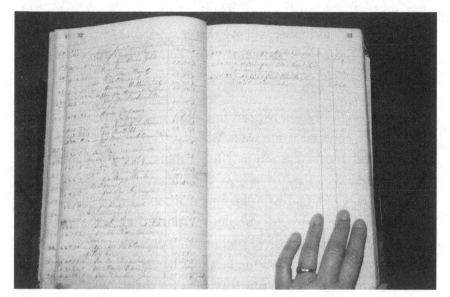

GASS HANEY FUNERAL HOME ACCOUNTING BOOK, 1879,
COLUMBUS, NEBRASKA

Comparing this to the cost of other coffins, I realized these must have been simple pine boxes. Katie, five, must have been the first to die, needing a smaller casket. Two beloved children gone, just days after Christmas. I closed my eyes and just sat there, my hand resting on the page.

I took a photograph of the page in the accounting book. There was no way to make a copy here. We thanked the receptionist for her help and went out to the car, both of us quiet.

Now that we had dates, Bob and I returned to the courthouse to look through old newspapers. It didn't take long. The *Columbus Era* reported on January 8, 1880,

Two of Mr. Farley's children have died of the diptheria [*sic*] within the last week. It was in the sickness and death of those two children and the grief and destitution of the family, that we witnessed the practical fruits of modern Christianity. In procuring a coffin and removing corpse to burying ground, A. J. Arnold and Charley Davis tendered them service. These were the only two male members of the church present, we believe. On our own motion we will say that many thanks are due Mrs. Ed Clark and Mrs. Hempleman for their kindly offices in the death and burial of these children.

Destitution? They'd only been in Columbus for a year and a half. Things must not have gone well. Was Patrick unable to find work? From a good and stable job at Miss Porter's in Farmington, what had happened that they were now considered destitute? The parish women, Mrs. Clark and Mrs. Hempleman, in their "kindly offices," had prepared the little girls' bodies for burial: washed and dressed them, combed their hair, lifted them from their beds and placed them in the plain pine boxes. Did the fact that Mr. Arnold and Mr. Davis had procured the coffins mean they paid for them? Was Patrick not able to afford his own children's coffins? Did he go to the burial, or did he stay at home with Bridget and the other children? Was he sick? Was she? Were the rest of the children sick? Why weren't more people there for the funeral? The family seems isolated, alone. Were people afraid? I had so many questions.

My dad had talked about a diphtheria epidemic. It was a rampant killer in the nineteenth century, an illness we don't even think about now that it's been eradicated by the DPT vaccine, the combined guardian against diphtheria, pertussis, and tetanus. My dad used to say that people who refuse vaccinations have never seen what diphtheria does to a person.

Sometimes called "the Strangling Angel of Children," diphtheria announced its arrival with a slight fever and a sore throat. At first it seemed like a simple cold. Sometimes a barking cough would follow. In the nineteenth century there was no cure, although people tried anything they had heard might help, including bleeding with leeches or swallowing turpentine or kerosene. It seemed to strike most often in the winter, probably because people were staying indoors. Children, especially those living in crowded situations, were more susceptible. A bacterial infection, it is spread by droplets in the air or direct contact with contaminated objects. As the disease progressed, a thick blue-white or grey membrane would develop and spread over the throat, tonsils, and airway. The membrane might bleed and turn greyish green or black. If the patient did not begin to recover and the infection raged unabated, the palate would become paralyzed, making swallowing and breathing difficult, if not impossible. Lymph nodes became swollen and the soft tissues of the neck would fill with fluid. Eventually the bacterial toxins would travel unabated to the heart, liver, and brain. Coma and death could come within a week. Some managed to survive its onslaught, although a long, slow recovery would follow.

Imagine the terror of a parent who heard their child cough or complain that their throat hurt. Was the whole Farley family sick? How do you grieve for the ones you've lost when your other children are still in danger? Or if you are? Sheer panic must have filled Patrick and Bridget's hearts.

Annie and Katie died as 1879 came to a close, but Bridget was very much alive. When did her mind break? When did grief turn into something else?

•

CHAPTER THIRTY-ONE

Identity

Now I had a lead on Bridget. Back home, I began my search for answers long-distance. Nebraska has very strict laws about access to mental health records. I was told it was impossible, but I decided to give it one more try. I composed a heartfelt email to the Platte County District Court, sort of a Hail Mary pass, stating that I had no intention of legal action and just wanted this for family history. I gave a brief bio of the family and added the fact that they were early settlers in Platte County. I mentioned the hard times that many women experienced on the plains.

Who knows if it was those words that made the difference, or if it was the fact that it was a woman with a compassionate soul who opened my email, but I received a prompt response: "Thank you for your inquiry. I will review my early court case indexes to see if we have anything under that name. We do have most of the original case files yet, so hopefully, if something was filed, we may still have it. I will be in contact with you after my review, hopefully by tomorrow afternoon."

True to her word, I got a follow-up email the next day.

Lois – I have found no court case files regarding your great-grand-parents, however, that doesn't surprise me as a mental health file generally would not be located in the court docket. Now, I have 2 mental health record books still on site—they are dated from 1911 through 1980. Book No. 1 which has the mental health records dated from 1874 to 1911 was transferred from our archives to the Nebraska State Historical Society on August 21, 1991—it is called the Record of Insanity / Book No. 1. I do not know if they have it microfilmed or if it is easily accessible, but at this point, you would need to contact them to see what they can find for you. I hope that helps in your search. I was so disappointed that we didn't still have that 1st record book, but at least it wasn't destroyed. Good luck & let me know if you have any questions. Thanks.

This, along with the email contact info for the Nebraska State Historical Society in Lincoln, was more than I'd dared hoped for. I wrote to the state archivist and curator of government and state records, repeating my heartfelt request. The first email response stated the Nebraska law that all mental health records are confidential "proactive and retroactive in regard to timeframe." I would need a court order to release any records. I'd gotten my hopes up just to have them dashed. But then, just minutes later, a second email from the archivist arrived: "I just looked for RG247, volume for Platte County, and can't find it. It may have been misspelled, but I tried other counties and couldn't locate this volume."

Well, at least she'd tried.

The next morning, a third message arrived from the archivist. She told me that earlier in the morning she and a female coworker, who happened to be an archaeologist, had searched the shelves and turned up the missing volume. Maybe it was a slow morning, or maybe they just wanted to help, but here's what she shared:

This volume was indexed in the front, and I did look at the information noted for Bridget Farley, page 38. However, it does not provide much information for you as to why Bridget was placed in the mental asylum. I also looked in some admissions information in Box 2, SG3, Series 2, folder 12. Platte County Insanity Board of Commissioners (1878–1891). People admitted into insane asylums were approved or denied by this county board.

The folder contained Auditor's statements for those admitted into the asylum. In essence, the county paid for Bridget's duration in the insane asylum. Bridget is listed on these forms from June 3, 1881 thru Dec. 1, 1888 (time charged for, weeks/days, and amounts to be paid by the county). Regrettably, many of the patient case files or hearings files do not exist for this earlier time period.

This was a lot—the closest I'd come so far to finding out what happened to Bridget. The archivist said she could send me a hard copy by mail. I called, thanked her, and said yes, please, send me what you have. I told her how grateful I was for this information and for the extra effort she had made to find it. I couldn't help but feel that these women had banded together with me to dig a little deeper for Bridget. How many women's lives and histories are lost somewhere on the Great Plains? Unearthing the minutes of an admissions meeting from 1888 might seem small, but to me it was no small thing. It was a gift from kind strangers.

A week later, a large envelope from the Nebraska Historical Society showed up in our mailbox. The packet of papers inside was titled "Bridget Farley, Insanity"—her identity defined and spilled out in a meeting of three men, members of the board of Platte County Commissioners of Insanity. Along with the minutes, the archivist had included copies of pages from an accounting book listing the people sent by Platte County to the Lincoln Asylum, including one Bridget Farley.

The minutes began, "Friday, May 13, 1881. The roll is called. A. C. Turner, S. A. Bonesteel, physician, and the clerk, John Stauffer. Dr. Bonesteel is the chairman." And then, in the clerk's neat cursive, "Affidavit of Patrick Farley in regard to Bridget Farley being insane is read."

My heart sank. I hadn't grasped the fact that Patrick would have asked to have her committed. But of course it would have been him. What did it take for him to get to that point? To need to remove his wife from their home—the mother of his children, the woman who crossed the ocean with him, both full of hope and excited to begin their new life. But by the day of this meeting, they had already buried three of their six children. Now Patrick had to face these men, his social superiors, in the town where he was a simple laborer, and say to them, "My wife is insane, and I can't manage it anymore." Mary, the oldest of their children, was just sixteen. George was ten, and Lizzie was five—all still children. For how long had they been living with their mother's illness? How did it manifest? What did they understand of it? For Patrick to do this, life at home must have become impossible. His heart, already broken, must have broken even more.

The *Columbus Journal* article about her suicide attempt was written several years later, when apparently she was living at home again. It said that Bridget had been suffering from "frights." And what on earth did the *Omaha Bee* article mean in the odd Brooklyn Bridge reference? Was it perhaps Patrick's attempt to make sense of her instability? Losing three of your children, the last two out on these lonely plains, cruelly just days apart after Christmas, seemed reason enough to me to lose one's mind. Did their deaths, so close together, awaken memories of the famine years she had lived through back in Ireland? I know so little of her earlier life. She seems only a faint apparition who materializes in record books, the ghost at family reunions. No photographs. No letters. Nothing in her own words.

Back in Ireland, she shows up in a few records. Her birth is recorded in the Moynalty parish book: Bridget, daughter, born October 20, 1835, mother Ann Tait, father, John McCanna (the old spelling of McKenna.) There are two sponsors on her baptism record, but it's hard to read their names: perhaps Laurence Farrelly and Betsy Mallon. She shows up again in the parish records as a sponsor of her sister's first child, Philip, in 1856, and four years later as a sponsor again, for her sister's son John.

The marriage records that Father Joe found for me in the old parish book tell a little more. In the winter of 1864, just before the beginning of Lent, Father Patrick Ginty recorded their marriage: "February 8, married Pat' Farrelly to Bridget McKenna, witnesses, Edward Lynch and Betsy Sheridan." It was the first year that civil records were required by the state, and they included more information: age and occupation of bride and groom, and their fathers' names and townlands. That's how I learned Bridget was from Skearke, where she was living with her sister and brother-in-law. Their fathers, "Pat'k" Farrelly Sr. and John McKenna, are both listed as farmers; Bridget is a spinster (as all unmarried women were), and Patrick is a laborer. But Bridget is still just a name on a page. A daughter, a sister, an aunt, and now a wife.

A few older members of my family floated the idea that Bridget might have come from a wealthy Protestant family that disapproved of her marriage to Patrick, a Catholic. I have learned that family stories are best taken with a very large grain of salt. They can be true or false or somewhere in the middle; even the biggest fabrications might hide a piece of truth. Most family stories are told for a reason, and that may have been the case here because in the early days of the small Iowa town where my grandparents lived, there was no Catholic church until the 1950s. It was not uncommon then to still find some prejudice against Catholics, especially Irish Catholics, who were often perceived as the Other. My grandmother's family was well respected, pillars of the town and founders of the local Baptist church. I have wondered if the handsome boy she married might have been more acceptable if he hadn't *really* come from an Irish Catholic family.

I always found the "Bridget was disowned" story suspect; it just made no sense to me. Bridget McKenna was clearly Catholic: born, baptized, and wed in her Roman Catholic parish. I'd been there, and I'd seen the records. But if you work your way through the haze of a family story, you might find something. On a recent trip to Moynalty, I met two McKenna cousins; we'd found each other through DNA. Eilish, the historian, told me more about the McKennas and how they fit into the local community. She gave us a little tour of various relevant sites and filled in the history.

Though definitely not Protestant, the McKenna family was successful and held strong social standing in the area. Movers and shakers, you might say. The name *McKenna* has a deep history in Ireland; its chieftains presided over a large barony for centuries until it was confiscated by the British in the 1600s. The McKennas were leaders and poets, and active nationalists in Ireland's War of Independence from Britain. Our mutual ancestor, Nicholas, was a farmer and owned a pub and inn on the main street of the village. Successful though he was, Nicholas was still a tenant like everyone else. He paid rent to Colonel Alexander Saunderson, a member of the British Parliament during the famine, who owned twelve thousand acres (including Nicholas McKenna's) and resided at the palatial Castle Saunderson on land taken from the O'Reilly clan.

Eilish said, with a smile, that today you might call Nicholas a *gombeen* man, a wheeler and dealer. He wielded influence, made deals, and arranged marriages. She wondered if Patrick and Bridget's marriage had been arranged by him. I wondered if they left for America so soon after their marriage because it *hadn't* been arranged; that Bridget married outside the family's approval. Maybe there had been someone they wanted her to marry, but she married Patrick instead. Or maybe it really was an arranged marriage, as Eilish suggested. Both scenarios are possible. Maybe they had planned all along to set out for America right away after the wedding. Or maybe they needed to leave because of family strife. I doubt that we'll ever know. But the disowned-by-her-family story could have held a seed of truth.

Whatever the motivation, she and Patrick came to America shortly after their marriage. Once they arrived, like many women of her time, she's virtually invisible. Her surname doesn't appear on the records, and even her husband's surname has been Americanized; now she's Bridget Farley. Bridget McKenna is her identity only in her mind. In the 1870 census, like many of her New Haven neighbors, she is an immigrant, Irish born, sharing a dwelling with other Irish families, the mother of three children, five and under. The youngest, three-month-old Elizabeth, would be dead the following September.

I found Bridget next in the vital statistic records in New Haven, where "Bridget Farley, mother" appears on the birth records of Mary in 1865 and Ann in 1867, and in 1870, on both birth and death records for tiny Elizabeth. She is "Bridget, mother" again on the birth record of George, on June 30, 1871. Then her paper trail disappears for nine years. I haven't yet found a birth record for Katie, but she must have been born right about the time they moved from New Haven to Farmington in 1874. Their last child, the second Elizabeth, who was known to the family as Lizzie, was born two years later in Farmington.

In the federal census of June 1880, the family is in Nebraska. But now the family is considerably smaller. It says Bridget is forty-three (losing or gaining a few years in age is not unusual on census records). Scrawled over something unreadable is "Keeping house" as her occupation. Patrick is forty-five, occupation: laborer. Mary is fourteen, George is six, and Lizzie is four. They are living in their own house. Their neighbors come from Switzerland, New York, Pennsylvania, Ohio, Prussia, Wurttemberg. I can find only one other person nearby from Ireland.

That census was taken less than a year before the May 14, 1881, meeting of the Platte County Board of Commissioners of Insanity. Several months earlier, however, on September 1, 1880, a small, ominous article in the *Columbus Journal* reported, "On Motion, the clerk was instructed to issue an order to St. Mary's hospital to receive Mrs. Farley and child as inmates in said hospital, until further orders of this board." Was Lizzie the child mentioned in the article? She would have been almost four. It had been only nine months since Annie and Katie died. Franciscan nuns had recently opened St. Mary's Hospital, which consisted of a few beds in a small house in town for their stated mission: "To care for the sick and to serve paupers."

This marks the beginning of Bridget's absences from home. Was she having trouble before they made the move west? Could that have been a factor in the decision to move? My cousin Dru, a clinical psychologist, suggested that Bridget's condition could have begun with postpartum depression. Bridget had given birth to Lizzie and given her the name of her dead sibling just a year and a half before they left Connecticut.

It's hard not to imagine that uprooting from an urban life of modest comfort and companionship and relocating to the isolated western plains was difficult for her. Women pioneers, especially immigrants, often struggled alone. And there's a hint that Patrick may have regretted his decision to bring them all out west. Many years later, in a letter to Mary, he wrote a wistful sentence about New Haven: "You were born in that City and it is a good City and there are good people living in it. I do not believe that I ever met with any kind of a bad person there and if I made up my mind to settle down there when I came into it, I think I would be better off today."

Bridget's stay with the nuns at their small hospital seems to mark the beginning of her downward spiral. The next spring, soon after the decision of the board, she was sent to the State Asylum for the Insane in Lincoln, eighty-eight miles away from her family. Wrenching as it had to have been for Patrick and the surviving children, it may also have been, on some level, a relief. I wondered what it was like for Bridget to leave her home in Columbus for the asylum. When she walked out the door that spring day of 1881, did she look back? What was it like for the family? Perhaps it brought calm to the household along with the emptiness.

The *Columbus Journal* article also notes that "Mrs. Clark assisted, taking Mrs. Farley to the Lincoln asylum." It's safe to assume that this was the same "good Mrs. Clark" who had helped to prepare Annie and Katie for burial. She was someone Bridget trusted, someone who could help manage this move. They probably traveled from Columbus to Lincoln by train and then by carriage out to the asylum. If they had done the entire trip by horse and carriage it would have taken a full day, but rail probably halved the time. The last time Bridget would have been on a train was the move west from Connecticut. Did she think she was going back?

I wonder whether she understood what was happening to her. Was she frightened or confused? Probably so, and certainly pained to leave her children. I wonder also how much the children understood. Teenaged Mary may have tried to help her father explain their mother's illness to her younger siblings.

I wish so much that we had a photograph of Bridget, or at least a physical description. Some way to imagine her. Sometimes I search the old photographs of Mary, George, and Lizzie for traces of her face. Does one of them have her eyes? Her hair? Is that cleft in George's chin a McKenna trait?

When the carriage pulled up to the gates of the asylum in Lincoln, it may have evoked an old memory. The workhouses of Ireland and the new Nebraska asylum shared an architectural design. They were impressive institutional edifices, large stone buildings with wings off to each side. The Kells workhouse, just five miles from where Bridget grew up, served a wide area that included both Moynalty and Mullagh, the two villages Bridget knew best. Did the building itself raise a memory of workhouses in Ireland and stories of people she knew, or whose names were known to her, who entered them a last resort? It was the place you most feared having to go. It meant separation from your family, shame, desperation, disease, and death. Most didn't come back.

Nebraska Territory had become the State of Nebraska just ten years before the Farley family arrived. Settlers flooded in as the railroads stitched the country together, which drove a flurry of institution-building as the new western states had to grow up fast, organizing themselves nearly from scratch. Shortly after the Civil War ended, the Capitol Removal Act allowed the sale of property lots in Nebraska to raise money. Among those lots was a parcel of land in Lincoln that would become home to the first Nebraska Asylum for the Insane. More lots were sold, and more institutions followed: a penitentiary, the Deaf and Dumb Asylum, the School for the Blind, and the Reform School for Juvenile Offenders, all established in the first ten years of statehood.

The Lincoln asylum was built quickly in 1870 and, in its first year, burned to the ground. A new, more structurally sound building went up two years later. This was the building that Bridget would enter. It contained thirty-nine sleeping rooms, a dining room on each floor, and bathrooms. Beds were four and a half feet wide with mattresses of hair supported by wire springs. Patients slept two to a bed. It was secure: the walls were thirteen inches thick, and metal grating covered the windows. Patients had access to outdoor courtyards with lawns and flowers, a library, and a chapel. Bridget's care was managed by a staff under the guidance of the superintendent, Dr. H. P. Mathewson. Treatment at Lincoln, as at many asylums at the time, was based on a philosophy called "moral management." It was a repudiation of the horrors of the confining, prisonlike places that many asylums had become on the East Coast. The goal of moral management was to promote a gentle approach to the patient, buttressed by the belief that a regular schedule with a simple diet, cleanliness, and fresh air would lead to well-being. It promoted occupational work, amusements, and an individualized approach to engender a healthy psychological environment. It was a wonderful abstract ideal. Bridget probably experienced this optimistic approach in her first year at Lincoln. Patients had postal privileges, and visitors were allowed. Did she have visitors? Did she get letters from Patrick or Mary? He was a letter writer. I want to believe that he wrote to her, or that Mary did.

Unfortunately, Lincoln's early optimistic approach didn't take into account the accelerating population growth and the stress of pioneer life. Demand for care increased rapidly because it had now become more acceptable to remove mentally ill people from family homes, where they often were hidden or neglected. As more and more patients were sent by county boards, moral management gave way to a focus on control and a pessimism that insanity could ever be cured. Staff were overwhelmed, and regimentation took over. What had been a commendable approach, seeing the patient as an individual, gave way to delivering medical treatment en masse. Purgatives (laxatives) were commonly used. There was a strong belief that repeated "cleaning out the intestines of the insane" by whatever means available was curative. As the need for control grew, narcotics were more frequently prescribed, particularly morphine, opium, and potassium bromide, an antiseizure and sedative medication, to induce sleep or make patients quiet and more manageable. In "The Nebraska Asylum for the Insane, 1870–1886," Klaus Hartmann and Les Margolin report, "Potassium bromide was given every one or two hours until sleep would occur. It was described as 'very good for hysterical and maniacal wakefulness.' It was also used with narcotics for insanity with excitement and insomnia" (*Nebraska History* 63 [1982]). Bridget may have been treated for those symptoms, as the *Columbus Journal* article reported "her mind from fright has been affected for several years."

Just two years after Bridget was admitted, the situation at Lincoln had significantly deteriorated. It was so dangerously overcrowded that patients thought to be of no harm to themselves or others were sent back home to make room for incoming patients. The administration had little recourse. The *Columbus Journal* reported, on May 16, 1883, "Sheriff Kavanaugh returned Friday from the Insane Asylum at Lincoln, bringing with him Frank Chambers, Henry Reige, Nicholas Mattia, Mrs. Farley and Mrs. Grip. The discharge is made on the grounds that the patients are incurable and harmless, and room must be made for new applicants. The removal of them cost Platte County about $55."

Suddenly Bridget and four of her compatriots were back in the world, to be received by families who were likely unprepared for their return. Did Patrick receive any guidance, or were he and the children left to deal with this transition as best they could? Had Bridget been routinely given narcotics or potassium bromide that she would now have no access to? Had her condition improved, and if not, how was Patrick supposed to handle her needs now if he couldn't handle them before? He would have seen soldiers suffering from forms of anxiety—what we now know as posttraumatic stress disorder—but this was his wife, the mother of his children. How did the family react to having her back home?

Mary—now eighteen—had stepped in as mother to her siblings (and perhaps had been doing that work for years before). Finished with her schooling, she may have found some extra work in dressmaking. But her primary responsibilities would have been making sure that six-year-old Lizzie and twelve-year-old George got to school and church, cooking breakfast and dinner, and keeping clothes washed and pressed and the house clean. Her mother's return, in a presumably unwell state, must have only added to her burden. It's hard to imagine that Bridget was in any better shape than when she left.

Incurable and harmless. Decreed not harmful to self or others. Room must be made. And then, two and a half years after she had returned home, on an evening toward the end of January 1886—by all reports a nightmare month of snowfall so heavy that impassable drifts blocked

train lines and cold so severe that telegraph systems shut down—
Bridget Farley held a knife to her throat and tried to end her own
suffering.

She did not die. She was stitched up and sent back to Lincoln, adding one more soul to its already overcrowded halls. Back to the place
that had no room for her, where patients were now sleeping three to
a bed or on mats on the floor, where they had infrequent baths and
overworked staff. The situation was ripe for contagion and abuse.

CHAPTER THIRTY-TWO

Norfolk

THE LINCOLN ASYLUM, once an answer to a problem, had become an urgent problem itself. Even after sending "harmless" patients back to their homes, it housed twice as many patients as was intended. When Bridget was readmitted at Lincoln after her suicide attempt, the numbers were even worse. The Nebraska Board of Health saw the desperate need for more space and proposed building a new hospital for the northern part of Nebraska.

At the same time, new ideas were emerging about how "insane persons" might be helped and cared for in better ways. The Lincoln asylum had become an embarrassment; the decision to build a new site gave them a chance to improve. The new institution was built in Norfolk, a day's wagon ride north from Columbus. This asylum would promote a progressive approach to mental illness, reviving much of the moral management philosophy and adding innovations. It aspired to be a self-sufficient institution where patients had meaningful work in cooking, sewing, and gardening. It was designed, built, and ready to open in early 1888. In what had to be a prodigious feat of organization and compassion, ninety-seven patients from the asylum at Lincoln—fifty-four men and forty-three women—were sent north to Norfolk by train to be the first group of "inmates" in the new asylum. Bridget was one of them.

The *Omaha Bee* reported the event on February 15, 1888, the day the patients would be transferred. (Their numbers were in error; there

or desertion by husband, destitution, fright, jealousy, lactation, loss of children, masturbation, menopause, prostitution, separation from friends, religious excitement, typhoid fever, and more. How was Bridget categorized? Was it under "fright" or "loss of children"?

Paroles and furloughs were frequently granted at Norfolk, with successful results. Mechanical restraints were prohibited. A daily report from each ward gave an account of the personal condition of each patient and their conduct and status. This was handed over to the supervisor and filed in the office. Those reports would have given us a glimpse of Bridget's life there, her physical and mental condition, and maybe even a sense of who she was. Unfortunately, the daily ward reports were lost in a fire several years later.

Bridget McKenna Farley died on October 19, 1888. There were six deaths at the Norfolk asylum in that first year—three men, three women. Of the women, one died of "organic disease of the brain" and two of "phthisis pulmonalis," an early name for tuberculosis. It's logical to assume she was one of the two females who died of tuberculosis. She probably acquired it at the Lincoln asylum, confined in crowded wards with three to a bed and little ventilation. Sometimes called "consumption" or "the wasting disease," its symptoms are fever, coughing up blood, chills, night sweats, and weight loss. It's a disease of poverty, closely linked to overcrowding and malnutrition, now so preventable with screening and antibiotics.

Bridget was simply born at the wrong time. Her depression, anxiety, or "frights"—whatever caused her mental illness—would have been treated with drugs and therapy today. Her death could have been prevented with care and medication. So far from home, she suffered and floundered in her new country. Before the move to Nebraska, from all accounts she appears to have been healthy, a good mother who loved her children. I continue to look for her in the photographs of her children. Even now, she's hiding somewhere in my own DNA, a ghost from beginning to end, appearing only fleetingly in various records. Her bones rest somewhere under the Nebraska soil. I so wish I knew where.

CHAPTER THIRTY-THREE

Reunion

THE FOURTH OF JULY WEEKEND brings another Farley family reunion. This time we decided to meet in Columbus. People arrived from all over: Iowa, Kansas, Florida, California, and Wisconsin, and Bob and I from Illinois. On the last day, after most of them had left for home, Bob and I and my cousin Erik had another day before our flights left. We decided to go up to Norfolk, maybe see what we could find.

We left after breakfast and headed north from Columbus on US 81. It's a ribbon of a highway, like the Woody Guthrie song says, rising and falling, a black line slicing through the green and golden fields. It was a nice drive in the height of summer, and heat rose off the road in waves. Bob drove, I rode shotgun, and Erik navigated from the back. We figured it would take us an hour or less to get to Norfolk. We were not sure what we would find, but we were committed to the goal.

My mind moved between two time frames. In one of them, it was October 20, 1888. Patrick had rented a wagon from Goss Haney, the undertakers in Columbus. (The previous day we had visited the funeral home and found in the accountant's book, "Wagon for Mr. Farley to pick up Mrs. Farley, died at Norfolk.") It would have taken him a full day by horse and wagon. The wheat would have been harvested and gathered up in shucks, standing in the fields. The fall air would be crisp, the corn long cut and stalks plowed under, the ground prepared for the winter. Dark soil prepared to freeze over, for snow to cover the roots. Everything was dormant.

In the other time frame, it was today, summertime, riding in this car in the twenty-first century. We had each other's company, so the time went quickly. I watched the small towns pass as we followed the map. Erik asked me if I thought our grandpa George would have accompanied Patrick. I said, "Possibly." He would have been seventeen, a help in lifting the wooden coffin, keeping it from sliding around in the back of the wagon, and then helping to lower it into the ground, shoveling the dirt over her. A prayer. Sign of the cross. Maybe he was there, but maybe not. Patrick had done this by himself so many times: as a gardener for the county, digging paupers' graves had been one of his duties. And there had been plenty of grave digging during the Civil War. This one was just one more—but so much more. The box would have been light. She had wasted away with illness. I imagined a tiny woman, coughing, flushed cheeks, feverish, vacant blue eyes, disheveled hair. She probably had had it for months, maybe years. People with tuberculosis wasted away, like they had wasted away in the famine.

Eventually we saw the sign for Norfolk. We watched for evidence of something that is no longer there: the first asylum building, where Bridget had lived, was destroyed by fire in 1901, thirteen years after it was built. The facility was rebuilt shortly after the fire and then, many years later, after the asylum permanently closed, most of the remaining buildings were torn down to prevent squatters and vandalism. But the property is still owned by the state, used now as a restrictive facility called the Norfolk Regional Center. There was only one new building, a residential site for sex offenders.

There was very little signage, but GPS led the way. A few months before the reunion, I found and purchased an old postcard of the Norfolk asylum in the early 1900s on eBay and brought it along in case it would be helpful finding the place. It was a little weird that postcards were produced of an insane asylum, but there you go. As we approached, the entry road was clearly visible and had the same gentle curve as the postcard. This was it.

There was no barricade, no guard or guard house, so we drove right on in, figuring we'd be stopped if we weren't allowed to be there. We drove past a newer building and parking lot and then around to the back, where there were some old, deserted buildings. Bob parked the car beside what looked like an old heating plant, and we got out. The warm summer wind had picked up. Bob and Erik walked along the road beside the heating plant, but I felt pulled toward a huge ancient oak tree standing alone off the road. There were traces of the foundations of old buildings nearby. As I stood there, I was overcome by a wave of regret, sadness, longing—tumbling emotions I can't describe. I took a deep breath, trying to hold back tears. It felt as if all the sadness of the world had come down to this small point, this empty place. Bob and Erik were up ahead talking to each other. The old oak stood alone beside a field filled with wildflowers. The wind had stopped, and now it was very quiet. *So strange*, I thought, *all these beautiful flowers growing here*. I had brought my good camera along, and pulled myself together enough to take some photos. I was focusing when I saw a red pickup truck coming up the road toward us.

Uh-oh, I thought, *we're in real trouble now*. The truck stopped, and a man and woman got out and came over to us.

"Do you have permission to photograph here?" the man asked as he stepped up to me, looking official and perturbed. The woman stayed back near the truck. Before I could open my mouth, Erik, the consummate salesman, came up behind me and said, "Let me tell you our story." He explained why we were here, that our great-grandmother had been among the very first group of patients, the ninety-seven who were moved here by train from the overcrowded Lincoln asylum in 1888. The first "class," as it were, of Norfolk's new Asylum for the Insane.

Suddenly their expressions changed, and they told us that they both worked here, that the man's father and grandfather had worked here before him. He told us that when this was still an asylum it was a model place, new and progressive for its time. Patients worked in the asylum's bakery and dairy farm, grew flowers and vegetables, sewed clothes and bedding, painted, and listened to music. The two of them showed us where the original buildings had been before the fire, where Bridget would have lived. Only the brick walkways are left from that time, they said, pointing to an area just beyond where we were standing. "Go ahead and explore; just don't take pictures of the new buildings."

As they walked toward the truck to leave, I asked about the wildflowers. The woman smiled and said, "Well, after they tore down the old buildings this land was empty and weedy, and we just decided to throw a bunch of seed out here and see if we could grow wildflowers instead. Like on the prairie."

They gave me the email address of the superintendent, who was interested in the history of the place and would want to know our story. "Don't forget to contact her," they said. "Great meeting you, you made our day!" And they waved, got back in the truck, and drove away.

Bob and Erik and I looked at each other, speechless and a little stunned. We walked further up toward the old walkways, and as we approached, I could see that the ground here was covered even more thickly with flowers. It was an artist's palette: yellow, red, purple, blue, white—everywhere you looked there were flowers. Daisies, poppies, Queen Anne's lace, cornflowers, sweet William, blue flax, lupine, prairie clover, baby's breath. It was a hot day, but now there was a soft breeze. It was so peaceful. All the sadness I felt before, the dark heaviness, was gone. In its place was a quiet kind of comfort.

We spent an hour exploring the grounds, winding our way through the walkways and not talking much. Then it was time to leave. We needed to get back to Columbus before dark, and it was a good hour's drive back. We planned to stop by the Columbus cemetery and clean off Patrick's gravestone before we left town. Our flight home was early the next morning.

I needed to tell him about this trip. I wanted to stop somewhere and buy flowers to leave on his grave before we left town, but it was obvious now what I should do. It was just a small bouquet. I know you're not supposed to pick wildflowers, but I think there are exceptions to every rule.

Back at the Columbus cemetery we got out of the car, armed with our cleaning supplies, and scrubbed down the gravestone. When it was clean and dry, I went back to the car and retrieved the little bunch of flowers, pink and purple and yellow and white, and placed them on Patrick's grave. I asked Bob if he'd say a prayer—he's a chaplain after all—but he said it had to be our prayer, Erik's and mine. Patrick was our guy.

Do the dead know we're here? Do they feel our weight above them?

A flood of thoughts raced through my mind. *I've been immersed in the life of this man for so long. I have his army records; I've been to the place where he was born and grew up and the church where he and Bridget were married. I've walked the roads he walked. His picture hangs on my wall, for heaven's sake. I know about the Great Hunger, the deaths, the landlords, the Atlantic crossing in the coffin ships. I've been to nearly every village, town, or city where he lived. I've stood on the battlefields where he fought. I know some of the terrible things he endured in the war and the family's hard life out here in the West. How three of his young children had died. And Bridget . . . oh, Bridget.*

I wanted to reach out to him across the thin space between life and death. I could feel the tears running down my face and the sharp, painful lump that stuck in my throat, but I managed a few words: "Patrick, it's me, Lois, and Bob and Erik—we're here. Erik and me, we're George's grandkids—your great-grandkids. We brought you flowers from Norfolk. From Bridget. They were growing all over the ground, so many colors all together, it was so beautiful, I wish you could have seen them. There's so much I want to say, I don't know how. . . . Thank you for everything you did. I am so sorry. So sorry for all the hard times you had. I don't know how . . . but I want to tell you. . . . I want you to know your kids turned out great. Mary and George and Lizzie. You took good care of them, you loved them, you never gave up. I want you to know, the family . . . we're still together. I want you to know . . . it's a good family, Patrick."

PART FOUR

Home

CHAPTER THIRTY-FOUR

Blessings

A YEAR LATER, Bob and I returned to Ireland. And as we often do, we spent the last week of the trip in Moynalty, arriving in time for the annual Steam Threshing Festival. We stayed at the Flanagan farm with Margaret. The festival is held on the third Sunday of August, the Feast of the Assumption, which is the feast day of the parish. It's a huge event for this village of eight hundred people, and every year it seems to grow bigger. Forty thousand people come from all over Ireland and England, Scotland and Wales for an all-day celebration of the rural life that many still remember from childhood or from stories passed down by parents or grandparents. There are demonstrations and re-creations of days when fields were cultivated by the hand plow or horsepower, and threshing was an event that gathered the whole community. A large field behind the village and beside the Borora River fills up with old steam threshers in action, vintage cars and tractors on display, a pig roast, boxty baked over a fire, an Irish soda bread competition, music, dancing, games for the kids, and a country music concert in the evening. Everyone in town is involved.

The night before the festival, the parish holds its annual Blessing of the Graves. The Saturday-evening Mass is held outside in the cemetery, just a few steps from the church. It's a tradition, part of the celebration of the Feast Day. For days before, the cemetery is full of life—people greet each other, sweep the paths, and place flowers at gravesites, while children run around the place, singing, laughing.

People return home from away to pay their respects. This one day a year, the extended family of the parish, living and dead, comes together again to mark the importance of each life, the linked chain of generations and community. People gather beside their family gravesites. The cemetery is packed.

Father Joe, who did not grow up here but knows the place as if he did, spoke to the reality of the communion of saints, an affirmation of these souls and our own, all one. Bob and I stood at the Flanagan graveside where Margaret's husband, Tommy, lies buried with others of the family.

After Mass and a long wait in a line of cars, we gathered back at Margaret's. Her daughter Maureen had brought over sandwiches, and we ate and talked and laughed and told stories. My heart filled with gratitude to be included as even a small part of this family, our American selves pulled into their circle.

After Maureen and her kids left, Margaret mentioned that she'd like to go back to "see the lights." A few years ago, people began coming back after dark on the night of the blessing to leave candles on the graves. It wasn't an organized thing. At first just a few families set out a candle, and then more people picked up on the idea and the next year there were many more. But Margaret had never gone back to the cemetery to see it at night.

I was so happy that she wanted to be there because I did too, but I hadn't felt right leaving her. So, after we cleaned up the kitchen, the three of us got in the car and drove back to the cemetery.

We parked along the road and walked in the dark. Margaret had brought her cane and held on to Bob's arm as we felt our way along the low cemetery wall. Soon we reached the gate and went into the cemetery. It was like entering another realm.

The sky was black as ink. There are no city lights here. Above us just a few wispy clouds floated beneath a field of stars. And here below, in this settlement of souls, the tiny lights shone in the night.

We walked down the path that divided the cemetery into sections. Margaret wanted to go all the way to the back and around, feeling more secure on her feet. As our eyes adjusted to the dark, we began to see that we weren't alone, that there were others here, their silhouettes barely visible in the night. No one spoke. It was so still, just the soft movement of people in the quiet dark, each step a step on holy ground. And the lights—all the tiny sparks of light, each an echo of the stars above, each one saying, "I am here. I am still with you."

Patrick and Bridget, you are with me too.

Here I am, one of your many great-grandchildren, standing here in the Moynalty cemetery, all these years later—coming home for you in a way. I have to smile, wondering at the unlikeliness of it all.

I am thinking of all that you experienced: the Great Hunger, the Atlantic crossing, the Civil War, life on the Great Plains. The two of you, married right here in this church. I am awed at how you mustered the courage to leave and tough it out in a new country that wasn't always the most welcoming. You persevered through joys and so many sorrows. You stayed and planted our family, and because of your courage we've thrived and spread out across the country. Your story is like that of so many others in Ireland, who have family far away in North America, England, Australia, New Zealand, and beyond. I hope that we make you proud.

Patrick, I think about that family reunion years and years ago at Aunt Ruth's house and my simple act of picking up your photograph, wondering who you were. I think of the words you wrote to your daughter Mary: "I am satisfied with the path that fate marked out for me. It might have been more smooth but it was not too rough to conquer me. If I met with adversity Heaven gave me hope to stand it. Prosperity does not try anybody. It takes adversity to do it. Notwithstanding that my path was a little rough betimes, it was not so bad as it was for thousands who were probably more deserving."

I tried to find your path and found so much more along the way.

That path, the one that "was a little rough betimes," opened a window for me into the whole wondrous world. The world of the immigrant, the world of hunger and war, the world of wealth and power, poverty and perseverance, the world of intolerance and acceptance, suffering and survival, the world of second chances.

Standing here under these stars, I know, beyond a shadow of a doubt, that this one thing is true: we are all connected. We are all who we once were, we are all who we have become. We are all family.

Epilogue

On Monday morning, we packed up. Leaving Moynalty becomes harder each time we go. The lump in my throat was raw and painful, and I couldn't talk as we pulled out of the drive onto the road and turned toward the bend away from the house and from all my rooted places.

It's mostly the pain of leaving Margaret and the whole Flanagan clan. But it is more than that, too—it's this whole place: Skearke, Moynalty, Mullagh, Curraghmore. The very land has made an imprint on my heart, and it is wrenching when I leave it. In just a matter of days we will be so far away.

What an unlikely thing, to find myself at this age so full of love for a small place on the other side of the Atlantic. All I have is a genetic connection to these people and a distant history with this one tiny spot on Earth. But somehow it feels more like home than almost any other place that I know.

Settled into my window seat on the Aer Lingus flight home, I craned my neck to watch Ireland recede as we gained altitude. I caught the tip of her west coast before she disappeared behind the clouds entirely. Now we were heading to Chicago, moving from one reality to another. Hurtling through the air, I thought of all the Irish souls on all those ships so long ago, my own Patrick and Bridget among them. Some made it to the other shore, some lay at the bottom of the sea below me. I think that we of the Irish diaspora carry a piece of their dream and a piece of their sorrow in our hearts always, even if we aren't aware. For some of us, it is a long invisible strand, like a Celtic knot unwound and stretched across the ocean, always pulling us toward home.

January 1, 1894

We are all well and hope this finds you all there well and in the enjoyment of good health. I will conclude this time by wishing you a happy new year, and many of them and may God in His infinite mercy watch over you and save you from all danger and harm.

Your Father,

Patrick Farrelly

Write soon.

Timeline

MARCH 19, 1836	Patrick Farrelly born to Ann Flanagan and Patrick Farrelly, Lurgan parish, Co. Cavan, Ireland
1845–1852	The Great Hunger, Ireland
1851/52	Patrick emigrates to United States
JUNE 5, 1858	Patrick enlists in United States Army and is assigned to Fort Ripley, Minnesota
APRIL 12, 1860	Fort Sumter fired upon; US Civil War begins
JULY 1861	Patrick's Company C, Second Infantry, reaches Washington, DC
JULY 21, 1861	First Battle of Bull Run
JULY 22, 1861– MARCH 1862	Second Infantry Regulars stationed as provost guard around the Capitol
MARCH 17– JULY 1, 1862	Peninsula Campaign: Siege of Yorktown, Battles of Mechanicsville, Gaines' Mill, Malvern Hill
SEPTEMBER 17, 1862	Battle of Antietam
DECEMBER 12–15, 1862	Battle of Fredericksburg
JANUARY 20–24, 1863	Mud March, return to Falmouth, Virginia
MAY 1–5, 1863	Battle of Chancellorsville
JUNE 5, 1863	First Sergeant Patrick Farrelly honorably discharged
JULY 1863	Patrick returns to Ireland
FEBRUARY 8, 1864	Patrick marries Bridget McKenn in Moynalty church, Co. Meath, Ireland

Spring 1864	Patrick and Bridget return to United States and settle in New Haven, Connecticut
April 9, 1865	End of Civil War
April 19, 1865	Lincoln assassinated
May 19, 1865	Mary Farley born in New Haven
March 9, 1866	Patrick Farrelly attains US citizenship
May 23, 1867	Anne "Annie" Farley born in New Haven
March 1870	Elizabeth Farley born in New Haven
September 4, 1870	Elizabeth Farley dies in New Haven
June 30, 1871	George Thomas Farley born in New Haven
1873/74 (est.)	Katherine "Katie" Farley born in New Haven
Summer 1874	Farley family moves to Farmington, Connecticut; Patrick begins work as gardener for Miss Porter's School
October 15, 1876	Elizabeth "Lizzie" Farley born in Farmington
Summer 1878	Farley family moves to Columbus, Nebraska
December 28 and 31, 1879	Annie and Katie Farley die in Columbus
October 19, 1888	Bridget McKenna Farley dies in Norfolk, Nebraska
July 22, 1921	Patrick Farrelly dies in Columbus
November 8, 1925	Erl E. Farley, son of George, marries Leah J. Gerhardt
February 16, 1945	Lois Farley Shuford born in St. Louis

Further Reading

General Irish History

Aalen, Frederick Herman Andreasen, Kevin Whelan, and Matthew Stout, eds. *Atlas of the Irish Rural Landscape*, 2nd ed. Toronto: University of Toronto Press, 2011.

Doherty, Gillian M. *The Irish Ordnance Survey: History, Culture and Memory*. Dublin: Four Courts Press, 2006.

Duffy, Séan, ed. *Atlas of Irish History*, 3rd ed. Dublin: Gill and Macmillan, 2012.

Killeen, Richard. *A Brief History of Ireland: Land, People, History*. Philadelphia: Running Press, 2012.

Ó Cadhla, Stiofán. *Civilizing Ireland, Ordnance Survey 1824–1842*. Dublin: Irish Academic Press, 2007.

Local Irish History

Farrell, Valentine. *Not So Much to One Side*. Cavan: Abbey Printers, 1984.

Mullagh Historical Society. *Portrait of a Parish*. Cavan: Anglo Celt, 1988.

The Great Hunger

Crowley, John, William J. Smyth, and Michael Murphy, eds. *Atlas of the Great Irish Famine*. New York: New York University Press, 2012.

Donnelly, James S., Jr. *The Great Irish Potato Famine*. Gloucestershire, UK: Sutton, 2002.

Kelly, John. *The Graves Are Walking*. New York: Henry Holt, 2012.

Kinealy, Christine, Jason King, and Ciarán Reilly, eds. *Women and the Great Hunger*. Camden, CT: Quinnipiac University Press, 2017.

Ó Cathoir, Brendan. *Famine Diary*. Dublin: Irish Academic Press, 1999.

O'Connor, John. *The Workhouses of Ireland.* Atlanta: Anvil Books, 1995.

Woodham-Smith, Cecil. *The Great Hunger.* New York: Old Town Books, 1962.

Immigration

Laxton, Edward. *The Famine Ships: The Irish Exodus to America, 1846–51.* New York: Henry Holt, 1996.

Miller, Kerby A. *Emigrants and Exiles: Ireland and the Irish Exodus to North America.* Oxford: Oxford University Press, 1985.

Miller, Kerby A., and Patricia Mulholland Miller. *Journey of Hope: The Story of Irish Immigration to America.* San Francisco: Chronicle, 2001.

Moloney, Mick. *Far from the Shamrock Shore: The Story of Irish-American Immigration through Song.* New York: Crown, 2002.

Irish America

Gallman, J. Matthew. *Receiving Erin's Children: Philadelphia, Liverpool, and the Irish Famine Migration, 1845–1855.* Chapel Hill: University of North Carolina Press, 2000.

Gribben, Arthur, ed. *The Great Famine and the Irish Diaspora in America.* Amhurst: University of Massachusetts Press, 1999.

Hogan, Neil. *The Cry of the Famishing Irish: Ireland, Connecticut and the Potato Famine.* New Haven: Connecticut Irish-American Historical Society, 1998.

Hossell, Karen Price, ed. *The Irish.* New York: Greenhaven Press, 2005.

Meagher, Timothy J. *The Columbia Guide to Irish American History.* New York: Columbia University Press, 2005.

Shiels, Damien. *The Forgotten Irish: Emigrant Experiences in America.* Dublin: History Press Ireland, 2017.

US Civil War

Gilpin Faust, Drew. *The Republic of Suffering: Death and the American Civil War*. New York: Vintage, 2009.

Goodheart, Adam. *1861: The Civil War Awakening*. New York: Alfred A. Knopf, 2011.

Gottfried, Bradley M. *The Maps of First Bull Run*. El Dorado Hills, CA: Savas Beatie, 2009.

Huston, James L. *The Panic of 1857 and the Coming of the Civil War*. Baton Rouge: Louisiana University Press, 1987.

Hutcheson, Austin E. "Philadelphia and the Panic of 1857." *Pennsylvania History* 3, no. 3 (1936): 182–94.

Reese, Timothy J. *Sykes' Regular Infantry Division, 1861–1864: A History of Regular United States Infantry Operations in the Civil War's Eastern Theater*. Jefferson, NC: McFarlane, 1990.

Sears, Stephen W. *To the Gates of Richmond: The Peninsula Campaign*. Boston: Houghton Mifflin, 1992.

Family History

Balhuizen, Anne Ross. *Searching on Location: Planning a Research Trip*, 2nd ed. United States: Ancestry Press, 1997.

Grenham, John. *Tracing Your Irish Ancestors*, 4th ed. Baltimore: Genealogical Publishing, 2012.

Kenneally, Christine. *The Invisible History of the Human Race: How DNA and History Shape Our Identities and Our Future*. New York: Viking, 2014.

Morgan, George G. *How to Do Everything: Genealogy*, 4th ed. New York: McGraw Hill Education, 2015.

Acknowledgments

THIS BOOK BEGAN WITH a simple question about a single photograph and grew into not only a search for the path of my great-grandfather Patrick Farrelly, but also a journey through the history of two countries over three centuries. It has opened my eyes to the resilience of people in the most difficult of circumstances and to the enduring human spirit.

I owe much thanks to the many guides along the way who pointed me in the right direction:

Helen Kelly, Accredited Genealogists Ireland, Dublin

The National Archives of Ireland and the National Archives, Washington, DC

The librarians, history centers, and B&B hosts in Ireland who offered vital information

The National Park Service staff of Bull Run, Gaines' Mill, Fredericksburg

The city clerks and vital records staff in Connecticut and Nebraska

Shirley Langhauser and Susan Tracy, archivists at Miss Porter's School, Farmington, Connecticut

Pat Heslin, Ethnic Heritage Center, New Haven, Connecticut

Gayla Koerting, records and state archivist at History Nebraska

Marlene Vetick, Clerk of District Court, Platte County, Nebraska

The Gass Haney Funeral Home in Columbus, Nebraska

The site caretakers at the former Norfolk Asylum for the Insane

My thanks to Patisserie Coralie for providing a perfect place to write (and the best pastries this side of Paris), and to Aer Lingus for smooth flights and a genuine Irish welcome.

Special thanks are due to author and playwright John Kearns for his generous and compelling foreword; to Tim Reese for invaluable insight on the Regular Army during the Civil War; to Lauren Etter, who first said this book was worth writing; to Nadine Kenney Johnstone, my wise and affirming writing coach; to Kellie M. Hultgren, who masterfully edited with grace and clarity and then organized with constant good humor as my project manager; to Julie and Ryan Scheife at Mayfly Design and to Jess LaGreca for the beautiful, evocative cover and interior designs; for Madeleine Vasaly's sensitive and exacting proofreading; and to Sue Garthwaite, writer, spiritual director, and dear friend, who never let me forget why I was doing this.

I owe the heart of this book and so much more to Margaret Flanagan and the Flanagan family, who welcomed me into their home and hearts, and to Clare, Catherine, Eilish, Caroline, the Moynalty community, Fr. Joe and Fr. Tom, and many Irish friends.

To all my Farley cousins, especially Erik, who nagged me to get this book finished and always pushed us to have one more reunion.

And, most of all, to my four remarkable progeny—Becky (who read every page in process), Gabe, Jes, and James, for their encouragement and joyful embrace of life—and to Bob, my first reader, my best traveling companion, my love and soulmate.

And of course, to Patrick Farrelly and Bridget McKenna, who started it all.

About the Author

LOIS FARLEY SHUFORD was born and raised in St. Louis, Missouri. Driven by a desire to know what and who came before her, she relishes history, travel, music, art, and of course baseball, and she carries a deep love for Ireland in her heart. She has had a rich and varied career in education, from teaching middle school and directing an early childhood education center to serving as assistant admissions director and program coordinator in the graduate program at the Medill School of Journalism at Northwestern University. Mom to Becky, Gabe, Jes, and James, Lois now shares an old house in Evanston, Illinois, with her husband, Bob—truly her best friend—and their cats George and Gracie.